Matinee Idylls

MATINEE IDYLLS

Reflections on the Movies

RICHARD SCHICKEL

Ivan R. Dee
CHICAGO

Library of Congress Cataloging-in-Publication Data:
Schickel, Richard.
    Matinee idylls : reflections on the movies / Richard Schickel.
      p. cm.
    Originally published: Chicago : I.R. Dee, 1999.
    ISBN 1-56663-318-4 (alk. paper)
    1. Motion pictures.   2. Motion picture actors and actresses—United States.   I. Title.
PN1994 .S3495 2000
791.43—dc21   00-043033

For Barbara

Preface: A Month of Sundays

A month of Saturdays, too. And no small number of weekday midnights. And, if I recall, some national holidays as well. All were sacrificed to writing the pieces collected here.

More or less gladly so. For the truth is that I like writing essays better than I like going on picnics or strolling the beach or doing chores in the yard. It is not a profitable sideline, which is why, of course, I've had to find the time for it around the fringes of the week, in those hours when I'm not reviewing new movies or making television programs or writing books.

About half these pieces I volunteered for. The rest I was drafted for. But all of them eventually came from the same pleasurable place—notably the ones that don't concern themselves directly with the movies but rather with that megamovie that so much of our public life has become, and the ones that are more or less uncritical portraits of friends I have made over the years.

That is to say, they come from a mind ruminating, recollecting at ease. That's the great thing about Sundays. The phone doesn't ring. You don't have some appointment or deadline looming distractingly over the day. Your mind is free to wander, to chase down those hints of ideas, those odd associations that occur to you in the midst of other activities. And, precisely because it is engaged with an essay, it is unburdened by the heavy load of research that something like a full-scale biography imposes on a writer. Some of these pieces required no more than reading and pondering someone else's book. Others asked only that I look again at the movies made by their subjects. A few required me just to focus some fairly abstract thoughts about general issues that had been chasing around in my mind.

These pieces are scarcely confessional, but they are more autobiographical than I realized until I began gathering them together for this occasion. That shouldn't have surprised me—it's what's supposed to happen when you write essays—but it did. I'm not someone to whom the first-person singular comes easily. Yet the kind of writing I like best is work that takes both writer and reader to places neither would have predicted at the outset, which are bound to be corners of the writer's mind that neither of them know all that much about.

I went to some of those places because many of these essays were written either as tributes or as obituary reflections. At such times one's thoughts naturally begin with those moments when the artist in question made his or her most memorable impressions on you, got themselves somehow entangled in your inner life. If you are of a critical turn of mind, it is equally natural, as you contemplate one of these careers, to try to understand the nature of that entanglement. This, of course, entails an attempt to analyze how an actor's or a director's main themes have been stated, and to try to figure out how they intersect with your own preoccupations. To some degree this approach applies to the more abstractly analytical pieces as well. If you've been involved with something like the movies as long as I have, the desire to look into that involvement—into topics like celebrity, genre, narrative—also arises, nags, gets temporarily stilled by writing something.

These pieces are more often about the movie past than the movie present. The simple explanation for that is that week in, week out, I supply first impressions of current movies to *Time* magazine. On my days off I find it rewarding—if only as a change of pace—to delve into less pressing matters, to try to put careers and issues into some kind of perspective, to see a body of work or an aspect of the movie past with a fullness that my usual journalistic rounds don't permit. Then, too, in my television career I've been given the opportunity to do programs about some of the great figures of the movie past—sometimes even to get to know some of them—and to work intimately with their films, selecting the scenes by which they are represented in our programs, trying to identify some of the themes that have shaped past eras, past careers. A number of the pieces in this book are attempts to distill the ideas that have arisen out of this work.

Finally, as our collective memory not just of movies but of this century's entire cultural history grows shorter and dimmer, it has come to seem more important than ever to me to engage the movie past in a manner that is more than merely nostalgic, to bring the same kind of rigor and passion to it that any good historian will bring to explorations of other aspects of the past. Too much of what is written about film history subtly (and not so subtly) patronizes it. It accepts its myths unquestioningly, refuses to examine its artifacts in a new light. And that says nothing about the gibberish of post-structural academic criticism.

All right, I won't go there. I'll content myself with this statement of belief: there *is* a usable, intrinsically interesting movie history that can inform us not merely about the movies we see today but about the lives we lead today. Virtually everything I've put into this book reflects that conviction.

Everything in it reflects, as well, a certain compulsiveness on my part. You can finish writing a piece on a certain subject, but that does not mean you are finished with the topic. Some previously unseen or forgotten movie resurfaces, or a new biography appears, or a friend makes a chance observation about an old film, or a new thought about one simply appears out of nowhere. Mental notes are taken, the corner of a page is turned down, a clipping slides into the files. And, eventually, more Sundays are devoted to revising and expanding your old pieces.

Aside from the first and last of them, which are attempts at broad generalizations, I've arranged these essays so that they form a rough historical chronology. In so doing, I've noticed a few recurring themes and ideas, and decided to let these repetitions stand on the ground that it is by his or her obsessions that we get to know a writer.

Right now I feel a little like a schoolteacher, lining up his kids for the graduation picture, straightening ties, patting down cowlicks, brushing lapels. Like that teacher, I feel I've done my best with this occasionally unruly bunch, and I send them out into the world hoping they'll lead useful lives. Or, at the very least, make a good impression on anyone they happen to meet.

RICHARD SCHICKEL

Los Angeles
February 1999

Contents

Preface: A Month of Sundays   vii

Mind Slips: Remembering and Disremembering Movies   3

King Vidor: Romantic Idealist   21

Garbo: The Legend as Actress   31

Frank Capra: One Man, Many Films   61

Irene Dunne: A Secret Light   79

Bette Davis: Marked Woman   94

Auteur of Our Misery   102

Charles Laughton: No Room for Genius   116

Laurence Olivier: The Master Builder   141

Time Out: Or, Love in a Cold Climate   151

Satyajit Ray: Days and Nights in the Art Houses   157

Fellini: Send in the Clowns   167

Cinema Paradiso: The Rise and Fall of a Film Culture   178

Sam Fuller: Movie Bozo   201

Richard Brooks: Tales Out of School   211

Real Reality Bites   227

Advantage, Andy   236

The Star on the Stairs   253

Clint on the Back Nine   268

The Narrative Crisis   279

Author's Note   301

Matinee Idylls

Mind Slips: Remembering and Disremembering Movies

There was a time, not too distant, when the lives of many of the people who created movies also encompassed the entire history of the medium. Such a man was my sometime father-in-law, John Whedon, who was writing screenplays for Disney at the time I was beginning to write a biography of D. W. Griffith. He helpfully described for me the hoopla attending the New York premiere of *The Birth of a Nation* when he was a boy—mounted men, dressed in Ku Klux Klan regalia, thundering down Broadway drawing crowds toward the Liberty Theater on 42nd Street—as well as the impact of Griffith's spectacle on his innocent, bedazzled eye. John was a kindly man of liberal temperament, and he was somewhat ashamed to say that the power of Griffith's imagery was so intense that it quite wiped out the film's noisome message.

Around this time, when I was also in my first years as a movie reviewer, many of my senior colleagues were roughly of John's generation, and critics like Dwight Macdonald regu-

larly summoned the shades of the silent masters like Griffith
and Eisenstein to witness the decline—as they saw it—of the
modern movie, often citing films like *The Crowd* or *Sunrise*
when they mourned the passage of what had been, for them, a
Golden Age. I thought there was something strained—or anyway distinctly unhip—about these comparisons. But writing
of this kind also drove me to seek out these older movies in
order to broaden my cinematic literacy, hoping that I could
enter into the critical dialogue on something like equal terms.

By this time—the early seventies—I was beginning to acknowledge that I was myself haunted by memories of my own
Golden Age, the 1940s, when I was approximately the age my
father-in-law had been when he first encountered *Birth.* Those
were the movies I reached out to when I was, as a young
critic, looking for comparisons. In this period I was engaged
to write a couple of television programs for Public Broadcasting and found myself interviewing some of the directors of the
films I had loved as a boy—Raoul Walsh, Howard Hawks, Bill
Wellman. In so doing I was romantically struck by the fact
that their careers, now over or winding down, had begun at
the beginning of the movies. Walsh had actually played John
Wilkes Booth for Griffith. Hawks first directed for Mary Pickford, briefly filling in, he said, for another craftsman laid low
by drink. Wellman was brought to the movies by Douglas
Fairbanks, Sr., who admired his record—and his dashing
spirit—as a World War I aviator. The first television programs
I produced were a series about these men and five of their
contemporaries. It was well received largely because their
reminiscences and their work put people easily in touch with
the entire run of movie history to that date. I suspect that,
like me, they found a certain comforting coherence in the way
these lives so neatly fit, and illuminated, that span.

I am not being idly nostalgic as I record these autobiographical notes. Everyone I've just mentioned is now gone,
which means that their memories are no longer recoverable, as

they so easily were just twenty-five or thirty years ago. More important, the passing of the generations who were our living links to the *entire* history of the medium betokens a larger phenomenon, namely that the history of this most democratic of art forms is no longer democratically available to us. In the comparatively few years I've been discussing here it has lengthened—and thickened—to a point where no individual can fully comprehend it. This means there will not be a successor to Paul Rotha's *The Film Till Now*—which may be no bad thing—but it also means that we, its devotees, will not be allowed to comprehend the medium without "expert" guidance, and that is a bad thing.

Or to put that another way: we have reached a point at which, when we try to think about the movie past, we can no longer just consult memory for the data. We will have to dig for increasingly obscure documentation, consult the archives, run from specialist to specialist in pursuit of whatever big picture interests us—the development of a genre, for instance, or the narrative history of a particular period. In short, what we're talking about now is an increasingly fragmented body of knowledge, presided over by academic specialists. The distinct possibility is that movie history is about to turn into something like Augustan poetry or eighteenth-century French painting—still more or less accessible to the curious amateur, still dotted with names a reasonably well-educated individual will vaguely recognize, but nevertheless a topic obscure enough that it will require a good deal of hard-won knowledge to pursue intelligently.

I'm learning—very reluctantly—to live with this situation, but I've still not quite gotten over the shock of discovery. We are, after all, dealing with a medium everybody—a few sullen literary mandarins aside—loves, a medium that could not be more agreeably approachable, a medium whose most significant American works (and not a few insignificant ones) are, generally speaking, available on tape, on the classics channels, in revival houses and university film series as they were not to previous generations, a medium that, with the growth of film education, now presumably has an enthusiastic and knowledgeable core audience. Hey, everybody I know reads *Film Comment*. What? You mean to tell me some people don't?

2.

The occasion for these gloomy reflections is another television project I've just finished working on. This was the ten-part series, broadcast on TNT, that was derived from the list of the one hundred "greatest" American movies created (through impeccably calculated democratic means) by the American Film Institute. As its producer, I am obviously at interest in the bristling controversy that followed publication of this list, but my intention is neither to defend it nor to add to the attacks on it. I guess you could say that, like everyone else in America these days, I am looking for closure on a matter that is close to my heart. Or maybe it's enclosure I'm seeking—a place finally to fence in all the stray thoughts that my intimate involvement with this project stirred.

The hubbub that greeted AFI's effort resulted, I'm convinced, from its perfectly innocent, perfectly understandable failure to understand how radically our recall of movie history has changed in the last few years. Its plan, which was to offer a panel of eighteen hundred people intimately involved with the movies—a cross-section of above-the-line and below-the-line individuals working creatively in the industry along with executives, agents, exhibitors, critics, and film scholars—a list of four hundred significant American movies and ask them to vote for their favorite one hundred, made perfect sense under the previous rules of the game.

Moreover, my impression is that the people AFI asked to join its deliberations were by no means flibbertigibbets. I have no insider information on the composition of the panel, but earlier this year I kept running into people who said they had participated, and they were all reputable and serious professionals—absolutely the right types for the job. Yet their work was deemed—let me put this as gently as I can—woefully inexpert by the baying band of critics who descended on it immediately after it was made public.

You remember, naturally, the chief points of irritation: the exclusion of Buster Keaton's work as well as that of Preston Sturges and Ernst Lubitsch, Busby Berkeley, and Josef von Sternberg, the absence from the final one hundred of films that starred Astaire and Rogers and Greta Garbo; the complete failure to acknowledge the importance (and the delights) of the early thirties' gangster cycle; the failure fully to acknowledge the delights of that decade's romantic comedies. Most obvious and perhaps most painful was the way the great works of the silent era—*Greed, The Crowd, Sunrise*—were ignored. Only three films from that period were shortlisted, and—bitter irony here—one of them was *The Jazz Singer,* the truly execrable movie that brought the era to an end. There was also considerable phumpheting about the way some recent films, which have yet to withstand the test of time—the likes of *Pulp Fiction* and *Fargo*—took places away from deserving classics. In general, much was made of the fact that seventy-one of the one hundred "greats" were made after 1950, the underlying supposition being that, either by accident or design, AFI had somehow contrived to serve youthful foolishness at the expense of mature wisdom.

Some of these criticisms are, I think, justified. Some are not. But in any event the reasons that things worked out the way they did are subtle and hidden. They cannot be explained simply by generational paranoia. It is time, I think, that we apply a little reasoned analysis to this case.

Let's begin by observing that the history of the American feature film—if you date its beginning, somewhat arbitrarily, from the release of *The Birth of a Nation* in 1914, and end it, equally arbitrarily, as AFI did for balloting purposes, on December 31, 1997—is not one hundred years old. It is eighty-three years old. Simple arithmetic tells us that thirty-six years of that span precede 1950, forty-seven years follow it. All other things being equal, it's obvious that post-fifties films are going to dominate any balloting of this sort, simply because they offered AFI's nominators and voters eleven more years of production to choose from.

But let's press our statistical analysis further. Let's first stipulate that because they no longer have a substantial living constituency, that because they are now solely the property of scholars and a few cultists, silent movies were, for purposes of this or any other such balloting, a lost cause and write them out of our calculations. Then let's turn to the numbers for the succeeding generations. Doing so, we find on the final list of one hundred, fifteen films from the 1930s, eleven from the forties, twenty-one from the fifties, seventeen from the sixties, nineteen from the seventies, six from the eighties, and eight from the present decade. Were you to plot these figures out on graph paper, you would have a slightly misshapen but still recognizable representation of that most familiar and comforting of statistical constructs, a bell curve.

Bell curves are reassuring because they tell us that nothing wildly outside our expectations is occurring within the realm of our data, and that, in my estimation, is the case here. For I hold this truth to be self-evident: when we try to analyze our tastes in movies, we nearly always find that our formative years were, in reality, deformative years.

By this I mean that the movies with which we forge our most potent emotional connections—connections that have nothing to do with educated taste or sophisticated critical judgment—are the ones we see roughly between the ages of ten and twenty. These films get into our heads in a way that those we encounter later, no matter how much we admire them, rarely do. They live there with an intensity that our childhood experiences with the other arts—much more forbidding, much less immediately apprehensible—do not. For these, obviously, are the years when we begin to see movies on our own recognizance, without "parental guidance," as it were. For my generation and the older ones, that meant being allowed to go to theaters alone or with a pal or two. For subsequent generations it meant being allowed sole command of the television set after school or after prime time, when the movies were on. In both cases this constituted a sort of sneak preview of adult autonomy, and it granted us a peculiar alertness to whatever stimulations the screen, large or small, offered. At the same time, our innocence granted us a peculiar susceptibility to whatever nonsense was being projected upon it by the machines of commerce. In short, we believed in what we saw with a concentration, a passion that most of us—even those of us who eventually made film our life's work—would only rarely achieve again at the movies.

In retrospect we see the movies we first encountered as defining experiences, individually and generationally. It is not uncommon to cement a friendship, later in life, on the basis of shared enthusiasms for movies. A little over a year ago a screenwriter and I bonded over *Gentleman Jim.* I don't suppose either of us would seriously propose it for the AFI one hundred, but on the other hand neither of us can think of a movie that more poignantly or romantically set forth the rules for old-fashioned masculine gallantry than the last sequence of Raoul Walsh's lovely portrayal of the nineteenth-century rivalry between the legendary boxers Jim Corbett and John L. Sullivan.

Maybe we're talking sheer sentiment here. But movies are a sentimental medium—more so than a lot of us care to admit when we are draped in our critical-historical finery—and I want to impose my disformative years theory on the AFI bell curve. I think it tells us a lot not only about how that list came to be what it was, but about the whole issue of, if you will, cultural recall. In order to do so I'm afraid I have to state one more assumption. That is that the movies—so different in many respects from other mature capitalistic enterprises—are very much like the others in one important respect: their most significant players are people—oh, all right, men—in their fifties. (If you don't believe that, just look at the guys you can reliably count on to "open" a picture.) The other really important group in the American industry are people in their thirties and forties. Positing, as we obviously must, that AFI made an earnest effort to solicit the most influential opinion makers for its panel, our bell curve begins to make a lot of sense. That big bulge—twenty-one titles—of fifties movies on the short list quite obviously represents the judgments of establishment people now in their fifties who grew up in the fifties loving the likes of *Rebel Without a Cause* (boo!) and *On the Waterfront* (yes!). Similarly, the preponderance of titles from the sixties and seventies demonstrates the almost equal weight thrown on this scale by the slightly younger Hollywood players— people whose impressionable years were passed in those decades.

This argument also explains the relative paucity of selections from the thirties and forties, the eighties and nineties. There are very few people in their seventies, people who grew up on 1930s movies, still active in Hollywood. There are clearly some folks in their sixties—the 1940s movie generation—clinging to power in the business, but they are inevitably beginning to thin out. These generations just don't carry the weight they once did. As for the younger crowd, they are still establishing themselves and were probably not as heavily represented in AFI's electorate as they will be when the next poll is taken.

I know, I know—this sounds terribly schematic. And maybe a little bit complacent. But I think both the contents of AFI's list and the popular response to it support my argument.

3.

I want to discuss that response first, mostly because it is so easy to dispense with. Indeed, the most serious sin of omission committed by AFI's panel—the inadequate attention it paid to silent film—is, of course, explained by the passage of the generations we've already mentioned. All I want to add here, by way of emphasis, is how quickly the constituency for the silent and early sound cinema has melted away. As late as the sixties and seventies there was still a lively, reliable awareness in the film world of the glories of its deeper past. For example, *Sight and Sound*'s once-a-decade international critics' poll for 1962 named *Greed, The Battleship Potemkin,* and *L'Atlante* to its list of the ten best films ever made. A decade later Buster Keaton's *The General* replaced von Stroheim's film, but Eisenstein's held fast and *The Passion of Joan of Arc* had come on and so had *The Magnificent Ambersons.* Okay, we're talking critics here, people who are duty bound to know, honor, and defend tradition. Still, I doubt that the next time *Sight and Sound* asks for their opinions it will get a lot of lists heavy with silent classics. Or, if the AFI poll is not an anomaly, lists that are loaded with films of the thirties and forties.

The reaction to the AFI panel's choices from those decades is, if anything, more amusing (at least to me) than what was said about the silent years. This is because, like the list itself, it proves my point about the potency of the impressionable years in forming popular taste. Russell Baker, for example, got himself cranked up over the omission of *A Tale of Two Cities* and *The Prisoner of Zenda,* as well as (more defensibly) *Gunga Din.* A correspondent to the *Los Angeles Times* (which, because the AFI's project was a big local story, devoted much space to the reactions it elicited) deplored the absence of *Goodbye, Mr. Chips; Jane Eyre;* and *How Green Was My Valley* from the winner's circle. Others proposed *Grand Hotel, Dinner at Eight, Gabriel Over the White House, The Thin Man,* and *The Ten Commandments.* Moving on to later decades, *Field of Dreams, Out of Africa, Roman Holiday, The Way We Were, Bullitt,* and *Rosemary's Baby* drew support.

I'm not arguing that all, or even most, of these were bad pictures. Many of them, in fact, are pretty enjoyable. What I am saying is that these choices are the products of precisely the same approach to the selection process as the one employed by most of the AFI panel—a trip down those memory lanes that wind through everyone's impressionable years—and that you can't reasonably claim superiority for the fool's gold you find on this trail over someone else's. One *Times* correspondent gave this game away when she stated that *The Night of the Generals* was the greatest movie she'd ever seen and gave her reason with touching forthrightness: "It is the first movie that just my dad and I saw together." To me, that opinion is inarguable. Worthless, but inarguable.

Needless to say, I think my opinions are worthier. Equally needless to say, I thought my fellow panelists treated my impressionable years—the late forties and early fifties—shabbily. All right, they somehow managed to get a couple of things right—*Casablanca,* which I once publicly chose as my favorite movie of all time, and which, upon mature reflection, I'm still not about to disown, came in second in the balloting while *Yankee Doodle Dandy,* which retains its ability to make me mist up in certain passages, snagged the one hundredth spot. Due deference was paid as well to *The Treasure of the Sierra Madre* and *Sunset Boulevard.* But if I were a letter-writing type I could have fired off some pretty nasty questions to the *L.A. Times.* What about *Air Force, They Were Expendable, White Heat, Out of the Past, Red River, All the King's Men*? Except for the first, which wasn't even nominated, I voted for the whole damn bunch and, despite my cool intellectual understanding of how this process worked, I'm cross that so few of my fellow panelists agreed with me.

4.

Cross, but tolerant—armored as I am in theory. Think about it a minute. AFI's panelists were busy people, more pressingly concerned with the future of their medium (and, more important, their places in that future, if any) than they were with its past. You have to remember, too, that the Scorseses and the Spielbergs, men who really do know movie history, are the exception, not the rule, among this game's players.

You really can't expect the Hollywood majority to be true-believing cineastes, any more than you can expect the majority of Americans to be. Truly, they are not going to know the edgy delights of the artists and roughnecks who worked the edge—Sam Fuller and Anthony Mann in their ways, John Cassavetes in his. They have not—curse them— seen *Detour*. And they can't probably be expected to know that it is *Bride of Frankenstein,* not *Frankenstein,* that is James Whale's masterpiece and the great work *King Kong* aside—of horror's classic era. It's fun to watch the cinephiles like the critics from the *L.A. Weekly* make their counterlists, showing off their familiarity with the exotic, especially since they made a bunch of dumb mistakes, too. No, guys, *Design for Living* is not the great early Lubitsch sex comedy; *Trouble in Paradise* is the right choice. And if you must have something by Douglas Sirk, *Written on the Wind* can't compare with *All that Heaven Allows* as a delirious document of the hysterical consequences of fifties-era sexual repression.

Details, details. But in the end this is the sad fact you can't escape: the industry is very like the rest of America at this time—increasingly trapped in the present, increasingly indifferent to the lessons, and the pleasures, of the past. Everyone I know who goes out to guest lecture in colleges comes back with the same horror stories. They mentioned Stalin or Einstein or Proust (or, yes, Preston Sturges), and no one knew whom they were talking about.

In this circumstance, what do people do? Well, if they're movie people they probably follow their first instinct and check the grosses. Movies that earn spectacular sums of money—the likes of *Gone with the Wind, The Sound of Music, Forrest Gump*—have afterlives longer than radioactive waste. Critics may go on nursing their grudges against what seem to them unaccountable popular favorites, but eventually even their outrage against movies that defied their judgment tends to dwindle into a sort of sociological sniffing at the objects of their disaffections, an attempt to see what they might learn about *zeitgeists* past. As for movie folk, they love to see their critics confounded at the box office. They are natural adherents to the notion that it's the only arbiter of success, the belief that any mega-hit must have something, else it wouldn't have broken all those records. It may be frustrating that they can't analyze what that something is, but they can honor it.

The same goes for a lot of Oscar winners, who often enough take home statuettes because they have already won the hearts and minds of the peasants. C'mon, guys! *Ben-Hur* (seventy-second on AFI's list)? The chariot race in the old silent was actually better, and the rest of the picture consists mainly of a lot of bad actors standing around discussing faith and morals. But—you can look it up—the thing won eleven Oscars, which means—this is the really good news—you don't have to see it again in order to place a confident check mark next to its name on a ballot. All those folks back in 1959 couldn't be that wrong.

Now don't get me wrong, as Sidney Skolsky used to say, I love Hollywood. By which I mean that there are plenty of box-office successes and plenty of Oscar winners—the aforementioned *All the King's Men, From Here to Eternity, Schindler's List,* to name just a few—that I think are great works. There are huge popular successes like *Star Wars* and *E. T.* that have Oscars in my heart, if not on their producers' mantels. But that's beside my present point, which is that the record books provide convenient cheat sheets for busy people possessed of only the dimmest sense of history.

There are, naturally, other ways of filling the gaps. One of them is consulting secondhand memory. Under the gun, you may recall a general history of the movies long ago skimmed, some film history course dozed through years ago because it had a local reputation as a snap, some clip show that danced by television. *The Birth of a Nation*? First American feature, first box-office blockbuster. Check—and never mind its racism, its lunatic sexuality, its laughably Victorian dramaturgy. *The Jazz Singer*? First sound feature, harbinger of a famously traumatic technological revolution. Check again. And forget—because you don't actually know from firsthand experience—that the movie is not merely bad but laughably so.

Then there are the cases I think of as unexamined premises, movies that have passed into legend as great works, mostly on the basis of good initial critical response, but which have not been much reexamined since their openings. Some of these pictures stand up quite well—*Double Indemnity,* for example, or *It Happened One Night.* But what about something like *Stagecoach*? It seems, well, stagebound now—all those folks crammed in the eponymous vehicle talking the journey away, mostly in a manner that reveals class prejudices and blindnesses in the peculiarly awkward way of 1930s movies that took their social responsibilities too seriously. But that's forgotten now. What the mind retains are John Ford's great shots of the tiny, vulnerable coach bucketing along against the vast panorama of Monument Valley. And, of course, John Wayne's beauty and earnestness in his star-making performance.

Something similar might be said about *The Philadelphia*

Story, which people think of as a sophisticated romantic comedy, but which is actually an all-too-earnest (and virtually humorless) study of class issues. If you're talking Philip Barry, I prefer the slightly more knockabout *Holiday.* If you're talking best-of-screwball breed, the retrospective winner is *The Awful Truth*—but the problem is that it lacks Katherine Hepburn, whose stardom glows on, thanks in part to her longevity, as the more lightsome Irene Dunne's does not.

Or let's take up a slightly more complicated case, something like *Modern Times.* Chaplin, of course, is a certified great man of the cinema, and this is a role that produced a still—The Tramp being ground through the cogs of that monstrous machine—that decorates not just most picture books about the movies but plenty of social histories too, the perfect emblem of dehumanizing modernism. What most people know about it now, because they haven't actually sat through it in a long time—if ever—are its *longueurs.* They are also unaware of how Chaplin's didacticism curdles his comedy. And besides, the man is still famous for being famous—probably he deserves to have three films on this list, and never mind that this is surely the one that's soaking up the place that by rights belongs to Keaton, who is famous largely for his austerity, his lack of the quality that is salient in Chaplin's work, which is sentiment.

Big mistake, Buster. For sentiment was also a refuge gratefully resorted to by a lot of AFI voters. It comes in two varieties, romantic and liberal-humanist, both of which tend to leave indelible impressions on adolescents, since both encourage us to test the large, idealistic emotions that come over us at that age. This is the time when we begin to learn that you can love and lose, but that that's okay as long as you treasure the memory. *Casablanca* is the great example in this regard. *Wuthering Heights, A Place in the Sun, West Side Story, Dr. Zhivago,* and, yes, that largest of unexamined premises in all of American movie history, *Gone with the Wind,* are the less-great examples. What these movies do, if they catch us or we catch them at the right age, is introduce us to noble, grown-up emotions, show us that they can have devastating consequences, then soften the impact with a soaring rush of music and some close-ups of brave, trembly faces confronting the lonely future—or maybe with a suggestion that the lovers will meet again in the great bye and bye.

Liberal-humanist sentiment is trickier, and maybe more socially dangerous. The great example here—and, to my mind, the other great unexamined premise in our movie history—is *The Best Years of Our Lives*. It is a paradigm of the breed, which is also represented on the AFI list by *It's a Wonderful Life*, *Giant*, *To Kill a Mockingbird*, *Guess Who's Coming to Dinner*, *Network*, *Dances with Wolves*, and, of course, *Forrest Gump* (which is a kind of twofer in that it provides us with a lost but inspirational love story, too). As I perhaps don't need to tell you, the film, made in 1946, places in peril the decent values that sustained us during World War II, the ideas we thought we were fighting for—most notably the diminution of class distinctions—then lets everyone off the hook in the most time-honored Hollywood fashion, by letting them find or rediscover true love, which not only heals all wounds but promises an untroubled future. I sort of see why people liked it at the time—it was so reassuring—but I find it hard to fathom why they go on liking it. I know, if I were to be faithful to my own theory—I was just the right age to be knocked out by all this bourgeois agitprop—I should love it too. But to be transgressively honest about it, I've always liked *The Magic Christian*'s scheme of rereleasing *Best Years* with a subliminal insert shot of Harold Russell's hooks disappearing up Cathy O'Donnell's skirt.

5.

This proves that if you stick with it long enough, the critical impulse can conquer generational sentiments. What a good boy I am. And about to prove myself still better by committing something like generational treason. For I'm obliged to admit, finally, that a rough democratic justice has been served by the preponderance of movies from the fifties, sixties, and seventies among AFI's chosen few—even though these films' supporters also have some premises they ought to reexamine. I've never, for instance, entirely understood why the fifties crowd so profoundly adores *Vertigo*. The story is just too strained and coincidental for my tastes. I much prefer Hitchcock's great work of my impressionable years, *Notorious*—so much more tightly wound, and so bleakly, disorientingly misogynistic. Similarly I've never fully embraced *The Searchers*. It has always seemed to me that for all its pictorial beauty, for all the furious power of John Wayne's performance, John Ford, trying to escape full acknowledgment of the film's dark subtexts by his resorts to low comedy and unfelt romance, fatally damaged it. I much prefer the somber, doomed dutifulness he celebrated in *They Were Expendable*. He was operating there in country in which he was completely at home. But these are arguments worth having.

And there are plenty more where they came from. Maybe I can't make the same kind of emotional connection that younger people do with, say, *The Graduate* or *Midnight Cowboy*, *M*A*S*H*, or *One Flew Over the Cuckoo's Nest*; maybe I can't find anything but desperate confusion in *Apocalypse Now* or *The Deer Hunter* or sheer, mind-numbing incompetence in *Easy Riders*, but I can appreciate their power as generational touchstones. And I'm happy to concede them their positions on AFI's list because there are dozens of movies from the last three or four decades on it that I do connect with just as powerfully as the latecomers do—*Bonnie and*

Clyde, A Clockwork Orange, The Godfather films, *Chinatown, Annie Hall,* even such late-starters as *Unforgiven, Pulp Fiction,* and *Fargo.* These are all, to my mind, great films, the qualities of which must, or should be, evident to anyone who cares critically as well as generationally about movies. If you love an art form knowingly and open-mindedly, it's always easier to come forward appreciatively than it is to go backward in the same spirit, trying to reimagine the mind-sets, the passions, of times past. That's hard work—stoop labor for that benighted minority among us who are cursed by the critical impulse.

It may be that in the future when someone undertakes a survey of the movie past they should create something like the Baseball Hall of Fame's veterans' committee, that body of creaky, caring sportswriters who make sure deserving old-timers whose achievements have grown dim in the minds of younger voters are acknowledged in Cooperstown. My sense is that if the AFI had formed such a committee, and it had added perhaps a half dozen titles to its final results, almost all the serious—as opposed to the merely nostalgic—criticism it received would have been stilled.

We are, let's face it, two nations now as far as movies are concerned. That's the largest lesson we ought to take from the AFI poll. It's up to us—the minority—to keep the memory of *Trouble in Paradise* alive. And *Shanghai Express.* And, yes, *Air Force.* It's up to us tend the fringe of the garden, where *Detour* and *The Steel Helmet* and Budd Boetticher's westerns struggle to live on. It's also up to us to keep the academic deconstructionists—far more dangerous than the AFI's panel—from distancing us still further from the movie past with their incomprehensible prose and their distorting ideologies.

We are—if I may refer to a movie that, as far as I know, I'm the only person in the world to admire—like those people wandering around in the snow at the end of *Fahrenheit 451,* memorizing old books, keeping them alive for future generations, hoping they may someday come to realize their need for them. In a certain sense, activities like the **AFI** poll are irrelevant to this enterprise. But they may not be inimical to it, either, if they direct our argumentative attention to the past, if they tell us something about the state of our collective memory, our collective forgetfulness.

1998

King Vidor: Romantic Idealist

King Vidor was, I believe, the greatest silent film director America produced. His highest achievements in that form— *The Big Parade, The Crowd, Show People*—rank, in my estimation, with the best work of his European peers, the likes of Lang, Murnau, and Eisenstein. Indeed, it is the central irony of his career that he remained a great silent film director through all the years he made sound films. For his best work in what was really an entirely new (and for him uncomfortable) medium were essentially wordless passages that expressed, often with great simplicity and economy of means, profound emotions in movies that never achieved the sustained visual brilliance or emotional resonance of his great silents.

I am thinking of the magnificently orchestrated sequence in *Our Daily Bread* in which members of a farm cooperative succeed in bringing water to their parched fields; of the slaughter of the Indian village in *Northwest Passage*, a wrenching portrayal of what we have since learned to call genocide, which brilliantly undercuts what was surely meant

21

to be a heroic climax by the studio; of the gathering of the cowboys to confront the railroad as it is about to penetrate the McCanles ranch in *Duel in the Sun.*

Right up to the end Vidor continued to create these astonishments in movies that were often, in many respects, risible: the long montage in *The Fountainhead* where Patricia Neal's high-strung heiress recognizes her attraction to Gary Cooper's loopily idealistic architect, and the rape sequence in which he brutally acknowledges her attention; Rosa Moline's dying moment in *Beyond the Forest,* in which Bette Davis, as the mortally stricken woman, crawls toward the train, symbol of escape from small-town constraint, in which Vidor visualizes its engine, all backlit steam and impatient snortings, as an eerie hellmouth out of a medieval mystery play; Henry Fonda's idealistic Pierre wandering the battlefield in *War and Peace,* a pacifist registering his horror at the carnage man has wrought; the climactic battle sequence of *Solomon and Sheba,* in which the outnumbered Israelites blind the attacking Egyptians with sunlight reflected off their polished shields, and send them over a cliff to their doom.

These are all, despite their context—Andrew Sarris called Vidor's postwar years his "delirious" period—highly privileged cinematic moments, and in their vividness they take up permanent residence in one's memory—alongside a question that is as indelible as Vidor's imagery: how could a man who retained the power to create such glorious sequences deploy them in such dubious battles?

I can't answer that question definitely, but when I came to know King in the early seventies, interviewing him for a television show about his work, I began speculating about it. And, curiously, I've gone on doing so, off and on, ever since. For King was like his movies; once he entered your imaginative realm he was not easy to shake off.

One day King showed me a copy of one of F. Scott Fitzgerald's short-story collections, which the author had autographed and presented to him. He was proud of the fact that Fitzgerald had used him as the model for the doomed director in "Crazy Sundays," a character to whom Fitzgerald attributed the only "interesting temperament" among Americans plying that trade at that time in Hollywood. It was perhaps a slight exaggeration, but one could certainly say that his sensibility was unique. There was more idealism in him than one found in most American directors of his time. And more individuality. And more romanticism, too.

These traits were doubtless natural to him. But they were reinforced by his experience. He arrived in Hollywood a self-taught moviemaker who was a constantly learning autodidact in other disciplines, too—philosophy, history, the traditional arts. Yet within a decade he was MGM's leading director, allowed pretty much to choose his own projects by Irving Thalberg, its head of production, as long as he held power there. Not obliged to compromise, very often indulged because his films, even if they failed commercially, were deemed by Thalberg to be good for the studio's image, King Vidor was, at a comparatively early age—his middle thirties—a man living the American dream of success, and doing so without having to temper his beliefs in any significant way. In other words, his own life taught him there was profit—anyway, no significant downside—in idealism, and whatever disappointments came to him later, he never wavered from this lesson of his youth.

He was lucky in that his inherent values were particularly well-suited to the serious silent movie. This medium was not essentially a realistic one. Freed as no other fictional medium was from dialogue and its chief imperative, which was to make characters speak in demonstrably authentic tones, which in turn obliged them to naturalistic behavior, silent film was impelled to take flight from the realistic. In the hands of someone like King, whose natural bent was in this direction, a silent film could not help but transform reality, sometimes poeticizing it, sometimes rendering it in expressionistic terms.

The war in *The Big Parade* is not portrayed realistically. When John Gilbert's James departs for the front, with Renée Adorée's Melisande clutching at him, then clinging desperately to the truck that is bearing him away, we are not in the realm of naturalism; the expression of loss is much more primal, universal than that. And King was proud of the fact that the great image of his convoy, stretching in a straight line to infinity, was disapproved by the film's military advisers. In modern war no army would move so openly toward its objective. But King, of course, had something else in mind—an expression of the weight of events and materiel dwarfing more human concerns. Later, the terrifying advance through the woods, the movie soldiers moving to the metronomic beat of drum (unheard, of course, by the audience) evokes a dreamlike terror far more potent than the usual muck-and-mire representations of World War I trench warfare.

The Crowd goes much further, much more openly, toward expressionism. And achieves something few films have ever achieved. Its protagonists, John and Mary, are representational figures, their very names suggesting in their commonness that they are a modern Everyman and Everywoman, their tragedies the ones we all endure, their triumphs the small ones that briefly sustain all of us in our modest passages through life. And Vidor's style subtly yet perceptibly distorts their reality through his choice of angles, lenses, and the occasional forced-perspective setting, intensifying the symbolic nature of these characters and their little adventures. Yet they tear our hearts out. The devices that one might think would distance us from them somehow enhance our identification with them. The sheer alertness of the moviemaking, the tension of Vidor's aesthetic striving, imparts to this quotidian world a significance that mere realism could never achieve.

The same thing is true, in a different way, of *Show People*, that giddy tribute to the primitiveness and childishness of early Hollywood, captured only a historical millisecond before it disappeared completely. No movie has ever more sweetly evoked the eternal romance of moviemaking, the innocence and openness with which show people strive to please, or their infinite distractability. This is a comic poem, but a poem no less than *The Crowd* in the way that it compresses and forces up experience, transcending the reality it evokes but does not slavishly copy.

Sound film is, of course, a prosaic form, not a poetic one. And the coming of sound changed all the equations of moviemaking. The new stars of this new medium spoke in the accents of the city's streets, and in Depression America a new toughness of spirit, an air of realism—eye-level camera, ping-pong dialogue, a certain briskness of pace—was prized. It wasn't true realism, of course. It was at its best tough-guy (and tough-gal) realism, that is to say, realism with a stratum of sentiment hidden not too deeply beneath its hard surfaces (see almost any Cagney movie).

This was not a time in which King Vidor felt entirely comfortable. He had no gift for gritty dialogue; the woozier poetics of the intertitle were much more to his liking. He had no great appreciation for realistic acting; the more general-ized expression of emotions required by the silent screen suited him better (which may be why there is so much of what seems to be overacting by the divas and heldentenors of his later works). He had no great love of realistic settings; he was always looking for the transforming angle on them (see the other great sequence in *Beyond the Forest*—Davis's drunken wanderings in Chicago, which King turns into a nightmarish night-town, its denizens clutching evilly at her). Though he eventually worked in most of sound film's major dramatic genres, he was never entirely comfortable within their con-ventions, was always trying to break out of them in some spec-tacular and interesting way, which is probably the chief

25

impetus for the sequences I listed earlier—all of which derive their power not from the values intrinsic to the script in which they were embedded, but to visual values King imparted to them on the set or the location or in the editing room, where he could work his untrammeled magic on them. When his visual imagination failed him, or the script proved utterly intractable, his work was often, ironically, flatter, more static, than that of less gifted directors.

He often, indeed, gave the impression of being impatient or bored by what he was doing, never quite understanding what was so important about realism when there were so many more interesting ways you could explore the world if you used this medium more metaphorically. Thus unengaged, he would at best manage his material in a rather straight-ahead fashion, wasting no time trying to shade it so its banalities were less evident. Sometimes his lack of duplicity worked for him. The over-the-top sentimentality of *The Champ* is curiously affecting. So is the all-encompassing ambition of *An American Romance* (King was good with roughnecks like Wallace Beery and Brian Donlevy, who starred in the latter film). It was about an immigrant inventor-dreamer who loses his way and is crushed by the very industrial system he helped create. Released in 1944, it creates an oddly mixed effect. On the one hand it seems to celebrate the might of American industry, the seemingly irresistible power of the entrepreneurial imagination, which was then in the process of winning the war for us. But the ambiguous fate of its protagonist—shut out of the company he built, and bitter about it, he comes back to aid in its war effort—may reflect some of Vidor's own feeling. For was he not, by this time, a man whose originality was partially suppressed by a system he had helped build but in which he was no longer a dominant figure?

By and large King Vidor in the sound era—which, after all, consumed most of his years in the business—was a restless and, I suspect, a dissatisfied man, subverting (without quite knowing he was doing so) the official values of his industry, the stated intent of many of his movies. Crazy Sundays! No. Rather, a succession of crazy evenings at the movies, in which there would suddenly arise out of a flat and barren landscape some magical edifice—and for a moment or two we would discover that we weren't in Kansas anymore (King directed a couple of weeks on *The Wizard of Oz,* and one can't help but think that if he had spent longer with the film its imagery might have matched its sentimental force).

Sarris wrote that Vidor's later work is no less deserving of honor than that of his "humanistic museum period" (i.e., the silent classics), and I think he is right, though my reasons are different. In the end, memory is the great deconstructer of movies. As the years pass, the overall design of all but the most beloved (and thus the most often reencountered) movies tends to fade. The plots begin to elude us, the dialogue we thought we'd never forget is, in fact, forgotten, or we improve upon it, remembering what should have been said instead of what was actually said. But the images remain, burned into consciousness, transcending their occasions, their original storytelling functions. And those King gave us in great plenitude. Again to quote Sarris: "He created more great moments and fewer great films than any director of his rank."

It could be argued, I suppose, that in some of his later movies King developed figures that projected some of his own unexpressed feelings. Rosa Moline and Ruby Gentry, for instance, are women of pride, energy and intelligence, trapped by dismal circumstances (and their own distaste for subtle maneuver) and desperate to escape them. Perhaps King felt the same way about a Hollywood that obliged him to suppress his natural imagistic gifts in favor of the mere professionalism that came awkwardly to him. Certainly one can see why Howard Roark, the unappreciated architectural visionary of *The Fountainhead,* appealed to him. Perhaps, by the time he made this film, Hollywood had become King's stone quarry, a

place to toil honestly, honorably, while he awaited another opportunity to assert his singularity. Perhaps he envied Roark
the mad courage he summons to blow up one of his buildings
when it is compromised by client demands.

Be that as it may, the women of these films were unquestionably more like silent-picture heroines than sound-film
leading ladies—full of self-destructive passions expressed
with hysterical openness, but preferable (if only as entertainment) to the tight-lipped sufferings of Jane Wyman, for example, endured in the "women's pictures" that Douglas Sirk
was making at around the same time. There is, finally, something endearing about Vidor's sometimes snarling, sometimes
seductively writhing vixens. And something irresistibly compelling in the feverish compassion King brought to their stories.

It is said that in his later years King became a devotee of
the anti-collectivist, radical libertarian philosophy that *The
Fountainhead* celebrated. I don't know that for certain, because we never talked political philosophy. But if he was—and
he was without question a resolute anti-Stalinist—I suspect it
was yet another of the abstractions that he enjoyed turning
over in his mind, playing with in his curious, quizzical, somewhat childlike way. For he remained in his person a sweet-
spirited man, humane and tolerant and unlike many of his
contemporaries (whom I interviewed at the same time) eagerly—almost boyishly—engaged in the world generally, the
movies in particular (though at that time he had not worked
in them for some twelve years). He did not think the movies
had declined since his day. Nor did he think his day had been
an especially golden one. Off camera he remarked to me that
if he had known people would go on looking at his films for so
many years, he would have made them better.

Most interesting of all, and again in contrast to many of
his directorial contemporaries, far from thinking the movies'
best days were behind him, King was convinced that the best

was still to come. He was working (through the American Film Institute, as I recall) on a short, experimental film, and he told me that he was also looking forward to seeing *Deep Throat* on the grounds that he hoped, from what he'd heard, that the porn film might help edge movies toward a freer representation of sexuality on the screen.

About that, about his generally optimistic feeling about where the movies were headed—this was the early seventies, remember, when young Hollywood, inspired by developments in the foreign cinema, was astir with hope for the medium— he was wrong. But this was a man who liked to talk about how eagerly he had studied the work of Eisenstein and the Russian greats of the silent film, how much the UFA films of Fritz Lang had meant to him and how he had tried to incorporate something of their spirit and vision in his work. You couldn't blame him for hoping that a new generation might now be profiting from the examples being offered by a new generation of foreign filmmakers.

When my series of director profiles aired on PBS in 1973–1974, I received a note from Woody Allen that was pleasingly complimentary about the programs, and contained this aside: "I liked King Vidor best." Despite the fact that the subjects that interest Allen could not be further from those that preoccupied King Vidor, the young director had obviously responded to the older man's romantic-idealistic-individualistic spirit and to his indomitable, curiously inspiring, and very sympathetic nature. More than that, I surmise, Allen saw in him something of what he saw—continues to see—in his beloved Bergman: metaphysical striving, we might call it, a desire to push the cinema into realms where it does not easily or comfortably live. As the years drift on, one begins to see, despite all the grand authorial posturings of our directors, how rare such aspirations are. And how necessary they are to this hasty, careless, self-regarding medium. In the end, I think, it doesn't much matter how we judge their individual works, or how much it "disappoints" some people who wish they had gone on doing what they had so pleasingly done in the days of their early acclaim. The important thing these rare figures do is keep faith in the possibilities they dream for their medium, risking absurdity (and contumely) in their pursuit of a sublimity they can't quite explain to the rest of us—or perhaps even to themselves.

1993

Garbo: The Legend as Actress

At some point in the early forties, Greta Garbo and I decided to go our separate ways. Her decision was apparently a conscious one. Mine, alas, was entirely unconscious. But both were consequential acts, for both had powerful inferential implications for our personal lives, for the history of the movies, and for social history as well.

Yes, I'm joking. For though, by chance, I had an extra's part in an insignificant scene in her later life, my role in this essay is intended to be symbolic. I see myself as typical of her latter-day audience. I imagine that by consulting my responses to her image after she left the screen, I can say something useful to readers—by now the vast majority—who, like me, know her almost entirely as a legend. Those of us who were not present at the creation of her screen self have to reimagine the singular hold she exercised on an influential minority audience—her hold on the American mass audience was never all that firm—in the 1920s and 1930s. We have to do that, of course, with any star who does not make an impression on us when we are most innocent, therefore most open to the raw power of a screen image. But her silence and withdrawal—and the lack of resonance most of her films have for a modern audience—makes that task peculiarly difficult in Garbo's case.

One of the legends entangled in her legend is that after the critical and commercial failure of *Two-Faced Woman,* a humiliated Garbo abruptly and finally abandoned the screen, the better to embrace the reclusive life that had always, obviously, held a vast appeal for her. But that drastically simplifies the case. As her most conscientious biographer, Barry Paris, makes clear, her withdrawal from the screen was, at least initially, tactical. She did need to nurse her wounded pride, but she was also aware of two more significant matters: that her screen character and the kind of movies in which she played that figure had been drifting out of style in the United States for some years, and that the European audience, on which her pictures depended for profitability, was now temporarily lost to her as a result of America's entrance into World War II, which occurred just weeks before the release of what turned out to be her last film.

In these circumstances, as Paris suggests, it was logical to take a hiatus. She was only thirty-six, the war couldn't last forever, and the time could be well spent exploring new options. It is not clear from the historical record if she thought all this out coolly and rationally. But no matter—it was a bold decision, one that few performers have ever been brave enough to make. Most retirements from stage or screen—even temporary ones—are forced, despite the face-saving publicity that is put about. In any case, it is hard to imagine Garbo realizing the most important implication of her decision, namely that she was seizing total control of her image, eliminating from the process of tending and trumpeting it the studio functionaries who had participated in its creation. She would now be obliged to test whether or not stardom could be converted into a pure idea. Or perhaps one should say, a pure ideal. She was in effect asking, could it be kept alive by *not* working at her profession, by *not* submitting to the hubbub and degradations of performance, publicity, and promotion, but simply by relying upon what David Thomson once called "the self-perpetuating mechanics of stardom"? And she was doing so at a moment when that mechanism was wholly owned by the studios, with the era of star-driven independent production still more than a decade in the future.

Of this, of course, I knew nothing. I was coming to the movies in 1941 just as Garbo was leaving them. I might have seen *Two-Faced Woman* that year, but it was not the sort of thing on which a hearty American boy of the time would choose to spend his weekly movie dime. Romantic comedies involving upper-class swells were not for us. Romance was a matter to be avoided and, if accidentally encountered, something to be hooted at. Comedy, for us, was farcical (Abbott and Costello made their first appearance on the box-office top-ten list that year) or wisecracking (Bob Hope was high on the list, too). We were also into action—westerns, crime stories, and, with war drawing near, the military adventure and espionage tales then starting to proliferate. To us, Greta Garbo was a rumor circulated by our parents, her "mystery" subsumed in the all-encompassing mystery of adulthood. Like cocktails and cigarettes, sweetbreads and the "Voice of Firestone" radio program, she was a taste we imagined—if we imagined anything at all about her—we would acquire when we "grew up" and attained the rights, privileges, and fancies of that remarkable status.

I'm sorry she decided not to wait for us. But she may have sensed that we were unlikely to be worthy of her. And that she was unlikely to survive, on screen, in a form worthy of her legend. Indeed, as I look back on her movies now, consciously attempting to isolate and analyze the essence of her appeal, it occurs to me that she had been drifting away from us for something like a decade, so out of tune was she, were they, with the prevailing spirit of American movies, for that matter, of American life, in the 1930s. Another way of putting this is to say that she was at this point shrewder about her past and the limited prospects it proposed for her future as an actress than anyone else was, including MGM, the independent producers who, over the next decade, continued to tempt her with projects, and the press, which avidly speculated about these enterprises as word of them leaked out.

What no one—except, conceivably, the actress herself—could see (or perhaps accept) was the possibility that her screen character would be totally irrelevant by the time the war ended. During that conflict young Americans would go to Europe by the millions. After the war we would continue to go there, as tourists, in even greater numbers. And we would see that it didn't look like the world she had inhabited on screen, would find no females of her sort there. Even if we did not travel abroad, the European movies we imported showed us in the persons of Bardot, Loren, and their ilk an erotic exoticism of a kind quite different from hers. There was now an exemplary overtness—a boldness, symbolized by the willingness of these younger women to do skin scenes—that was quite different from her more romantic sexuality.

But these changes merely made obvious what was implicit throughout Garbo's career in sound pictures. For during the eleven years from her first, somewhat belated talkie, *Anna Christie* in 1930, to her final film, the strain of finding vehicles that were at once suitable for her and reasonable commercial propositions was obvious to at least a few contemporary observers. Graham Greene, for example, serving a five-year term as a movie reviewer, twice likened the prospect of attending a Garbo movie to picking up a work by Carlyle—not something to thrill the heart with anticipatory joys. "Retarded," was his word for the typical Garbo sound film, as it awaited "the slow consummation of her noble adulteries." If that was true for a man of Greene's sophisticated and patient interest in sin, sinning, and sinners, think of the impatience such movies would have engendered in us of the forties generation untutored in the high romantic style of the silent film, the manner most of her sound productions tried to ape. The movies now featured women who were almost uniformly seen as peppy good sports, loyally, chastely standing by men deeply preoccupied by the military necessity and by their own problematic heroism. Later, to be sure, the movies introduced a more fatal sort of femme, the spiderish creature luring males, often seen as psychologically weakened by the war, to their doom in *films noir*. But they were trampy types, and the motive for their dark doings was always money, never love. If they usually came to ends as gloomy as Garbo's generally were, they uniformly deserved them. One cannot imagine her playing one of these roles—nothing noble about their adulteries—any more than one can conceive of her as a pinup girl.

All of these circumstances support the logic of her withdrawal from the movies, even if it is a somewhat suspect *ex post facto* logic. And they somewhat demystify it as well. Is it possible to do the same for her screen image? Is it possible, at last, to blow away that cloud of gaseous speculation, much of it generated by intellectuals of a temperament less brisk than Greene's, and more anxious to claim their iota of immortality by definitively solving her famous mystery? Is it possible, in short, and at this late date, to see her plain? Not entirely, perhaps, but it is a worthwhile exercise nonetheless.

She was always a creature of withdrawal, of silence—thus, ideally, of the silents—an actress who from the first moments she appeared on the screen defined herself by her refusals. This was an inescapable condition for her, a point that is reinforced by all the biographical delvings into her childhood and adolescence that we have.

She was not astonishingly beautiful in her formative

years—"nice looking," one thinks, glancing at photographs of the young Garbo. The chubbiness of her early years had to be melted away by maturity before the classical fineness of features, inherited from her father, could emerge. Her body, long, slender, uncurvaceous, was her mother's genetic contribution, as was her odd gait, rather mannish, rather predatory (at least to some observers). In other words, there was nothing about her appearance in her early years that would inspire notable confidence or outgoingness. And, as she would later testify, the poverty of those years, encouraging withdrawal into dreams of success, obviously made its contribution to the formation of her essential shyness.

Yes, shyness. After so many decades of complex and fanciful writing about Garbo, one hesitates to introduce consideration of such a commonplace condition into the discussion. But it was, indeed, the most basic element in Garbo's character, both off the screen and on. It is a basic element, ironically enough, in the characters of many performers. Film is the perfect medium for performers so afflicted: you can work in near privacy, surrounded by the familiar, supportive faces of a relatively small cast and crew—your trusted colleagues—and you do not have to face an unpredictable audience of strangers night after night as the stage actor does. Garbo was notorious for her insistence on closed sets and on working with people she had come to trust (Clarence Brown, a man of no more than routine gift, directed six of her movies; William Daniels photographed no less than eighteen of them).

Equally important, the screen performer is free to study her work as long and as often as she likes, for film is, among other things, a mirror, capable of reflecting back its subjects' self-images. Actually it is an improvement on a mirror, for it retains those images permanently, permitting one to study them at leisure—for a lifetime, if you like. As in fact Garbo did: after her withdrawal from pictures, she was known to book screening rooms at New York's Museum of Modern Art in order to run her old pictures, and, later, to watch them on television.

Returning to her first feature, *The Saga of Gosta Berling,* for purposes of his "Portrait" of Garbo (1980), Alexander Walker, the English critic, found her "somnambulistic power" already fully developed. Drifting through a garden, gliding through the halls of a castle, lit only by the lamp she was carrying, she suggested, in Walker's words, "an infinity of emotion while registering only abstraction." Perhaps "self-absorption" might have been a slightly better word, but no matter, the point is made. Even at the beginning of her career she felt no obligation to the reigning traditions of movie acting, which in silent days necessarily involved the physicalization of very basic emotions in the broadest imaginable terms. Nor did she feel an obligation to the lunatic narratives of the films in which she appeared, these tales of forbidden lusts and awful retributions—no obligation, that is, to the conventional hyperactivity of their plots. Her business was to illuminate the effect of all those comings and goings on her "spiritual interior," as Walker would have it.

Narrative, one feels compelled to add, is a public matter, a composition of events even humble journalism, not to mention routine moviemaking, is capable of adequately rendering. It is also an essentially masculine concern. Men are always hurrying heedlessly past the emotional nuances of a story in order to reach its point. They want to know who won and who lost—in love or war, in sports or business or politics. Women, as Garbo never tired of reminding us, prefer to linger over the state of their feelings, are quite willing to risk everything they have in order to experience the rush and glow, the fervor and avidity, of the romantically heightened moment. To experience such moments *is* the point of the story. And if the narrative conclusion of experiencing them is death or disgrace or poverty, so be it.

This escape from narrative, which also implies an escape

from the ruling generic conventions of the movies when Garbo came to them, is of enormous significance in analyzing the grasp she exerted on both the popular mind and the critical imagination. Until her arrival, women in the movies were always the playthings of plot, their characters determined by its requirements, their fates worked out by its usually melodramatic, often implausible, always conventionally moral dictates. They were good (Lillian Gish or Mary Pickford) or they were bad (the vamps, from Theda Bara onward), and everyone they encountered in the course of the stories they appeared in were as conscious of their moral condition as they were themselves—and so was the audience. It was the fate of the good woman to assert her goodness against all manner of assaults until every challenge had been defeated. It was the fate of the bad woman to assert her badness until her victims recognized her evil intent and she received her comeuppance—no exceptions allowed, no special dispensations permitted.

Until Garbo claimed the right to both. Oh, all right, she would accept whatever punishment plot and morality demanded of her character. But it was a matter of supreme indifference to her. Indeed, she always seemed to know instinctively, from the start, that she would eventually have to pay the price of death, disgrace, or exile for her passions. Therefore these final exactions came as no shock to her, and so the idea of a last-minute recantation never seemed to enter her mind. She merely smiled—a secretive, ironic smile—at the final fadeout, and accepted whatever fate morality and the screenwriters doled out to her.

We can now see that this acceptance of fate's blows was a remarkable achievement in integrative psychology as well as the actor's art. For consider what we know about the two most significant men in her life, her father and her discoverer and first director, Mauritz Stiller. The former was a simple, sickly man, given to drink and though apparently affectionate

enough with his children, not an entirely trustworthy reposi-
tory for a young girl's love. His death, when Garbo was fourteen, can be seen as a kind of desertion, and her account of her
reaction to it, reprinted in the Paris biography, makes one
think she saw it as such. She claimed to have cried herself to
sleep every night for a year and to have fought a constant desire to visit his grave to make sure he had not been mistakenly
buried alive.

As for Stiller, who was something of a surrogate father to
her, his masculine failures were equally serious: he could not
defend her against MGM's rather crass and often preemptory
management of her career; he could not defend himself
against the studio's unmanning contempt for his gifts; he
abruptly deserted her in America in order to try to pick up
the pieces of his shattered career in Europe; whereupon he
died, if anything more untimely than Garbo's father had.
After such experiences, cynicism, and of a rather coldly self-
protective sort—true vampishness—might have become her
romantic essence. And there was in her silent films an element
of what Alistair Cooke once called "disdain." For her to have
evolved a screen character based on the opposite quality—on
compassion—to have become by the time she was making
such later sound films as *Anna Karenina* and *Camille* the
great exemplar of a near existential acceptance of the pain
and loss one must absorb in the name of love, is nothing short
of astonishing.

Assuming we are correct to believe that she was drawing
deeply on her own history, her own feelings, to project this
complex of emotions, we may perhaps have stumbled on a
simple, partial solution to the enigma of her early retirement.
She spoke often of the exhaustion that visited her when she
was making a film, which is odd considering her physical stamina. Obviously this was psychological in origin, the result of
intense confrontation with herself in order to play her parts.
It is akin to the debilitation that modern method actors like

39

Brando have spoken of, and it may be responsible in his case—as in hers—both for the self-protective evasiveness of some of his work and for his withdrawal from the acting that seriously taxed him.

Be that as it may—and obviously other factors were at work in her—what she was doing may well strike us, from today's perspective, as unremarkable, as no more than good, realistic, psychologically acute acting. We now see it all the time. But in the context of her moment, it struck critics and the ordinary audience with something like revolutionary force. Pola Negri and the rest of the dark, vampish crowd, the only types to whom Garbo could logically be compared, took things much harder. The effects of their ups and downs were visibly manifested in unmistakable terms. Garbo couldn't, and wouldn't, indulge herself so broadly.

This was the source of her mystery. Very simply, no one had seen anything like her before on the screen. And the initial response to her was puzzled. Reviewing her first American film, *The Torrent,* Richard Watts, Jr., wrote, "She seems an excellent and attractive actress, with a surprising propensity for looking like Carol Dempster, Norma Talmadge, Zasu Pitts and Gloria Swanson in turn." Having thus misdefined the indefinable, he added: "That does not mean she lacks a manner of her own, however." With that breathtaking analysis behind him, he turned in haste (and obvious relief) to the work of her costar, Ricardo Cortez.

There is, at least, a commendable modesty in such retreats from judgment. For after *The Torrent,* the torrent—of unhappiness for her screen characters, of critical guff about the sublimity of effects. For the remainder of the silent era, and most of the rest of her career as well, she was condemned either to a life of adultery or to wistful dreams of it. In the former category are *The Temptress, Flesh and the Devil, Love* (an adaptation, but with a happy ending, of *Anna Karenina*), *A Woman of Affairs.* In the latter we may list *The Kiss, Wild*

Orchids, and *The Single Standard.* In only two of her American silent films did she avoid this fate: *The Mysterious Lady* and *The Divine Woman.* But the former involves her in a sort of symbolic adultery. She plays a spy who must finally betray her spymaster (or husband surrogate, if you will) because she falls in true love with the soldier he has assigned her to seduce. It appears that only in *The Divine Woman* (no print or negative of which now exists) does she avoid messy romantic entanglements. In it she plays a Bernhardt-like actress who rises from the peasantry to greatness on the Parisian stage. But even this story, as almost all Garbo stories had to, involves a renunciation: she must give up the stage career for which she struggled so hard in order to claim permanently the man she loves.

To be sure, her talking-picture debut was something of an anomaly. In *Anna Christie* her surroundings were uncharacteristically inelegant. And all of her bad behavior (as a prostitute back home in Minnesota), occurred before the main action of this adaptation of Eugene O'Neill's lugubrious and sometimes risible drama opened (in a New York dockside saloon). But from here to *Ninotchka* she continued to suffer in her well-established, increasingly old-fashioned way. If she was required less often to die for her sins—she did so only in *Mata Hari,* in her second try at *Anna Karenina,* this time with Tolstoy's tragic denouement intact, and in *Camille*—her renunciations are legion.

She gave up a young clergyman (*Romance*), a young diplomat (*Inspiration*), and Napoleon himself (*Conquest*) rather than blight their promising careers. To maintain her better self, she gave up John Gilbert in order to claim a throne (*Queen Christina*), John Barrymore in order to maintain her career as a ballet dancer (*Grand Hotel*), and George Brent in order to save her marriage and fight a plague (*The Painted Veil*). In this decade she was allowed only two more-or-less happy reclamations: in *Susan Lenox (Her Fall and Rise)*, she was permitted to flee an arranged marriage with a brute and find happiness in Clark Gable's arms; in *As You Desire Me* (based on a work by Pirandello, no less) she was an amnesiac who recovers her memory and, as a result, her first, true love.

Are we talking tosh? Yes, we are largely talking tosh. Though, of course, the productions were all first-class in the MGM manner. That is to say, the decor, the costuming, the hairdressing were ravishing, much of the acting talent the best that money could buy. The air of *luxe* surrounding these productions was quite overpowering. But the scripts were either smooth reductions of complex sources or, conversely, polish jobs, in which subliterate forms and ideas were toned up, given a little literary glow. A screenwriter at MGM in those days was a person charged with creating the rich, creamy centers for a line of assorted chocolates, which were, in turn, lavishly packaged by directors who knew what Mr. Thalberg and Mr. Mayer wanted, which was no expression of individuality on their part but rather restatements of the one great message this organization wanted to impart to the public in those days: that it, unlike its rivals, spared no expense to please its customers.

In the broad flow of American film history, MGM in the thirties and forties represented a cultural and intellectual backwater, saved from total stagnation by the forceful personalities of its stars and by the occasional freshening influence of talents acquired after they had developed elsewhere (the Marx Brothers, for example, or Spencer Tracy and Katharine Hepburn, or Ernst Lubitsch, who enters Garbo's story too late). Concentrating heavily on adaptations of second-rate literature, historical spectacles, and romantic melodramas, the studio did not attract the best directors of the day, the liveliest writing talents, the craftsmen for whom the coming of sound released enormous creative energies and whose work gave the best American movies of the time their fizz and spunk. They were at Paramount doing light, sophisticated romance, at Warner Bros., where something of the fast-paced spirit of an urbanizing America was caught in brash, darkly witty melodramas. Columbia, economically downtrodden, had no compunctions in taking a chance on Capra's social commentary comedies and the screwball cycle, since it had no dignity to defend. RKO, the other economic fringe-dweller, was an important contributor to that cycle, and like Columbia it became a place where independent spirits like Howard Hawks, George Stevens, Leo McCarey, and, ultimately, briefly, Orson Welles, could find shelter for their quirky projects and singular talents.

Out of this ferment which was highly verbal, in response to the new sound technology, a new woman—usually a working woman—smart of style and of mouth, able to hold her own with man dialogically and sexually, emerged. She might be brassy like Harlow, ironic like Colbert, dizzy like Lombard, wry and elegant like Dunne, brainy like Hepburn, but she was never a victim—not for long, anyway. Even Dietrich, in a sense the new era's successor to Garbo, since she too projected a slightly androgynous subtext, stated her desires with a boldness and wit that would have been quite foreign to Garbo. Indeed, the movement of the typical Dietrich movie was not from virtue to fall but from fall to regeneration through a new or reclaimed love, quite different from that of the typical Garbo picture. Over at Warner Bros., Bette Davis suffered many a sad fate, but there was something feverish, openly neurotic about the way she dealt with circumstances that seemed more modern (even when she was in period costume, as she often was), and a lot more entertaining than Garbo's way.

That Garbo continued to give herself intensely to her films, that she was often effective in them, is not in question here. But contemplating the full Hollywood context of the 1930s leads one to contemplate what now seems to be the central issue of Garbo's career as an actress (as opposed to her career as a celebrity). Namely, would she have prospered better had she not been so closely bound to **MGM**? Is it possible that under contract elsewhere, or as a freelancer, she might have found projects that would have extended her range, stimulated her imagination, thus encouraging her to lengthen her career? Is it possible, most important of all, she would have obtained immortality as an artist rather than as a curiosity, a phenomenon, if she had not been locked into films that were already anachronisms as they were being made?

These questions are not simply answered. However unhappy Garbo was with **MGM**'s management, it was mainly money, rarely roles, that sent her into sulks and suspensions. And if the studio's father figures sometimes distressed her, the rest of its "family" was, as we've seen, invaluable to her. Moreover, given that self-absorption which only grew more intense the longer she resided as a stranger in a strange land, it is doubtful that she was aware of the alternatives available to her elsewhere. Or, even if she was, that she would have explored them.

For one cannot help but speculate that the silliness of her movies may have served what she imagined—with what degree of conscious calculation it is impossible to say—a larger purpose, which was utterly to dominate her texts and contexts. This began with the phenomenon we have already observed, her lack of full emotional obligation to her films' story lines. But it finally went much further than that. There was literally nothing in these pictures to distract the audience from contemplation of "The Divine" (as the catchphrase of the day, doubtless adapted from the title of her 1928 silent film, had it). All their great moments are unequivocally hers. And excepting *Ninotchka,* no line from any of the screenplays ever permanently attached itself to memory, and no strong directorial hand ever asserted itself in her movies. No male lead or, for that matter, powerful supporting performance—with the possible exception of the all-star *Grand Hotel*—ever challenged her domination of the screen. It was, seemingly, a perfect arrangement. she evaded all responsibility for the twaddle surrounding her, yet all eyes were always focused on her, because there was no place else they could profitably rest for very long.

As a result, her career became, finally, a little anthology of treasured moments, assertions of her "genius" against a lowering background of mediocrity. One recalls the communion scene in *Flesh and the Devil* where, presented with the chalice, she solemnly turns the cup so that her lips will touch it at just the place her secret lover's lips recently vacated. Or the moment in *A Woman of Affairs* when, sick unto death, she physicalizes forbidden passion by embracing a bouquet of flowers exactly as she would the lover who sent them. Of course, the moment in *Queen Christina* when she wanders the room she has shared with her lover, touching the objects it contains, committing them to tactile memory because she knows she will never see them—or him—again, is justly celebrated. And *Anna Karenina* is full of such moments, wonderful bits of business at a ball, at a race track, on a croquet ground, as slowly she acknowledges the fact that she has fallen into a forbidden love. Then, too, because the renunciation she is called upon to make in this film is of her son, her scenes with him (he is played by Freddie Bartholomew) have a natural poignancy which she realizes through the most delicate playing. A typical moment: she is in a garden, where her son disappears up an alley of shrubs in one direction while her lover, Vronsky, played by Fredric March, disappears in the opposite direction, and the camera catches and holds her, twisting and turning amongst the greenery, a befuddled animal, her conflict symbolized by the anguished flutter of her movements. Her next film, *Camille,* is similarly rich in unforgettable actor's moments, the most notable of which is perhaps the one in which, to drive away her young lover, Armand (Robert Taylor), she pretends decadent attachment to an older man. The way she throws her head back in wild laughter, the way she sustains her merriment, at once persuading the youth of its genuineness and the rest of us onlookers of its brave falsity, the way she brings it to near-hysterical pitch but does not lose control of it, constitutes great and subtle acting.

Camille's director, the wise and tasteful George Cukor, would later comment that it was precisely her refusal to play the title courtesan as a victim, her insistence that the character be the self-aware author of her own misery, that redeemed the film from its origins as romantic popular nineteenth-century fiction (and drama). He believed that Garbo, like a handful of other great stars, had an instinct—an instinct supported by the medium's great tools, the close-up and montage—that enabled her to find, as he put it, "the human truths, the human experience" that always exist beneath highly conventionalized material, no matter how hoary it is, how laughable it may seem to literary sophisticates.

So it seemed at the time, certainly. Her public, which had grown up with her, or were growing up with her, found her mere presence sufficient to animate a respectful attention to antiquated dramas and to an antiquated vision of a woman's lot they might have hooted off the screen if another actress had attempted them. They were joined with her in the agreeable, unspoken conspiracy that she bore no responsibility for the nonsense in which she habitually appeared, and that her presence on the screen in anything at all conferred on the vehicle dignity enough to make it worth their time. In any case, they could be pretty certain that she would for a shot here, a sequence there, transcend whatever it was that had brought her out of her famous seclusion, them out of their houses.

In this view, the best critics concurred. Or maybe they invented it—impossible to say at this late date. In any case, if one goes back to sample the written record of her career, one discovers an astonishing lack of specificity about the films themselves. More often than not, in reading the typical review of a Garbo film, one is left in the dark as to what, precisely, its story might have been. But about the actress herself there are always several yards of dubious generalities.

One day in 1932, for example, Stark Young, unquestionably the leading drama critic of his day, lowered his eye from contemplation of the then-lofty (in its own mind, anyway) theater and fixed it upon Garbo. Possibly influenced by her appearance that year in film adapted from a certifiably great writer (the Pirandello piece), he found that "She presents an instance of the natural and right progress of the poetic: from the concrete toward ideality." What he meant is what we have just been talking about, that air of removal from the contexts in which she was presented. "Elevation" and "distillation" were also words that occurred to Young in contemplating her work, and he spoke of "the remote entity of her spirit, a certain noble poignancy in her presence" as well as "a sense of mood that is giving and resisting at the same time." All of this, he claimed, combined to "defeat and break down the poor little common theory of naturalness and prose method" which ruled the reviewing of theater and movies at that time.

Young established, in this piece, what amounts to the main line of professional Garbo-watching. Some two decades later, Kenneth Tynan was still saying the same thing, though in livelier, more sexually charged prose: "What, when drunk, one sees in other women, one sees in Garbo sober. She is woman apprehended with all the pulsating clarity of one of Aldous Huxley's mescaline jags. To watch her is to achieve direct, cleansed perception of something which, like a flower or a fold of silk, is raptly, unassertively and beautifully itself. Nothing intrudes between her and the observer except the observer's neuroses." And so forth, with the usual dismissal of her roles ("Through what hoops, when all is said and done, she has been put . . ."). Around the same time, Roland Barthes brought to our subject his highest mandarin manner, that uniquely Gallic blend of shrewd observation and woolly generality. Garbo, he wrote, "belongs to that moment in cinema when capturing the human face still plunged audiences into the deepest ecstasy . . . when the face represented a kind of absolute state of the flesh, which could be neither reached nor renounced." She offered, he wrote, "a sort of platonic ideal of the human creature . . . descended from a heaven where all things are formed and perfected in the clearest light." And so on, with no clear indication that he has lately seen anything of hers but a rerelease of *Queen Christina*.

We might term writing of this sort "impractical criticism," criticism as detached from contexts as its subject was. It does more than free Garbo from responsibility to her vehicles; it implies that no vehicle made by man could ever be worthy of her. Tynan, to be sure, moons regretfully that she never essayed Masha in *Three Sisters*, but there is something obligatory in the remark. It partakes of the ritual regret men of the theater, even as late as the 1950s, felt they had to express over the way movies wasted and misused talent, as if the stage were never guilty of that sin.

Gush of this sort has its dangers. Especially for its recipients. The more their singularity is insisted upon, the more they tend to isolate themselves, not only from the world but from the original sources of their talent. And the more abstract their work tends to become, the more detached from reality. This was both true and untrue of Garbo's work in sound pictures, and a certain irony is to be found in this dichotomy. It is certainly true, as Barthes observed, that as the years wore on, her makeup tended to grow thicker and whiter, more masklike, which reinforced everyone's sense of her as woman idealized. At the same time, though, there grew in her work, in her attitudes, that new compassion that we spoke of earlier. So far as I know, the first critic to remark on this fact was a highly practical one, Alistair Cooke, doing some youthful time as a weekly movie reviewer. Engaging with her 1935 *Anna*

Karenina, he found not the "old, bold slick disdain" of her previous work but rather "a sort of amused grandeur." In this film, he thought, she became "a tolerant goddess" wrapping everyone "in a protective tenderness." He added, acutely: "She sees not only her own life, but everyone else's, before it has been lived."

Fatalism, Cooke thought this might be; knowledgeability of a simpler, more instinctively acquired kind, I think it might have been. He seems to have thought it might have come upon her of a sudden in this film; I think I detect hints of it even in such otherwise goofy enterprises as *Mata Hari.* But it doesn't really matter. It is there, it is the good side of maturity (as opposed to makeup masks), and it is surely the quality that enabled her to achieve the transcendence that Cukor spoke of in *Camille,* for is it not precisely "a protective tenderness" that she extends to Armand in that film?

It is also a source of frustration. For this achievement of art is swaddled, muffled, in yards of period costume, trivialized by the fake historicism and the turgid literariness of the films in which Garbo appeared, and further distanced by the growing Garbo legend. As early as 1929, in *The Single Standard,* a subtitle had her repeating a variation on the "I-want-to-be-alone" theme that she had first enunciated to importunate newsmen who cornered her in New York in the course of one of her trips home to Sweden. "I am walking alone because I want to be alone," the title card read, and the film emphasized her solitary nature; it often showed her taking long walks in the rain. Thereafter the famous phrase, twisted this way and that, turned up in *Grand Hotel* and even in *Ninotchka.* More important, almost all the stories concocted for her stressed her isolation. As Tynan pointed out, it was generally necessary, given her accent, to cast her as precisely what she was: an exile, arriving alone in some strange port of call, either escaping from or in pursuit of love. If she survived whatever amorous adventure the script took up, she was then typically seen at the end departing as she came—alone. The famous last shot of *Queen Christina,* standing alone at the prow of the ship carrying her into exile, is the emblematic shot of her career, the one by which future generations, encountering it in compilation television shows or picture books, know her. To put the matter simply, everything possible was done to mystify, to obscure, the plangent, poignant human truth—that reality beneath convention that Cukor was talking about—that Garbo was constantly illuminating in her work. Tosh scripts, in short, encouraged tosh journalism and a tosh legend.

As the 1930s wore on, a price began to be paid for this. Through *Camille* her films continued to be profitable, but apparently at diminishing levels and with ever-increasing reliance on the foreign market for the largest share of that profitability. Then, in 1937, disaster struck. *Conquest,* the story of the doomed love of a Polish countess, Marie Walewska (by whose name the film was known outside the United States), for Napoleon, ran catastrophically over budget. According to Walker, no less than seventeen screenwriters (among them F. Scott Fitzgerald) took whacks at a project that eventually cost over $3 million to produce, only a million less than *Gone with the Wind,* which was twice as long and incalculably more enriching to the studio two years later. Obviously it was finally time to bring Garbo into the twentieth century. It was also time for her to embrace, as well, what were by now the established conventions of the sound film.

Hence *Ninotchka.* By this time Garbo's long-term MGM contract had run out, and she signed a one-picture deal with the studio for less than half what she had received previously. But Ernst Lubitsch, whom she later—incorrectly—described to a friend as the only first-class director she ever had in Hollywood (she omitted Cukor), had been wanting to make a picture with her since the early thirties. It was a happy collaboration and, as it turned out, one that restored her to favor at the box office

The script, a collaboration between the great comedy writing team of Billy Wilder and Charles Brackett and an old friend of Lubitsch's, Walter Reisch, represents a brilliant adaptation of her screen personality to the purposes of comedy. She plays, of course, a Russian commissar come to Paris to investigate the bumbling and bungling of a highly comical trio of trade commissioners. She falls under the spell of the city and of a womanizing con man (Melvyn Douglas), who seduces her out of habit, then genuinely falls in love with her. As a new Russian woman, it is natural for her to travel alone on business and to conduct it in a mannishly independent manner. In the film this becomes an almost parodistic comment on the solitary ways of her former characters. It is the same when it comes to sex. When Douglas goes into his seductive routine, she eyes him coolly and calls it "a natural impulse, common to all," thereby openly stating the calm acceptance of the physical act which she had only been able to imply in her previous roles.

Thereafter, in a speech since much quoted, she makes, if you will, her most famous plea for privacy, for the individual's right to surcease from exactions of public responsibility in the age of mega-politics: "Comrades! People of the world. The revolution is on the march. Bombs will fall. Civilizations will crumble. But not yet, please. Wait. What's the hurry? Give us our moment." Again, this is an open statement of one of the most common implications of her previous screen incarnations—a deployment of her image for witty as opposed to lugubrious effect. And somehow the more touching as a result. *Ninotchka* even contrives to give her a renunciation that cheers instead of depresses. For in order to claim her true love, it becomes necessary for her to abandon what has heretofore sustained her, her political beliefs—and this too represents a distinct improvement on her former sufferings.

All of this says nothing of the lovely context in which she appears: the funny low comedy of comrades Iranoff, Buljanoff, and Kopalski, the trade commissioners she comes to chastise and stays to indulge; the sharp satirical thrusts at Communist, aristocratic, and capitalist habits of thought and manners; the combination of worldliness and sweetness, so characteristic of Lubitsch, in the romantic interludes; the sheer smartness and pace of the whole enterprise. In a single, gracefully sweeping gesture, its creators lifted Garbo out of anachronism and placed her in the center, at the height of what history now correctly sees as one of the great American filmmaking traditions, that of romantic comedy as it was practiced in the 1930s and early '40s. In sum, they did for Garbo what has had to be done for every actress—names like Harlow and Marilyn Monroe come to mind—who makes her initial impact as a sex symbol of great and exotic force: they gave her the opportunity to practice humanizing self-satire. For though distance lends enchantment to such figures in the beginning, it creates estrangement as time goes by.

Unfortunately, however, *Ninotchka* turned out to be a signpost on a road not taken. To be sure, the studio executives saw what it had accomplished for a star who represented a huge investment and who was still youthful, therefore still valuable to them. They would try to find something in a similar vein for her. Unfortunately they came up with *Two-Faced Woman.* It was a scrimpy production, put into work after the outbreak of the war in Europe, with a budget that was minuscule by her standards (she took another, more modest, salary cut to make it). And though Cukor was an effective director of romantic comedy (*The Philadelphia Story, Holiday,* and many of the Tracy-Hepburn collaborations), he was certainly not Lubitsch. Far worse, the writers, S. N. Behrman and Salka Viertel, who had worked on many of Garbo's heavier romantic epics, and George Oppenheimer, who had not, could not compare to the *Ninotchka* team.

The result was not, perhaps, as bad as its reputation. Indeed, it was not unlike hundreds of other studio products, capable of generating mild pleasure and instant amnesia—nothing to work yourself up over. Otis Ferguson, who was the only great American movie reviewer of this moment, shrewdly noted the difference between this film and its predecessor: the director had patiently shot everything the writers had churned out, instead of pruning and pointing their work as Lubitsch, who always worked closely with his writers, did. The result, as he observed, seemed draggy despite a lot of good lines and despite Garbo's "nice, dry" talent for comedy. As he said, "Unless you are determined to be grumpy you will probably enjoy it."

But *Two-Faced Woman*—in which Garbo plays a wife trying to rekindle her husband's flagging romantic interest (he's played by Douglas) by pretending to be her sexy twin sister—was greeted by a chorus of critical outrage. And some moral outrage, too. The Legion of Decency hated the adulterous implications of Douglas's pursuit of her in the sexy twin role; after all, he didn't know she was really his wife, even if we did. But that was beside the point, as far as the critics and the knowing audience were concerned. They believed the goddess might laugh, but only when directed to do so by an acknowledged master of sophisticated wit, and only in a film whose budget clearly reflected the artistic status to which the smart set had long since elevated her. Or as Ferguson shrewdly noted, "Serious people naturally want Miss Greta Garbo to be serious," and the relative insubstantiality of this movie led to an outcry about the shame and waste of their idol. Or, again to quote Ferguson: "Serious people object with high contempt to what they call Hollywood typing, and then turn around and issue the exact sounds that make shrewd movie producers keep as many actors as possible in as nearly the same part as possible, to keep the paying dumb public from squinting and shuffling its feet. Serious people of the kind I mean feel them-

53

selves above the dumb public, but cannot be differentiated in the matter of squinting and shuffling feet."

In other words, one might be disappointed to a degree by something like *Two-Faced Woman,* but it was not—or should not have been—a cause for vast alarm or a great reexamination of everyone's premises. Alas, however, the outcry over it reached the star's ears. She had always had her doubts about the project, reluctantly choosing it over an even more lugubrious alternative, *A Woman's Face,* which did its bit to turn Joan Crawford into box-office poison at the time. And she had been rendered unhappy by the studio's refusal to assign her favorite cameraman, William Daniels, to the picture, one of those minor stupidities Hollywood executives are always insisting upon in order to assert their petty authority over "talent."

Now the excesses of outrage visited upon her by the critical press seemed to confirm for her the studio's lack of gratitude for past successes as well as its long-standing habits of patronization and erratic minginess in its dealings with her. Worse, this failure obviously loomed larger to her, an actress who made a picture only every year or two, than it might have to a performer who made, as most did in those days, three or four a year. Her films had always been events; she was not in the habit of forgetting the easily forgettable and pressing on to the next project. Still worse, it seemed to cancel out the promise *Ninotchka* had held out to her. Perhaps that had been just a onetime sensation. Perhaps there was not, after all, a future in lighter, more contemporary romantic vehicles. Perhaps she had better reclaim her distance while yet she could. Perhaps she had better increase that distance, if possible.

And so the beginnings of her withdrawal. One can, of course, see other appeals in this strategy. Shall we put it mildly? She cannot have been unaware of her extraordinary beauty and the fact that sooner or later she would either have to withdraw its "maturing" charms from the crowd or consent to letting the *hoi polloi* observe its inevitable decline. Barthes puts this matter very well. "the essence was not to be degraded, her face was not to have any reality except that of its perfection, which was intellectual even more than formal. The essence became gradually obscured, progressively veiled with dark glasses, broad hats and exiles; but it never deteriorated."

In one way, however, she miscalculated—disastrously. One has to believe that Garbo counted on her films to buttress the legend that she had created around herself, counted on them to bear interestingly enigmatic, endlessly reinterpretable evidence on behalf of her life and her achievements. Isn't that precisely the kind of gnomic material other people we are pleased to think of as gods, heroes, exemplars leave behind? Even if she were not thinking quite as grandly as that, she certainly had reason to suppose that the films would serve her as their legacies—their books and poems and paintings— had served other artists.

But the movies failed her. Or perhaps, in fairness, we who came along later failed her, in that we could not make the imaginative backward leap her work required of us, could not, would not dig the reality of her achievement out of the antique dramatic and emotional conventions encrusting it. The world was hurrying on past all that, redefining its aesthetics in ways she could not have imagined. By 1964 Susan Sontag correctly identified "the haunting androgynous behind the perfect beauty of Greta Garbo" as one of the touchstones of the camp sensibility, which overturned all the cultural assumptions of her work.

In any event, there is this irony to consider: of all her movies, the only one that remains alive for us today, the only one that is not the sole property of her ever-dwindling cult, the only one we can contemplate reseeing with pleasure or recommend to younger people with confidence, is the movie in which she and her colleagues so artfully satirized her screen persona. That movie, of course, is *Ninotchka.*

It is not enough. Maybe in the end all great star careers are reduced to the dimensions of a televised tribute, a compilation of film clips, reminiscences, antique critical opinions and secondhand gossip. And, heaven knows, every movie actor's life includes many films—generally a majority—that he or she might wish evanesced like a failed stage play. But the fact remains that all of Garbo's contemporaries who might be considered her peers left behind at least a half-dozen movies that we can profitably and pleasurably return to at any time. These pictures are the anchors of their immortality, works that retain their freshness across a half-century and more, permitting newer generations to see not just their high moments but the full range of their personalities and gifts in enhancing—not to say delightful—contexts. These movies allow us to take stock of a player at leisure, to form our own impressions of him or her, free of legend, free of the cultist's odd enthusiasms, the historian's opinions, or the clip-show producer's tastes.

Garbo, in short, paid a price for her self-absorption, for her egoism, for her curious passivity when it came to choosing roles. Useless to complain, years later, that she had had only one great director in her career. She was in Hollywood when it was at the height of its creative energy, and she had the power, if she had used it, to insist on its greatest directors, its finest writers. But she fought only for money and the minor prerogatives of stardom—like the cameraman whose light bathed her most attractively. Many performers with far less clout had struggled for—and got—parts that sustained their careers not merely into middle age but onward into a future that is not yet finished. Sadly, one concludes, she had a peasant's shrewdness but not an artist's high instincts. A legend in her time, she was not a legend for all time. With each passing year she becomes more and more a curiosity.

Think of it! Something like a half-century's existence as—to vary Daniel Boorstin's famous formulation—someone

known for her unknowness. Or perhaps one should say her unknowability. The public saw much of her in the newspapers
and magazines during the early part of that period. She was
wraith to the world, glimpsed slipping in and out of airports,
restaurants, theaters, hidden behind dark glasses, swathed in
a veil, her hat pulled low on her forehead. Some cultists took
to following her about on her walks in Central Park or her
strolls through the shops of her neighborhood on Manhattan's
East Side. Occasionally enterprising journalists joined in
these stalkings and reported the unilluminating comments of
the tradesmen who did business with her. For years, New
Yorkers reported to one another their chance encounters with
her on their streets, though few dared speak to her. The pseudonym under which she booked airline and steamship tickets,
"Miss Brown," became almost as well known as her own
name.

Those who knew of her only through the gossip press assumed she was a recluse, but she was not. She actually had a
fairly wide circle of friends, and she exposed herself to the
ever-lurking *paparazzi* mainly because she wanted to join her
rich pals at their play. Indeed, she was something of a free-
loader, always glad to accept an invitation to the South of
France or the Caribbean as long as someone else was picking
up the tab. Once ensconced in villa or exclusive resort, she
participated freely, if quietly, in her friends' activities.

One would like to think that in these years she carried
out the plan she had once contemplated, of making and sustaining relationships with the best minds and spirits of her
time, world figures in the arts, politics, intellectual life. As she
surmised, her status would have assured her access to these
people, just as she might have had access to Hollywood's best
and brightest in her active years. But the evidence is that the
only artists she saw were those she naturally encountered in
the social circles she preferred—Tennessee Williams, Truman
Capote, Cecil Beaton. Many of them were homosexuals, there-

fore safe escorts for her (though, famously, she lured Beaton across the line into a brief and, on his part, impassioned affair with her). There is no evidence whatsoever that she reached out beyond this quite narrow cut of life toward a wider artistic world, let alone toward the worlds of politics or intellect. She remained, one may kindly guess, too shy, too insecure intellectually, to make that effort. Unkindly, one may speculate that she remained all too conscious of her legendary status and dared not risk placing it too close for comfortable comparison to legends of comparable standing in other fields. In any event, and for whatever reason, she passed most of her time not just with the idle rich but with the stupidly rich, people who continued to defer to her stardom as hurrying youth, preoccupied with new fads, could not and would not. Her set's interests in ideas and art was confined to what was comfortable, settled, approved by all the right authorities. And, of course, its members could provide her with those comfortable, carefully controlled environments where she could rest from her restless travels. Little that was new, youthful, challenging was permitted to penetrate their lives—or her life.

For all her restless comings and goings, her life after she left the screen—and it consumed by far the majority of her years—was an empty one, unrelieved by altruism or by any sense of obligation to culture or to history. It was, truly, among the most selfish lives ever lived by a public person in modern times, and one that is not redeemed by any posthumous benefactions. One can read her last years as analogous to the last reel of so many of her pictures, that is to say, as a renunciation, mournful and noble, this time not of a man but of a woman—her former self.

This creature, half fiction, half fact, was (largely) Garbo's invention, and she had a right to do what she wished with it— to protect it from time's ravages, to protect us from witnessing its inevitable decline. But she forgot that life is not a movie, that it has a way of drifting on past its emotional high points, its logical climaxes, carrying us into the becalmed absurdities of age. So although she avoided the pity we sometimes feel for the idols of our youth when we glimpse them in their late infirmities on some talk show or making a cameo appearance in an ill-calculated movie or TV show, all her efforts could not prevent Garbo the idea, Garbo the ideal, from deteriorating into a kind of silliness—on those rare occasions when we thought about it.

Yet there was still a kind of magic in her presence, if you could penetrate to it. I said at the outset that I played a walk-on role in one of these entirely forgettable scenes from her leftover life. It was her habit to spend a month or so every year with Gayelord Hauser, the eccentric nutritionist. He too was a homosexual she had enticed into a heterosexual fling, maintaining a friendship with him after their ardor had cooled. Clever with money, Hauser was generally rumored to have been responsible for guiding some of her real estate investments—so she had reason to be grateful for his contributions to the comfort in which she was able to maintain herself so long into retirement (her estate exceeded $32 million). He lived in Los Angeles in a handsomely decorated house built around a pool just off Mulholland Drive, often complaining about Garbo's exigent ways when she was his house guest (she was fussy about her meals and their timing). We had a mutual friend, and one day he called her to ask if we would like to join him and Garbo at a small party other friends were giving. This was, needless to say, an offer we could not refuse.

She was introduced under her "Miss Brown" pseudonym, but she was, naturally, fooling no one. Her face was remarkably unlined (except, if you looked closely, around her mouth), her body slender, her movements calm, graceful, vigorous. Predictably, she did not have much to say, but on the other hand she was very much a part of the party, following the banal conversation with perhaps more alertness than it deserved.

I felt, or thought I felt, a slight impatience in her, an unspoken hope that she might hear something she had not heard before, some news or gossip from the outside world. But even if these people had been capable of providing that, the constraint of her presence imposed on everyone precluded any ruffling of the surface. At one point, though, I found myself involved in a conversation about investment strategies far too technical for me to follow. My eye wandered, and caught hers across the room. She smiled broadly—and winked. I winked back. For just a second I was Armand or Vronsky, a whole generation of males, caught in that all-knowing glance, our otherness, our waywardness, our peculiar devotion to plot and ploys at the expense of the infrangible moment exposed, accepted, indulged. In the lengthening history of the movies, only this woman had the gift for imparting this gift. It is a sadness that she made it so difficult for the future to find it.

1988

Frank Capra: One Man, Many Films

The newspaper and television obituaries all stressed the heartwarming aspects of Frank Capra's work; his love of ordinary people and his—as they saw it—genially, perhaps naively calculated manipulation of events in their fictional lives so that they ultimately achieved improbable but inspirational triumphs over rich and powerful malefactors. Indeed, many of the obituaries made it seem that his entire career, stretching over forty-two years and embracing thirty-six feature films, had only one point—the creation of the film that most vividly summarizes the most obvious of his virtues, 1946's *It's a Wonderful Life.*

It has become over the last two or three decades perhaps the most widely beloved of all movies, the one film of its era that just about everyone, regardless of age, cinematic sophistication or station in life, knows well and cares about greatly. It is now, as the annual ads remind us, "A Holiday Tradition." But that tradition is rooted in accident and hard commercial reality. The film fell into the public domain in the early seventies and as a result became for television programmers a source of (quite literally) cheap Christmas sentiment. If that had not happened—if it had not been so convenient to impose it upon the television audience—it is dubious that it would have achieved its present status.

Not that one should begrudge it anything. Familiarity has surely diminished its impact, and our need for its nostalgic view of small-town life and its last-minute redemptions has even more surely whited-out for many the several quite astonishing passages of blackness and rage that precede its giddily inspirational conclusion. But even so it remains—if only for its hellish imagining of Bedford Falls as it might have become without George Bailey's wonderful life—a remarkable film. The most vivid complaint we may lodge against it is that it has imparted a cruelly ironic spin to Capra's famous motto, "one man, one film."

The fact is that this one man made more than this one film. It is for the span of his career, the richness of what he accomplished within that span, and the moral ambivalences of his work that he should be remembered—especially in the near-decade of his ascendancy, which dates from 1932, when he made *American Madness,* to 1941, when *Meet John Doe* was released. In that time I believe Frank Capra may have been the greatest of American directors.

I offer this claim in full knowledge that we are talking about what may be the best years of Hollywood's life, and that Frank's competitors in those years included the likes of Lubitsch and Ford, Hawks and Hitchcock, Mamoulian and Wyler (among others). Nor do I base my argument entirely, or even most significantly, on the fact that his characteristic themes were so in tune with the needs of his audience during the depression decade, though certainly they were. Nor do I rest it on the large commercial success of his movies in this period, though that was vital in sustaining his freedom to choose his material and to realize it in his own untrammeled way. What I'm talking about is sensibility and technique.

Sensibility first. It was much more ambiguously poised than most people now think it was. An immigrant lad, Capra liked to say that he learned in his early days as a traveling salesman to respect the kindliness and common sense of the common man. That was doubtless true. But he sold, among other things, self-improvement books and dubious stocks, and sometimes worked as a professional poker player. A man following these lines inevitably learns something else about ordinary people, which is that fed a smooth line they are easily (and often quite literally) sold a bill of goods—hustled, hoodwinked, hosed. And if he's bright and ambitious and somewhat declassed (Frank held a hard-won but economically useless degree in chemical engineering), he stands in a similarly ambivalent relationship to uncommon people, at once awed by and envying those who have made it—to social stability, to worldly power.

I've always imagined Frank in those days as a character out of Dos Passos: "The young man walks by himself, fast but not fast enough, far but not far enough . . . head swimming with wants. . . ." And I've felt for a long time that we have to reimagine his films critically in the light of that eager, needy background.

Put it this way: his movies were consistently more uncomfortably class conscious than anyone else's, not least perhaps because to a young man in a hurry his movie apprenticeship—as lab technician, as silent-picture gag writer, as a director both fired and failed—seemed to him so lengthy. It was 1930, and Frank was thirty-three, before he made his first sketchily "Capraesque" movie, *Ladies of Leisure*, in which a rich artist (Ralph Graves) picks up a gum-snapping party girl (Barbara Stanwyck) and warily, edgily tests with her the possibilities of trusting each other despite their differences in accent, attitude, wherewithal. This is a matter Capra (and Stanwyck) took up in more tragic terms in two powerfully melodramatic (and nowadays quite neglected) films of this period: *Forbidden,* which may be the best of the "Back Street" romances so popular in the early thirties, and *The Bitter Tea of General Yen,* that exotic, visually potent study of the miscegenous romance between an American missionary and a Chinese warlord.

I think it is worth pausing over these films, for each in its way says something important about their director. At least one student of screwball (or romantic) comedy, Elizabeth Kendall, somewhat eccentrically sees the beginnings of the 1930s, most characteristic form in *Ladies of Leisure*—even though its tone is almost never humorous. It does however, establish the genre's basic conceit—lovers from opposite sides of the tracks overcoming the objections of the rich one's family (chillingly personified here by Nance O'Neil, a once-famous star of the touring stage, in whose company the young D. W. Griffith once played, and who later in life—irresistible historical tidbit here—became Lizzie Borden's lover)—and achieving, with a good deal of winching about, a happy ending.

Graves, who was a Griffith discovery, was something of a stiff as a society artist, but Stanwyck, in the role that brought her stardom (and Frank Capra as a lover) was a revelation—a beautiful young woman (she was twenty-two at the time) whose toughness was as authentic as her vulnerability. Their first tryst—he picks her up dripping wet after she swims to shore from a yachting party that has got out of hand—has a marvelous dark romanticism: a stormy night, an artist's *atelier;* she undressing in silhouette behind a screen; he coming to her later; she wearily prepared to accept his advances; he simply covering her with a blanket; she chewing its corner to prevent him hearing her sobs of gratitude as he turns away. There is in this passage a tense, blunt awareness of underlying class issues—girls like her expect to be used by swells like him—

that we don't generally find in movie romances of the time, whether comically or dramatically stated.

The same is true of *Forbidden*, which Capra made with Stanwyck two years later. It is an altogether more melodramatic and, I think, accomplished picture. Stanwyck, as a spinsterish librarian named Lulu Smith, meets wealthy, dashing Bob Grover (Adolphe Menjou) on a cruise ship, moves to his city, and takes a newspaper job in order to be near him despite the fact that he is indissolubly married (his wife is an invalid), waiting faithfully for his clandestine visits to her apartment. As a political career opens up for him, their relationship is sundered, and she marries one of her editors (Ralph Bellamy) and allows him to believe he is the father of Bob's child. Eventually, of course, the truth wills out; the newsman jealously threatens to publicize it and spoil Bob's chance to become governor—never mind the cost to his wife. She murders him before he can do so, her lover pardons her just before he dies—and also leaves her half his estate. The film's last sequence shows her tearing up the will, throwing it in a trash can, and being swallowed up in a heedless city throng.

Sounds like romantic nonsense, of course. But it doesn't play like it. There's a marvelous scene, for example, in which Grover appears at Lulu's door wearing a Halloween mask and bearing one for her which she wears as they banter their way through what will turn out to be their last tryst. The mask symbolism, given their hidden relationship, may seem obvious, yet it is also very powerful—and to my knowledge unique in the history of such scenes. So is Capra's staging of the murder, with Bellamy's character raging outside Stanwyck's door, she raging uncontrollably on the other side until she fires repeatedly through it. Again, staging, not to mention Stanwyck's playing—no actress I can think of has ever more fully given herself over to animal panic than she does in this scene—transforms banality. And, lest we forget our theme, there is a class issue at work in this movie: the newsman's working-stiff resentment of a wealthy and powerful man's ability to have, seemingly casually, all that he cannot— celebrity, power, and the unquestioning love of a splendid woman. We should also remember that the movie's pioneering consideration of the relationship between private morals and public life prefigures *Citizen Kane*'s exploration of that issue by a decade—to say nothing of our own more recent, still more avid, preoccupation with it.

The Bitter Tea of General Yen, with Stanwyck as a missionary who falls in love with the eponymous Chinese warlord (Nils Asther) who has imprisoned her, can also be read without much strain as a love story that crosses class lines—this time with tragic results. The picture was a flop despite its extraordinarily handsome realization, and for the rest of his life Capra would claim to have learned valuable lessons from it. He made it, he said, because he lusted for an Academy Award and was sure he would never receive one if he continued to make the kinds of modest comedies and romances he had been doing. Its failure, he claimed, taught him not to overreach in such a naive and obvious way. It also taught him to stay close to people and situations he knew more intimately.

But despite its setting and the fact that it ends with a love-death Puccini (if not Wagner) might have admired, Stanwyck's missionary is a classic Capra woman—smart, spirited, a little bit wrongheaded in her idealism, and near-to-writhing with suppressed sexual longing. And there is in the presentation of her story a powerful anti-pietistic, anti-hypocritical quality, with the general's elegant realism contrasted very effectively with the missionary cant that Stanwyck comes to him mouthing and leaves him regretting. Whatever the state of Capra's belief in the Catholicism he was born to, there was in much of his work an active skepticism about conventional religious belief. Only once, in rather desperate narrative circumstances, did he resort to religious sentiment of the kind that his contemporary, Leo McCarey, an equally sophisticated craftsman in the comic-romantic vein, descended to ultimately. This represents, I think, wholly admirable restraint, given Capra's many leaps to somewhat dubious populist conclusions.

Indeed, one cannot leave these most fecund years of Capra's career—he made nine movies between 1930 and 1933—without mentioning two films that still more obviously prefigure the more famous work to come. The first of them, *The Miracle Woman* (1931), probably owes something to Sinclair Lewis's *Elmer Gantry* and something more to the life and career of Aimee Semple McPherson, in that it recounts the rise and fall of a sexy female evangelist, or "hot spieler" as she's called in the film. Stanwyck's Florence "Faith" Fallon, a conventional minister's daughter, finds her calling as she denounces her father's congregation for its hypocrisy, which she blames for his premature death. There's a promoter in the crowd who senses her gift for inspirational preaching, and soon enough he's made her a star on the revival circuit. The love of a good, blind man, who has been saved from suicide by her inspirational words, makes her wish to confess the fraudulent cures she has been trafficking in, but the promoter cuts the electric power in her tent, causing a short circuit and a fire, allowing her and her lover to escape into anonymity (she is last glimpsed playing in a Salvation Army band).

What we see for the first time in the revival meetings is Capra's unrivaled gift for portraying the volatility of the masses under the pressure generated by delusionary promises of salvation. One of Fallon's gimmicks is to enter a lion cage armored only in her faith, but big cats or not, all these passages have an operatic power—a frenzy—that you do not find in other American films of the time, or for that matter of any time.

You can find the same power in 1932's *American Mad-*

ness, which I believe to be Capra's first truly great film. It's the story of a populist bank president, Thomas Dickson (Walter Huston in one of his foxiest performances), who lends money to people on the basis of their character rather than their balance sheets. He is also a primitive Keynesian, believing that in bad times it is the duty of financial institutions to get money into circulation, not hoard it. Under pressure from his board—they're thinking merger—to mend his ways, he is also confronted with peculation by one of his officers. Exaggerated rumors of the losses he has created led to a run on the bank and to some of Capra's greatest scenes of mass hysteria.

His trick in such sequences was to pack a large crowd into a tight space, using the resulting claustrophobia to heighten panic. His camera placements fill in every inch of the frame with excited humanity, and his editing, generally a little faster than was customary at the time, further intensified the sense of agitation he communicated with such visceral force to his audiences. But technique aside, the obvious importance of the film is its first presentation of what we would come to identify as the quintessential Capra hero—an intelligent, compassionate figure who has risen to prominence from modest beginnings and has not lost his faith in the common sense and common goodness of the common people. Along with that goes a very vivid sense that the triumph of those virtues is always a near thing; that the assertion of that faith requires a leap, which may require a man to physically face down a dangerously misled crowd, as Huston's character does when a mob invades his bank demanding their deposits—as, later, a smaller but equally hysterical group will bring George Bailey to the edge of ruin and suicide.

While he was making these films, Capra was also doing pictures of a more conventional, more commercially successful sort, like *Platinum Blonde* and *Lady for a Day,* in which class issues, though present—there are plenty of rich ninnies and raffish lower-class characters being snooted before emerging triumphant—are very lightly stated. Indeed, taken as a group, the films Capra made in the early thirties offer us a picture of a talented, energetic man making up for lost career time while at the same time groping for his main line, grasping it occasionally, but letting go of it in the rush of doing studio business. It was a pattern that was broken in 1934 by the surprise success of *It Happened One Night.*

Historically we think of it, correctly, as the movie that definitively established romantic comedy's ruling conventions, the begetter of the genre that survives—and in a way defines—its historical moment better than any other. We also think of it, thanks to Frank Capra's latter-day autobiographical nudgings, as a movie whose success was rather like that of a Capra hero. It was a little guy that thanks to his good humor and common sense eventually triumphed over the big guys.

As Frank liked to tell the story, *It Happened One Night* was dismissed by reviewers and failed in its first run at Radio City Music Hall; but then it was transformed into a hit by enthusiastic word-of-mouth passing from one ordinary moviegoer to the next and the next until eventually it became the first movie to sweep all the major Oscars. Doubtless there is a certain amount of truth to this tale. And the film's charm, as we all know, holds up across the years, not least because of the playing of its stars, Clark Gable and Claudette Colbert, both of whom were obtained by bottom-feeding Columbia because the grander studios that controlled their contracts wanted to punish them for rebelliousness.

The movie is—*Arsenic and Old Lace* aside—the least ambiguously comic of all Capra's sound films. It is also the most artful in disguising his major preoccupations. But they are there, lurking beneath the larking story of a tough-guy newsman who finds a runaway heiress who is trying to avoid marrying a fool, then tames the giddiness out of her in the course of bringing her home.

The class issue is obvious—the spoiled child brought down to earthiness by the roughneck guy, tough and no-nonsense and getting a little help toward the end from her father, a self-made man who turns out to share the good values of low rather than high society. The film takes up, with similar charm, that other great Capra preoccupation—the relationship between the media and the mass public. For remember that Gable's reporter meets Colbert's heiress not because he is looking for romance but because he is looking for a scoop. The marriage she is running from is a tabloid sensation, and her disappearance becomes even more of one. The distorting pressure of publicity, the avidity of the media and the public it feeds to penetrate her privacy, is one of the things driving her crazy.

This is a matter Capra would return to frequently, though never more brilliantly than in this film's last scene, the wedding on her estate where she deserts her twit bridegroom at the altar to run off with the newshawk. Aside from the fact that newsreel cameras stand in for today's television cameras, this masterful sequence—all swish pans and rushing crowds—eerily predicts the media feeding-frenzies that attend celebrity ceremonials of every kind today.

The success of *It Happened One Night*—it was the first Capra movie to become not just a hit but a social phenomenon—provided his career with a main line. Or perhaps one should say, gave him and his studio the confidence to pursue his preoccupation—until now intermittent—with the relationship of the individual to the mass in an age when the media were beginning to change that relationship radically. He might divert from it with films like *Lost Horizon* and *You Can't Take It with You*, but it is unquestionably true that the *Deeds-Smith-Doe* trilogy represents his most vivid and significant work, hailed as such at the time and offering a continuing historical resonance. No documentary history of the depression era is complete without some reference to these films.

Of the three, *Mr. Deeds Goes to Town* is the cheeriest as it recounts the attempts of a small-town greeting-card versifier to give away a surprise inheritance to the deserving poor so they can start small farms. This turns him into a media sensation, a celebrity, and the scenes of desperate men storming his mansion to obtain his largesse are, of course, wonderfully handled. You get a very powerful sense of their precariously balanced hopes and fears. Remember, too, that Jean Arthur's newspaperwoman—a figure who would recur more dangerously in the person of Barbara Stanwyck in *Meet John Doe*—is drawn with similar ambiguity. Yes, she comes to love Longfellow Deeds. But she is present initially to get the inside dope on him, to find any chinks in his saintly armor. Remember, as well, that when his plan is challenged by establishment lawyers and bankers with an insanity hearing, his beneficiaries turn into something pretty close to a mob in order to support him. Eventually he gains his ends by a resort to comically stated courtroom violence.

In *Mr. Smith Goes to Washington*, James Stewart's idealistic young man is appointed to fill a U.S. Senate seat, and finds corruption in that body—represented by the senior senator from his own state (Claude Rains, that silkiest of villains), who is also something of a surrogate father figure to him. Arthur is again present, this time as a worldly-wise secretary who is won over by Smith's gulping idealism. Her best friend is an affable, skeptical newsman (Thomas Mitchell), who sets the tone for his colleagues' treatment of Mr. Smith as a comical, possibly even dangerous naif. When Smith challenges the bosses in his state over a land deal that would enrich them, the local press is shown to be entirely in their pocket. He fights this establishment in part by demagogic means—he is the head of something called the Boy Rangers, politicized Boy Scouts, if you will, who are mobilized to support him—and are brutally treated by the establishment's hired thugs. The melodramatic filibuster sequence offers more hysteria in a tight space—the well of the Senate—though this time it is personified by only one man, the brilliantly raging Stewart. It leads to the suicide of Rains's senator, and Smith's redemption brings the movie to a satisfyingly idealistic and boldly melodramatic conclusion. But this ending does not entirely vitiate the potent, populist criticism of American democracy's workings that precede it. Again, as one goes back to this film, one is struck by the continuing relevance of its social criticism, especially its portrayal of media complicity in overheating public opinion for dubious ends.

By the time he made *Meet John Doe* in 1941, Capra placed on the screen a media baron (Edward Arnold, who had played a similar role in *Mr. Smith* and had no peer in playing menacing men of power) who is also a full-scale native American fascist. Capra showed him controlling a small private army—the thugs of *Mr. Smith* are now menacingly uniformed and given to paramilitary rituals. The press lord is also secretly financing and aiming to corrupt the seemingly benign sociopolitical organization John Doe has been recruited to front so that it will subvert democratic values while pretending to advance them.

The movie turned out messily. Capra and his most faithful writing collaborator, Robert Riskin—they had first joined forces on *Platinum Blonde*—had trouble with the ending. Their eponymous hero has threatened to commit suicide if people don't start treating one another more decently; it is a gimmick cooked up by Stanwyck's newspaper reporter, who works for one of Arnold's rags, and it is what has made Doe a celebrity as the leader of the publisher's quasi-religious mass movement. Should their script permit Doe to embrace the martyrdom he has promised? Should it rescue him? If it did, how could that business be plausibly managed?

They never came up with an entirely persuasive solution to their dilemma. Part of the problem lay in the characterization of Doe, who is just a little too dumb and a little too passive for his own good. Ultimately, if belatedly, Mr. Deeds and Mr. Smith take charge of their own fates. Gary Cooper's John Doe does not. By the end of the film he is pretty much a Christ figure, mocked and scorned by the crowd that formerly worshiped him, but willing to die to redeem their sins. That, however, is too much mythic weight for Cooper, Capra, Riskin, and the rest of us to bear, and they hastily shuck it by having some of his followers come to their senses and rescue him. The filmmakers cover their tracks with tolling bells and a quotation from Beethoven's Ninth—perhaps on the grounds that if you pump up the volume on false sentiment it will briefly ring true—and here Capra does embrace a queasy, discomfiting religiosity.

Andrew Sarris correctly saw that all of Capra's most important work "implied a belief in the innate conformism of the common man," and wrote that in *Meet John Doe* he "crossed the thin line between populist sentimentality and populist demagoguery." It's impossible to disagree with his generality, and his specific charge against this film is at least partially correct; that Christ business is scary.

On the other hand, all Capra's best films are tense with his awareness that the good nature and innocence of ordinary people leaves them vulnerable to manipulation from above, that their naiveté and geniality is both saving grace and Achilles heel. It is, as we've seen, the source of his greatest imagery, which reaches its heights in this film's great rally in the rain, in which in a few cuts Capra transforms the crowd's happy anticipation of John Doe's appearance into murderous frenzy. It is one of the truly privileged, truly alarming moments in all of movie history. And it is pretty close to unique in the popular fictions of its time. Who else in film, or for that matter in literature, even hinted at the dangerous possibilities of popular gullibility in an age when everywhere the people were being unambiguously celebrated for their goodness?

Certainly it is difficult to think of other filmmakers who

so consistently achieved that curious, riveting mixture of terror and exultation that Capra did in set pieces of this kind. To me, this is his signature sequence, the one I think of first when his name is mentioned. Perhaps perversely, and perhaps largely because of this astonishing sequence, I think of *Meet John Doe* as his greatest work—anyway his most courageous one. For it is the movie in which he brought to the surface, with fewer comedic distractions, all of the dark implications of his previous films and did his best to confront them. I acknowledge his failure, in the end, to resolve his conflicted view of mass man. And I suspect that failure exhausted him in a way that he did not see for some time (his war service, in which he threw himself into the *Why We Fight* series, allowed him to escape self-confrontation, as did his attempts to become a full-scale independent producer in the postwar years). But the effort is mighty, and it is reflected in the feverish brilliance of his filmmaking.

Another critic, David Thomson, went even further than Sarris, speaking of Capra's "rosy witless complacency," of "the doctrinaire use of illogical happy endings" based on a too-easy belief that "rottenness can be neatly excised." I suppose we have to concede his point, if not the curious outrage of his language. But having come to know Capra late in his life, when I produced one television program about him and participated in the making of another, I never believed that he embraced these conclusions out of commercial expediency. They were, rather, assertions of will, leaps of faith that all religions—and Frank's populism, as we have seen, did have a religious overtone—require. In other words, they were statements of a morality tested time and again by terrible doubts yet ultimately proved by his own experience.

Yes, experience. Frank understood the power of film, understood it better, that is to say more consciously, than any of his contemporaries. He was wise enough to understand that he—any director of great gift—has within him a power to lull and gull the audience that is no less than, say, that of Edward Arnold's press boss. He was aware that this power had brought him fame and wealth, and he was determined to use it for good—even if that meant pulling away from the darkest implications of his work. In his later years, when he achieved the status of a beloved icon, he cheerfully went along with official, award-giving America's view of him as a simple sentimentalist, accepting without demurrer a reduced, if convenient, version of himself and his work. It was, of course, satisfying to an ego that was not a modest one. But more important, it served what seemed to him a larger good, for his story, his legend, could be used to bolster democratic faith.

That may seem to us a strategy as naive as any employed by Frank's populist heroes. It may also represent a certain desperation on his part, an attempt to reclaim his historical place as he endured the many failures of his later years, the slippage into has-been status that his critics were not shy about discussing. But I have never distrusted the authenticity and decency of the impulse behind it.

Many now do, of course. A year after Frank's death (and the appearance of this piece in its first version), Joseph McBride published the first full-scale biography of him, *Frank Capra: The Catastrophe of Success*. Its title, in its way, tells you all you need to know about this enterprise.

McBride, too, had known and worked with Frank in his late years, and he wrote about him in the tone of a dismayed lover. He found that Frank in his best-selling autobiography, *The Name Above the Title*, had reinvented a good deal of his personal history. He found that he had grabbed a good deal of credit from his collaborators, mostly from the gifted and self-effacing Riskin. McBride also found him to be less than brave in his response to Hollywood blacklisting, claiming that he even did a bit of informing in an attempt to stay in the good graces of the witch-hunters. He implied, finally, that Capra's sharp postwar decline and his premature retirement could be traced to a deeply flawed nature, of which these transgressions are evidence. Sometimes he seems to be suggesting that decline was a sort of moral punishment for those sins.

I am obviously less convinced than McBride on this point. Like him, like everyone, I'd like to believe that artists are moral exemplars, that good work is the product of great spirits. Unlike him, I don't believe that is very often the case. Liking Frank as I did, I still had no trouble imagining him as a difficult case in his earlier days, hustling and bustling his way to fame, riding roughshod (though maybe with some guilty thoughts) over people who got in his way. Similarly, I can also understand the rather desperate self-assertions and self-denials of his long decline and even longer exile from the power he once enjoyed. Against that background, McBride's charges strike me as quite minor.

Most people—and especially show people—tend to improve their life stories when they recount them. It is a forgivable, even sometimes an endearing trait. Most directors tend to downplay the contributions of their collaborators, and though that's a little less forgivable, I hold to a sort of modified *auteur* theory. The director is, if he asserts himself as Capra did, the final arbiter and orchestrator of what appears on the screen, and unquestionably the creator of those images that are what we mainly recall of most movies after memory has played its deconstructive tricks on us. Riskin may have written the rally in the rain, but he did not realize it imagistically, and that, finally, is where its greatness lies. As to Capra's behavior during the blacklist days, it seems to me that it can be explained—if not entirely explained away—by the fact that, as he told me, he had always been a passionate anti-Stalinist, unable to understand how artists could surrender their autonomy to ideology.

All that aside, it is impossible to deny that this proud man panicked as he lost touch with his audience, the new spirit of the time. The ghastly "cluster" headaches Capra describes in his autobiography are surely the psychosomatic symptoms of that panic (they disappeared when he retired). More than most directors, his sense of himself was based on his ability to identify with his audience in the most profoundly instinctive ways. He couldn't hide from himself the evidence that he had lost that ability—his late films are a succession of flaccid entertainments, adaptations of supposedly hot properties, and remakes of his own past successes, realized without energy or conviction. There was, as well, a large irony about his career that was probably not lost on him either. His credo—"one man, one film"—was a statement of the *auteur* theory long before the French cinephiles formalized it. Now, just as it was beginning to gain general credence, he was ceasing to be an *auteur,* was very close to becoming a director for hire, his autonomy threatened by the stars to whom creative power over the shape of movies was now flowing, by an industry in a state of flux he could no longer comprehend.

Whether or not he saw this irony I cannot say. What I can't imagine at all is Frank accepting the truism that many authors, especially those working in the popular forms, have only a relatively short, highly accidental moment when they are perfectly in tune with their audience, that if you are such a person, you can only shrug, move to the side, and wait patiently for the tide to turn your way again—probably posthumously. That sort of silence and cunning was antithetical to his nature.

But that said, I still find it impossible to see the final unhappy years of Frank's career as a moral judgment visited upon him. Whatever McBride thinks, it was just bad—though possibly predictable—luck. Beyond that, I find it difficult to accuse the gallant old man, reveling in the acclaim his autobiography had brought him and the new life he had found as an inspirational speaker, of living a desperate lie. It was, at worst, a saving one—and who can begrudge a man his salvation, particularly when it does no great harm, and perhaps even does a bit of good here and there?

To put the matter simply, it is time now to set aside the kind of moralizing biographical speculation in which McBride indulged. I'm ready to stipulate that Frank was a tricky, complicated character, possibly no better than he should be, but no worse than most men and women of ambition and achievement are. It is time instead to assert that his work was richer and far more complex than it seemed then—or than it yet seems to be to that handful of critical historians who still care about it and the interactions between movies and the culture at large. It cries out for a revisionism that restores Frank Capra's films to nuanced controversy—and to centrality not only in the history of his medium but in the social and intellectual history of an era on which he left an indelible mark.

1991

Irene Dunne: A Secret Light

He has been bored to tears. His life has been in need of saving. He has begun to wonder, "Don't beautiful women ever travel anymore?" The object of this smoothly practiced seduction—Charles Boyer's delivery is almost languid, hinting at a boredom with the verbal conventions of womanizing that he has yet to admit—eyes him quizzically, an amused yet tolerant light in her eye. She too has been here before. "Have you been getting results with a line like that?" she asks.

This shipboard encounter in *Love Affair* is, I think, the quintessential Irene Dunne moment. The mock incredulity of her line reading is impeccably judged. She always knew how to put a man in his place but at the same time leave him room to maneuver out of it—the best method being to join her in good-natured laughter at the all-too-transparent stratagems, the all-too-obvious posturings of the male animal. The customary (or real life) alternatives—sulking, self-pity, indignant reproach—were not options when she was around.

If this image from Leo McCarey's 1939 film is the first that comes to mind when her name is mentioned, others, sim-

ilar in character, tumble quickly upon it. For example, her delicious response to the bumptious presence of Cary Grant,
playing her estranged husband, Jerry, at her genteel song
recital in *The Awful Truth*. Tipping dangerously back in a
spindly chair, deliberately trying to break her up, he manages
only to break up his chair, eliciting from her a delighted giggle
but no loss of pitch or dignity as she completes her aria. Her
laughter is only partly at his deserved discomfort; it also acknowledges her continuing appreciation of the prankish spirit
that drew her to him. It also promises the reconciliation that
is sure (and soon) to come.

Perhaps better still, there is the almost wordless exchange between Dunne and Grant near the beginning of
Penny Serenade. He has bought a phonograph record from her
in the music shop where she works. Now, having walked her
home, he asks if he can come in and play it on her Victrola.
Puzzlement scuds briefly across her face, then recognition of
his ploy; if he doesn't have a machine of his own, there can be
only one reason he bought the disk. He smiles shyly; she emits
an almost imperceptible chuckle and beckons him into her
house, into her life.

These transactions are both an acknowledgment and an
invitation. The former, stated without dither or evasion (but
without blatancy or cynicism, either) is of her own grown-up
sexuality. The latter encourages the man to join her on this
(to him) new level of self-awareness. It is a test, perhaps, but it
is never a tease. Never.

Her playing grounded the conventions of romantic comedy in a sort of idealized reality. Maybe one didn't—doesn't—
meet many women like Irene Dunne in life, but because her
reactions (and everything we've discussed so far *is* a reaction)
were so unforced, so free of mannerism, one felt—feels—comfortable in her presence, as one often does not with a more
overtly "screwball" woman like Carole Lombard. To put it an-

other way, Dunne makes you think she is less unusual than she actually is.

Her directness bespoke capability, the capacity to handle any situation—comic, romantic, tragic—life (or a screenplay) presented in a sensible and simplifying way. That capability, in turn, bespoke experience. And maturity. In her interesting, eccentric book on romantic comedy, *The Runaway Bride,* Elizabeth Kendall observes that Dunne came to the movies older than most female stars of her era; she was thirty-two years old when she made her screen debut, with a solid career as a working actress in the theater behind her. In other words, she was what so many stars are not, a woman who had lived a bit in a hard-knocks world before life-threatening stardom came to her. It is an overlooked but—now that it has been made—obvious point about her, one that made all the difference in her approach to comedy and romance.

But that said, there remains something elusive, mysterious about the source of the wisdom she wore so charmingly. Her upturned nose suggests a pert sense of fun. Her powerful jaw suggests strength of character. And her eyes enigmatically mediate the conflict we read in her face. As late as 1978, when she granted James Harvey, the expert historian of *Romantic Comedy,* what appears to have been her last extensive interview, he observed in life what he had observed on the screen, "something funny and secretive at the center of her eyes." But he, no more than anyone else, was able to penetrate to its source.

Most of her movies made no attempt to explain her subtly knowing air; they simply accepted it (and trusted the audience to accept it too) as the most salient quality of her screen persona, as defining in its way as Hepburn's hauteur or Davis's imperfectly suppressed hysteria. Other characters responded to it, obviously, but they never commented on it openly, and it was never turned into a plot point.

In her interview with Harvey, Dunne's attitude toward her work was just what one might have hopefully imagined: she remembered what she chose to remember, and she was in charge of herself and the situation, just as she had been on the screen. She looked back on her past with a kind of matronly forbearance. Neither living in it nor rejecting it, her attitude toward her former life is perhaps best described as distantly affectionate.

She sounded only one slightly off-key note. When Harvey asked if she had watched actresses like Jean Arthur and Carole Lombard, she replied rather abruptly (by her standards): "I didn't admire them. . . . I never admired a comedienne." That was, she said, because comedy had come so easily to her, and because she preferred, in any case, "the heavier things."

Preferred *Back Street* to *The Awful Truth*? *Magnificent Obsession* to *Theodora Goes Wild*? *I Remember Mama* over everything? Curious! Perhaps more curious to us than to her, since the conventions of romantic comedy have, if anything, grown yet more appealing with the passage of time while those of the weeper now require a strenuous imaginative exercise to apprehend appreciatively.

It's possible she did not always think so unkindly of comedy. She once told an interviewer, "for my career, I cry," implying that the darker emotions were not entirely natural to her, that perhaps her true spirit was a laughing one. On the other hand, two of the films in which we've noted her wry take on masculine duplicity—*Love Affair* and *Penny Serenade*—are not finally comedies. Each shows her enduring bitter losses and triumphing over them in inspirational ways. Each implies that their producers understood her emotional flexibility, her ability to downshift from the giddy to the gloomy without jarring our affections.

Indeed, consulting her "heavier things," one can see that in her playing Dunne made no distinction between comedy and melodrama. Her emotional directness, that straightforwardness that redeems her comedies from implausibility, generally redeems the soap operettas from sentimental excess. Dunne does not deny her emotions—they're right there, entirely visible—but she is always in control of them. She accepts cruel fate with the same steadiness of spirit that, in other contexts, she accepts masculine posturing.

Take, for example, the first of her sad stories, 1931's *Back Street*. When we first meet her Ray Schmidt in turn-of-the-century Cincinnati, she is regarded as "fast." She isn't, of course. She's just a gal who likes to kid around with the traveling salesmen as they pass through town, have a dance or a drink with them in a beer garden. She always knows, though, that she can manage these oafs, keep them in line. Indeed, she's so strong in these scenes that she subverts the rest of the film. We just can't believe that this confident woman would abandon her career, however modest, and allow herself to be unprotestingly kept in a "back street" apartment. Not by Walter Saxel (played by the same stuffy and inattentive John Boles who would soon prove to be Stella Dallas's unlikely undoing). And not for her entire life. A couple of years is the most we can imagine our Irene devoting to him before she recovered her senses. Yet, somehow, the picture works. Having subverted it, Dunne then redeems it with something unspoken in her performance. You believe that whatever her outward circumstances, an imaginative and sustaining inner life is being lived as she awaits, with uncharacteristic passivity, her lover's rather perfunctory visits.

Her *Ann Vickers* of 1933 coordinates Dunne's spirit and a fictional situation much more persuasively. In this adaptation of the Sinclair Lewis novel, she plays a prison reformer who falls in love with a casually corrupt judge (Walter Huston), bears his child out of wedlock (he is married when they meet), then bears loss of job and social standing when their liaison is discovered after he is sentenced to prison for his peculations. Theirs is a remarkably adult relationship, more good-humored than passionate, full of respect for the quality of each other's minds. Huston's judge is, indeed, one of the few plausible white-collar criminals in movie history—and one of the few presented objectively, without resort to moralism. We are encouraged to see him as a confident but not arrogant or cynical man, gracefully carrying a complex understanding of how the social and judicial systems interact, convinced that his manifest intelligence should guarantee his fundamental honesty against any inquiry. How could anyone think a man of his temperament would ever permit a few stock-market tips to cloud his judicial integrity?

The press and public, always eager for simplified understandings of human motives—in the age of gotcha journalism the picture has a powerful, continuing relevance—refuse to take him on his own terms. And he is too proud—or maybe just too smart—to try to explain himself to them. He contents himself with Ann's perfect understanding. Waiting for him to serve out his prison term, raising their child in severely straitened circumstances, she is serenely busy, earning her living in a new career as a writer. There's no time for self-pity in her life and no room for it in Dunne's playing.

Ann Vickers is a movie that, unlike her other thirties films, permits Dunne the dignity of a serious career and an opportunity to demonstrate how misery can be blunted by getting busy. It prefigures her wartime pictures, *A Guy Named Joe* and *The White Cliffs of Dover,* as well as *Anna and the King of Siam* and *The Mudlark.* In all of them she sustains more permanent and devastating losses (she is a widow in three and loses her fiancé in the fourth), but soldiers on, alone and sublimating, improving her own lot and the world's through hard, useful work. Her Mama in 1948, though spared widowhood, is the ultimate statement of that ethic. Practical, self-denying, taciturn at first glance, warm and fiercely protective of her numerous family on longer acquaintance, this Norwegian immigrant woman artlessly summarized the values Dunne's generation had been taught to revere in a film whose only business was to soberly (and lengthily) propagate them.

No one much cares for these later movies now, despite Dunne's regard for them. And no one much sees the two musicals that served, more or less, as the transitions from her sober screen beginnings to her giddy, late-thirties heights. But they are in some ways more revealing of her nature, and of her background, than most of her other work.

She had been raised in modestly prosperous circumstances until she was eleven. Then her father died, and her family was forced to live with grandparents in what Kendall calls "threadbare gentility" in Madison, Indiana. The way out was—need one say it?—hard work. Dunne was a church soloist, an earnest music student, a failure in an audition at the Met. For nearly a decade she pursued a theatrical career that was active and aspiring but only modestly successful, its height being Magnolia in the road company of *Show Boat*. That's where, when the company played Los Angeles, the talent scouts finally found her. Somewhere along the way she married a Chicago dentist and commuted between that city and Los Angeles during the first years of movie stardom, after which he joined her on the West Coast, where they settled into a comfortable, bourgeois existence, very much at odds with the fallen-woman roles she had been playing or the smartly comic ones she would soon begin to play.

She had not sung on screen before she was asked to reprise her *Show Boat* role in the well-mounted, well-directed (by James Whale) movie adaptation of the musical. Her part required her to age from stagestruck teen, whose mother is determined to keep her off the wicked stage—very hard to do since the family business is the eponymous floating opera—to a mature woman dealing with the consequences of marriage to the wayward gambler, Gaylord Ravenal, whose desertion of her obliges her to seek, and find, stage stardom. If Dunne's own romantic life was infinitely more placid than this, it is clear that she knew something about the genteel poverty her character was obliged to endure, something about the possibilities for rescue, however raffish, that show biz can provide a woman down on her luck. There is, in her work here, an emotional seamlessness, a calm yet spirited acceptance of life's ups and downs, that is very appealing. She is a good American sport about everything that happens to her. She can work a low-down dive if she has to and not dirty her skirts. Similarly, she can embrace success without denying her past—the goodness, fun, and, yes, romance she knew roughing it on the river. And, finally, she can forgive her wayward husband, despite the hurt he's done her.

High, Wide, and Handsome—a movie *Show Boat*'s composer and lyricist, Jerome Kern and Oscar Hammerstein II, concocted—offered her similar opportunities, though the script, which Hammerstein also wrote, is altogether loopier—a sort of halfway point between *Show Boat* and *Oklahoma!* In it Dunne is discovered working as Sally, the short-skirted soubrette in her father's medicine show, an enterprise far more modest, and farther down the social scale, than a riverboat was. Working a small town in western Pennsylvania in the years just before the Civil War, their caravan burns down and they are offered refuge on a farm while it is repaired. Its matriarch (Elizabeth Patterson) is a version of Magnolia's mom, prim and proper, but is ultimately won over by Sally's sunny nature. So too is her grandson, Peter (Randolph Scott), whose nature is nothing like Gaylord's—he's a hardworking visionary, determined to find and pump oil on the back forty, but he is romantically careless in other ways. Once he brings in the field, which encourages his neighbors to do the same, he turns into a workaholic, leaving Sally, whom he has by this time married, to fend for herself emotionally.

What particularly preoccupies Peter is a war with the railroads, which are determined to drive the oilmen into bankruptcy by raising their shipping rates. This leads to a heroic and suspenseful attempt to build a pipeline to circumvent the transportation barons (led by Alan Hale) against a court-imposed deadline. Sally has by this time left and, like Magnolia, found success as a singer (in a circus this time). But with time running out on the pipeline and railroad thugs trying to stop it, she rejects an offer from P. T. Barnum, no less, and leads her troupe to the rescue of the beleaguered oilmen—its elephants proving particularly helpful in the final battle.

I know—it sounds ridiculous. It *is* ridiculous. Except that it is also one of the most interesting movies of its moment (it was released in 1937). It is interesting first because its director, Rouben Mamoulian, was a man determined to move musicals away from the backstage settings everyone thought audiences required if they were to accept people suddenly bursting into song and dance; a man determined, moreover, to move them into down-home settings in which vernacular lyrics and folkish music would be appropriate (he would eventually stage the Broadway musicals that fully granted the genre this freedom, *Oklahoma!* and *Carousel,* for which Hammerstein supplied the books and lyrics). It is interesting because, despite its many disparate elements, Mamoulian's energetic conviction and his flair for action compels our attention, no matter how hard disbelief tugs at it. It is interesting because of the way Hammerstein looks backward and forward to preoccupying themes. Here we have the distracted male and the young woman finding the resources of spirit to redeem herself from his romantic fecklessness just as we had in *Show Boat,* just as we would have in *Carousel.* Similarly, the oilman-railroader conflict prefigures the cattlemen-sheepmen conflict in *Oklahoma!* And for good measure Hammerstein even throws in a sketch of that show's dark, sexually twisted villain, Jud Fry, in a character played in *High, Wide, and Handsome* by Charles Bickford. One also has to take note of his endemic populism, his notion that good, simple souls can, by banding together in the democratic spirit, overcome any problem—in this case the machinations of rogue capitalism. It is interesting, finally, because of the way it fits into a nearly forgotten genre of the thirties: pictures about workingmen who defined themselves by the rough, often dangerous, jobs they did—as railroad engineers, long-distance truckers, mail pilots, electrical linemen, or, yes, wildcat oilmen. Those who criticized Hollywood in those days for its lack of social consciousness tended to overlook these movies—perhaps because in celebrating working-class virtue they stressed comradely, communitarian values over ideological ones. Be that as it may, *High, Wide, and Handsome* is, so far as I know, the only musical of that period to partake of that generous, egalitarian spirit.

Its problem is that it is not very musical—its songs are scattered and perfunctory, lacking the shimmering grace of Kern's best work, the lyric intensity of Hammerstein's best. And, try as he will, Mamoulian doesn't successfully integrate them with the rest of the film's business—seems finally to abandon the effort, in the process somewhat abandoning Dunne. She has all of the songs, but her numbers often seem to be truncated. Worse, as the production, in its making and editing, shifts its attention away from her, Sally's character begins to come and go rather abruptly.

Yet here, as in *Show Boat,* one divines the secret of Dunne's appeal more clearly than one does in the comedies that covered shorter time spans or the dramas that tended to stress a single, self-sacrificial note. One sees in both these musicals her entrancing capacity to hint at the strong woman who was to come in her more girlish passages, to remind us of the eager younger woman who was in her more mature scenes. It bespeaks, I think, a stability of spirit, an acceptance of the self as a given, not as something one must tinker with or try to transcend, that is rare among actors.

It is interesting that between these two musicals there fell the one project about which she registered a temperamental aversion. Her first out-and-out comedy, *Theodora Goes Wild*, would also turn out to be one of her most delightful films. But when Columbia first proposed it in 1936, she rejected it. When the studio persisted, she actually fled to Europe in an attempt to avoid it. Why? We know she wasn't frightened of comedy, had already gracefully handled funny passages in a number of films.

I think it is possible that the piece cut discomfittingly close to the bone. Theodora is a small-town girl, living demurely with her aunts. Her life is not unlike what Dunne knew as a child. Under a pseudonym, however, she writes a wicked best-seller exposing the hypocrisies of small-town life. Her anonymity is then threatened by the pursuit of the womanizing New York artist (Melvyn Douglas) who drew the book's jacket. Dunne's character can, of course, handle him. Indeed, he's a man just dying to be handled by her.

What Dunne couldn't handle—or didn't want to handle—was a character who had rather obviously broken with the inner logic of her life, had sought, embraced, a bold discontinuity. In some part of her Catholic, Republican soul she just couldn't understand that kind of behavior. And we must remember too that she was brought up in a period when funny girls were not encouraged and intelligent ones were taught to suppress that quality—especially in small Indiana towns.

So it was natural for her to think long and hard over *Theodora*. And perhaps equally natural of her to come to the right decision about it. Maybe her character does flout the cautious conventions of small-town behavior, maybe her book does criticize the hypocrisies of small-town life, but implicitly so had Irene Dunne when she took to the stage, embracing thereby a life the girls she had gone to school with would never know. Put it simply: Irene at least knew where

Theodora was coming from even if she did not entirely approve of where she was going or how she was getting there. And she was lovely in it—that slight secretiveness of hers admirably suiting a woman who has a big secret she needs to keep.

Still, I have the feeling that despite her success in this film (it brought Dunne her second Oscar nomination and the beginnings of a new career path, just when she needed one, as the fad for weepers faded) she was determined never to break the rules quite so rudely again, and that is why she spoke so disdainfully of "comediennes" and their knockabout ways. *The Awful Truth* involved her in some very silly situations—a custody case involving a dog, a three-door farce sequence, abduction on a motorcycle, a reconciling consummation with her ex while he's wearing a Santa Claus suit—but she's always the reactor in these sequences, not the comedy's prime mover as she's obliged to be in *Theodora,* and that suited her better.

The outright rebelliousness of the runaway brides was simply not for her. The only time she got spectacularly lost was in *My Favorite Wife,* but that wasn't her fault; she was an anthropologist, shipwrecked on an expedition, who returns home, like Enoch Arden, to find that her mate (Cary Grant) has remarried but is also cranky when he discovers that her desert-island companion was handsome Randolph Scott. Dunne plays good-naturedly with Grant's suspicions about what they may have been up to all those years, and Scott's character is portrayed in a distinctly unthreatening way. But Dunne is uncomfortable with this farce, perhaps because it is rather leadenly directed by Garson Kanin. Her best scene is in fact a sober one—a rather touching encounter with her young daughter who no longer recognizes her.

That was her last full-out comedy—unless you count *Life with Father,* which she (correctly) hated because of the ditsiness required by her role as the wife of a curmudgeonly husband and the mother of a too-numerous family. However much one admires her appraising reserve in responding to the advances of Boyer and Grant in *Love Affair* and *Penny Serenade,* both pictures end with her coping resolutely, inspirationally, with glumly melodramatic circumstances. Thereafter, resolution is her salient quality, and though she played it appealingly enough—particularly in *A Guy Named Joe* and *Anna and the King of Siam*—her singularity was rather submerged in these roles. She was, as David Thomson has remarked, entering Greer Garson territory, a place where upper lips were not allowed to tremble, particularly in laughter. Or to soften with the hint of sexual availability if the approach was smart enough.

I Remember Mama aside—it was one of those strangely persistent properties that succeeded as book, play, movie, television series, before finally coming a cropper when Richard Rodgers tried to make a musical of it after its time had finally, blessedly passed—most of Dunne's later films were no more than mildly successful. She left the screen when she was only fifty-four, quitting if not at the top, when she was still near it. She did a little television, joined the board of Technicolor, did some political errands for Eisenhower Republicanism, and toyed with an autobiography but decided her life was too dull to interest most readers. She lived out the remainder of her days quietly, but not reclusively, and with no apparent regrets about any aspect of her life.

And why should she have entertained any? It was an entirely honorable life, unmarred by scandal or deep disappointments, sustained by solid, professional, well-regarded work. If a small-town girl, born just before the turn of the century, was obliged by circumstances to surrender her privacy and make a living in a public career, this was surely the way her parents and her peers would have wanted her to conduct herself. Yet I think there was, quite briefly (for not much more than a decade), something more than she cared to acknowledge (or perhaps fully realized) in the persona she projected—a spirit she could not quite suppress when she was in her first maturity and freed by her success from the genteel evasions endemic to her native ground. This was an intelligence that was not quite rebellious but was distinctly independent in its judgments. Writing about her, trying to analyze her peculiar appeal to me, I start thinking back on the women of her time and class who were the mothers of my middle-class generation. When they were young (and I was even younger), I recall seeing the light that shone in Dunne's eyes shine briefly in their eyes, eyes that never faced any camera bigger than a box Brownie. It was always quickly dimmed because the knowledge it bespoke was a private knowledge, a knowledge that if fully vented might have subverted the right order of things, an order that did not depend on specific political beliefs or religious conviction but was founded on the sense that the conventions of middle-class morality must be publicly upheld, whatever one's private knowledge of their failures and foolishnesses. They were what kept chaos at bay.

For me, Irene Dunne, who never played giddy and rarely played rich, caught the quiet delight these shrewd, curiously tolerant women, the ones who avoided harsh judgments and stern retributions, found in the world's waywardness. It was never something they spoke openly about, and certainly never endorsed—shh, the children might hear you. But it was a good thing to learn, and not a bad way of being.

Now, of course, everyone is free to criticize middle-class order as shrilly as they like. And, threatened, it responds in kind, with among other weapons, fundamentalist fanaticism. Now, of course, the war between the sexes, exacerbated by ideological posturing, is near to nuclear in its intensity. Yet the world is not appreciably better for the caterwauling.

But perhaps it's best not to go there. Better, perhaps, to content ourselves with the observation that the art of screen acting—which offers one way of measuring the state of our civility—is appreciably poorer now because on the whole it lacks the kind of tact, delicacy, and, yes, slyness with which Irene Dunne, among others, let certain undermining but never fatal truths about our social and, above all, romantic transactions slip forth between the lines of the highly conventionalized narratives she so entrancingly served.

1990

Bette Davis: Marked Woman

The brisk way she clipped her words and the singular pauses she often made between syllables—nobody took command of the language in quite the way she did, bending it to her inner rhythms rather than submitting to its tyranny. The abrupt gestures that accompanied her speeches—it was as if she were brushing aside the gnats of insincerity and indecision that so often distract ordinary mortals. The impatient twitch of her shoulders, indicating something less than gladness in the face of foolishness, even on occasion her own—it strongly implied she could bear tragedy, if that's where fate was leading her, more readily than she could stand dither.

No actress more boldly flaunted her mannerisms than Bette Davis, or earned more gratitude by so doing. For we sensed that her style reflected an authentically seething substance. And that is precisely what the movies in which she made her first, indelible mark needed. "Women's pictures" was the patronizing term for them, it being their business to encourage the female audience to bleary contemplation of the seemingly infinite ways in which their sex could be victimized.

Talk about dither! These movies, often arustle with pe-riod costumes, always agurgle with fancy talk, were generally ponderous with self-importance and literary (not to say Oscar) aspirations. With their ceaselessly moaning scores, their portentously shadowed lighting, their cameras endlessly inching in for lingering close-ups of the heroine's suffering features, they typified the high Hollywood style of their day. But they were not typical of its best (or best beloved) manner, which was all quick cuts, brash dialogue, and bustling movement through the frame. Edgy, wayward, domineering, Davis daringly supplied the equivalent qualities for the lugubrious genre that had claimed her. And made it her own. Her pictures all ran on her energy and stand the test of time because of the tensile strength, that inimitable electroplating of heedlessness and vulnerability, her soul's chemistry provided them.

The creation of this screen personality was no easy matter, and her battle to develop and establish it was a matter of public record when she fought it; there was a notable court case (which she lost) when she ran away from Warner Brothers in 1936 to try to make a picture in England she liked better than the lumberjack drama the studio wanted her to do (in which she was ultimately replaced by that towering figure, Beverly Roberts). Her fight to assert herself—"I . . . am ambitious to become known as a great actress," she dared to write Jack Warner just before decamping—also forms a significant part of the historical record. For in effect it guaranteed the truthfulness of her febrile screen presence, reassuring us that it was something more than mere star acting, a set of mannerisms she could shrug off, like a costume, at the end of a day's work. It is one reason she is a legend and such sometime competitors as Ruth Chatterton, Miriam Hopkins, and Kay Francis are not.

One wonders. Would she have succeeded so well if her path had been easier? There is no question that penny-wise

Jack Warner, who disguised his shrewd peasant's paranoia under the flashy manner of a carny huckster, at first impeded the development of Davis's screen character. But it is possible that his permanent opposition to her ambitions and the corporate culture that he created at the Warner studio—it was essentially that of a nonstop alley brawl—did wonders for the development of her moral fiber.

Her presence at Warner Bros. was something of an accident. She had done a few roles at marginal Universal and had been recruited by George Arliss to play opposite him in *The Man Who Played God.* Arliss was the studio's one and only (upper) class act at the time, a middle-aged English stage star who, in the early days of talkies, became an unlikely international movie star by "humanizing" famous historical figures and millionaires in an avuncular, confidential, and well-spoken manner. What he was doing at roughneck Warner Bros. is almost as much a mystery as his popularity, but the young Davis, not conventionally pretty but slender, energetic, and able to exchange dialogue with Arliss on equal terms, suited him.

She did not, however, suit the rest of the studio's output, which was not all gangster films and Busby Berkeley musicals but was definitely biased toward urban, working-class melodramas. Especially when Darryl Zanuck was head of production, these pictures tended to be smash-and-grab jobs, short in length, produced on two- and three-week schedules, full of fast cross talk, fist fights, and sudden death but with no leisure for, shall we say, the nuanced development of character. Particularly female characters. At Warner Bros. the guys—Robinson and Cagney most famously, but just about everyone else in pants as well—got most of the screen time, and most of the good lines. Joan Blondell fit in gorgeously with this crowd, but it was more typical of women on this lot to stand around watching the men strut their stuff. And since Davis did not yet have the credentials to be given leads in the occasional weeper the studio added to its product mix, she found herself doing things like *Parachute Jumper* and *Bureau of Missing Persons* and, most unlikely title in her filmography, *Fashions of 1934.* Yes, she would draw the line at *The Case of the Howling Dog,* in which she was supposed to play Perry Mason's secretary, Della Street, and (humiliation upon humiliation) she would accede to Jack Warner's order to "wrap up her bulbs" (breasts), but still most of her roles in these years could as well have been essayed by such interchangeable Warner girls as Patricia Ellis, Mary Brian, Marian Nixon, or, yes, Beverly Roberts. Indeed, one imagines the studio kept picking up her option mainly because its stories occasionally called for a classy dame—i.e., *Cabin in the Cotton* and *Jimmy the Gent* (which was, at least, a smart Cagney comedy, if not exactly a breakthrough for Davis).

It was a loanout, to RKO for *Of Human Bondage,* which firmly instructed Davis, and moviegoers, in her true worth. The trouble was, Jack Warner was slow to take the hint. Yes, she got *Bordertown,* which foreshadowed glorious neuroses to come, and *Dangerous,* which was in the same vein and brought her first Oscar, and *The Petrified Forest,* adapted from Robert E. Sherwood's play, an upscale project by the studio's standards but in fact a pompous, talkative movie in which a doomed poet and a doomed gangster—Humphrey Bogart in the role that established him in movies but did not make him a star of the first rank—threaten to talk each other to death in a desert restaurant. Still, these enterprises were surrounded by a lot of the same old stuff, and it was after an inept adaptation of *The Maltese Falcon,* which the studio called *Satan Met a Lady,* that Davis made her famous and ultimately effective bolt to Britain.

When she returned she got *Marked Woman,* a crime story obviously suggested by New York District Attorney Thomas E. Dewey's pioneering investigation of the Mafia. It sounds like standard Warner stuff, but it gave her excellent opportunities for character transformation (she played a call girl who testifies against her mob bosses) and colorful suffering (she was scarred for her troubles by the gangsters).

By this time the world was changing and so was Warner Brothers, where smooth, shrewd Hal Wallis, who had replaced Zanuck, was now firmly in charge of production. His literacy was of a different order than Zanuck's—people could speak in paragraphs and metaphors in his pictures—and his visual taste was different, too—darker, more expansive, with less quick cutting. Neither costumes nor psychology frightened him either.

He had, in short, a natural affinity for the kind of material that suited Davis, and he found like-minded talents around the studio—notably writer Casey Robinson—who could serve her gifts admirably. In effect, Wallis and his courtiers presided over her coronation as Queen of the Lot while the boss sulked in the corner of the abby, refusing ever to be seen kneeling at the royal ankle.

It was *Jezebel* in 1938 that announced her new status to the world. For it, Wallis brought in William Wyler to direct, and his fussy, time- and budget-consuming ways drove the producer almost as crazy as they did Jack Warner. But Wyler was to become Davis's lover and, more important, the only truly first-class director she collaborated with more than once. The picture also drove David O. Selznick crazy, for he saw her character—a New Orleans belle, maddened by love and determined to rebel against the gentilities of high society—as a direct competitor to *Gone with the Wind*'s Scarlett O'Hara. Indeed, he darkly suspected that Warner was trying to undercut him by rushing *Jezebel* out while Selznick was still in production on his all-consuming venture.

It would not have been out of character for Jack Warner to try something like that. And everyone was aware that Davis, surely the most logical choice for Scarlett, had been passed over for the role, possibly, she would later say, because

she and George Cukor, *GWTW*'s original director, had clashed
many years ago when they were both working in a provincial
stock company; more likely because Selznick's famous international search for a fresh face to play Scarlett could scarcely
end with the engagement of such a familiar one.

Her disappointment in this matter rankled Davis for the
rest of her life—justifiably so. She was robbed of a role in the
faux epic and ultimate woman's picture that somehow
serenely sails on, resisting all changes in critical fashion, popular taste, and historical perspective. On the other hand,
Jezebel is a much better movie—darker, nuttier, much more
tightly wound. Moreover, it brought Davis her second Oscar
and forever established her feverish screen character. Partly
by accident, partly by design, it offered a shrewd reading and
projection of her essential nature.

For the next decade, the years when she became a dominant movie presence, she would be the victim of many a dire
or miserable circumstance. But she would never be required
openly to acknowledge her victim's status. The women she
played would be—because they refused to heed the conventions and cautions that bind more sensible, less headstrong
folk—the authors of their own misery. And we were encouraged to tremble in the dark on their behalf, our minds shouting silent warnings to them.

But all the logic of the Freudian age (just now beginning
to be broadcast in the popular arts) and the actress's own firm
belief in what *she* was doing, dictated that these ladies be the
last to comprehend the full consequences of what they were
doing to themselves. As a rule their troubles came home to
them precisely because they refused to be the passive playthings of standard morality and social rules. Boldly they
grasped at romantic fulfillment. Bravely they accepted the
consequences of that boldness.

The price could be colorful but redeemable humiliation,
as it was in *Jezebel,* or a narrowly avoided murder conviction

(*The Letter*); madness (*Jaurez*); or, indeed, a death penalty (bitterly ironic in *Dark Victory,* thoroughly deserved in *Beyond the Forest,* in which for King Vidor she uttered her signature line, "What a dump"). Sometimes, to be sure, she settled moral accounts through long suffering (*The Old Maid*). Occasionally, to our delight, she got off scot-free (*The Little Foxes*) or received the unexpected benison of a happy ending (*Now, Voyager*). But her usual fate was melodramatic or at best melancholic, and always she embraced it without murmur of pain or protest, her fierce spirit unbowed, the core of her being intact. So deep, finally, was our faith in her spunk, her inner resources, that Bette Davis, alone of all actresses, could make spinsterhood seem like a bearable conclusion for a movie—or a life.

That was her glory. She refused to yield her essence under pressure. "High-spirited" (popular fiction's genteel synonym for neurotic) she entered the little world any movie is. "High-spirited" she departed it. This was no small gift to the women in her audience. Symbolically she claimed for them the right to yield to their own impulses (which movie males had always enjoyed), to live by their own standards (which movie males had usually dictated). It was no small gift to the rest of us either. For her conviction, her wit, her capacity for self-revelation constantly redeemed improbably tall tales and emotions for believable humanity.

It was no small gift, at last, for herself. Her insistent assertion of her singular reality on the screen, her refusal to project some democratic or corporate version of it was the habit that insured her against gentility's later enfeebling insinuations. And against self-pity or our pity when the great days passed and she found herself with a leftover persona to employ in generally unworthy vehicles. Precisely because her ego proved to be as shatterproof in age as it had been in youth, she compelled attention even when the picture did not. And occasionally she was able to bestow upon us the rambunctious rage for attention (and the heartbreaking insecurity) of *All About Eve*, or the close-to-the-bone pathos of *The Star*, the unjustly neglected 1952 film in which she played a self-destructing movie star, or the cracked grandeur of *Whatever Happened to Baby Jane?* in which amidst the Grand Guignol she manages somehow to touch us with the accumulated madness of thwarted ambition. These were privileged moments she bought for us long ago, paid for with the sound, glowing coin of her youth, and which, any time we want to, we can bring out of the trunk—that is to say, the videotape box—where they are stored, to remind the grandchildren what star acting in all its crazy glory used to be.

1987

Auteur of Our Misery

Cynicism? Sophisticated disdain? Satirical derision? Or just good old-fashioned liberal outrage? Hard to decide which tone offers the best hope of offsetting the depression that finally settles over a reader confronting *The Dame in the Kimono,* a carefully researched and well-written record of institutionalized self-censorship by the American motion picture industry. All of the above are, one way or another, appropriate to the subject; none is entirely adequate to it.

Perhaps wisely, its authors, Leonard J. Leff and Jerold L. Simmons, have opted for straightforward objectivity in their intimately detailed account of the rise to near-tyrannical power, and the fall to well-deserved ignominy, of the old Production Code Administration of the Motion Picture Producers Association. This tiny but ironfisted bureaucracy was widely, but less than accurately, known to the public as the "Hays Office" (after the alleged movie "czar") when its influence was at its height, more precisely referred to in the industry as the "Breen Office" (after its chief censor and guiding spirit). And I must say at the outset that Leff and Simmons are better men than I am, for they actually muster a certain amount of human—though rarely intellectual—sympathy for Joseph Ignatius Breen, his cohorts and assigns, a temptation I found it singularly easy to resist as I turned these pages.

For it was the duty of this small group of willful men to vet every script every major studio proposed to shoot, and to screen every movie before release prints were struck, to make sure it did not violate the list of taboo themes and treatments set forth in the Association's "Code to Govern the Making of Talking, Synchronized and Silent Motion Pictures," first promulgated in 1930 and revised on several occasions. From 1934, when Breen came on board and rigorous enforcement of the code began, until 1968 when, already much battered by changing law, custom, and (most important) pressures from the economically distressed studios, it was replaced by the present rating system, the power of Breen and his associates over the final content of American movies was absolute.

That power was based on their virtually unchallengeable right to give or withhold a seal of approval for every movie made by Producers Association members, which included every major studio. Without it a movie would not, could not be played in the major American theater chains. In other words, with a single stroke "the Breen boys" (as they were known around town) had the means to render a film essentially valueless. Given the industry's traditionally pusillanimous business style, it is perhaps superfluous to observe that Breen only rarely had to apply—or even threaten to apply—his ultimate sanction. For most of his career Joe Breen had but to raise an eyebrow or cough delicately behind his fan to bring the mightiest moguls around to his way of thinking. He became, in fact, the American movies' great, unacknowledged, and totally unqualified *auteur*.

A sometime coal company press agent whose appearance and manner belied his dour later calling, Breen was a large, affable man who could take a joke and tell a joke, and he enjoyed negotiating with studio executives over excisions. He often proposed alternatives to material he found in violation of the code, permitting the studios to imply ideas or story points without saying or showing things that bluntly transgressed the rules. He was also often open to trades—all right, you can keep the décolletage here but that dialogue in reel six has gotta go. By and large the studio people who regularly dealt with him liked him, despite the fact that he performed his duties in a niggling and literal-minded way that will surely make the soul of the modern reader cringe and his mind reel.

The spectacle Leff and Simmons spread before us is of a grown man spending the better part of his life arguing over matters that should not detain an adult for more than a minute. Should Mae West be allowed to say things like, "It pays to be good—but it don't pay much"? Could the juvenile delinquents of *Dead End* use words like "punk" and "louse"? And what about Rhett Butler's famous, "Frankly, my dear, I don't give a damn" tag line in *Gone with the Wind*? It took producer David O. Selznick months to argue Breen into that one—and then only at the cost of toning down the movie's brothel scenes. Not that details of dialogue were Breen's only concern. He insisted on the elimination of *Anna Karenina*'s illegitimate child in Selznick's movie version, but, in another tradeoff, permitted her climactic suicide. Breen could have written a novel of Tolstoyan length in the amount of time he spent fussing over Jane Russell's cleavage and the jiggle and sway of her breasts in *The Outlaw* and *The French Line*.

It is possible, though, that he actually did more damage to movies made before his reign than during it. For his office was charged with editing films made prior to 1934 when they later went into rerelease. In her autobiography Myrna Loy justifiably complains that her role as the title figure's mistress in the 1931 *Arrowsmith* was reduced to incomprehensibility by Breen office cuts when it was rereleased. Moreover, the only time she ever sang in a movie, in Rouben Mamoulian's

Love Me Tonight in 1932, is also now lost because of retrospective moralism. Her filmy costume for that sequence revealed the outline of her navel, and so her contributions to it were removed. (Female navels were not seen in an American movie until 1962, *Town Without Pity* being the breakthrough film.)

The largest mischief of this type that I know of is an obviously mutilated scene in the extraordinary *Baby Face* of 1933, which recounts the story of a woman, played brilliantly by Barbara Stanwyck, coolly sleeping her way to the top of a large bank. Early in the film we more or less gather that her father has been forcing her to work as a whore in his very sordid saloon. More remarkably, however, there's a scene that seems to imply that he is also forcing his own attentions on her. Or not. Impossible to tell from the picture as it now stands. But if one's suspicions are correct, that would account for the coldly vicious way she uses men in her subsequent career. It would also, of course, make *Baby Face*—a very modest little Warner Bros. programmer (in which John Wayne has a small role as one of the middle managers Stanwyck's character uses to get ahead)—into a movie of large historical importance, just possibly the first American movie to bluntly take up the issue of incest and to show, in almost clinical fashion, one of the common consequences of this crime for its victims.

One could go on and on with horror stories of this sort. Indeed, one must conclude that the only discernible good produced by Breen's assaults on screen history was the unintended one of giving Leff and Simmons a catchy title. "Who is that dame in my kimono?" Eve Archer cried when she dropped in unexpectedly on Sam Spade in the first (1931) version of *The Maltese Falcon*. Bad enough that the private eye already had one visitor in dishabille. But that the second one—the wife of Spade's partner, no less—implied by her question that she visited so often that she found it convenient to keep a negligee on the premises—was too much for the censor. Out it went. And out of history as well, since the studios

105

had no archival sense in those days. Censored film, as a rule, was simply junked, lost forever.

These examples of what we might call the "Breen touch," I assure you, are chosen at random from a rich store of nonsense. Doubtless they puzzle people too young to remember movies of the code era. For everything we have mentioned could today be shown on prime-time television without raising fuss or eyebrow except among those religious fundamentalists who more or less impotently carry on the good fight. Moreover, the language, imagery, and activities alluded to were no less within the common experience of most people in those days than they are today. Believe it or not, children, brothels, adultery, navels, and bouncing boobs were not invented by the sexual revolution of the sixties, and such problems as they might have presented in movies before that could easily have been addressed by posting some simple warnings on them for the parents of younger children.

Indeed, it must be said that there is no evidence that the majority of Americans in the 1930s and '40s felt any compelling need for Breen's ministrations. There is nothing in the record to indicate mass disgust with the moral tone of movies before his arrival in Hollywood or mass anxiety that without censorship they would become a vast affront to decent people. On the contrary, customer satisfaction with the movies has never been higher than it was in this period, when they were unquestionably the most powerful and the most beloved of all the mass media.

If there is a criticism to be made of *The Dame in the Kimono* it is that its authors are so transfixed by the variously horrid and hilarious details they have dug up of the Breen office in action that they fail to state as forcefully as they might the reasons for his rise and for the peculiar policies he pursued. To put the matter simply, he was a man with a carefully hidden agenda, the result of which was to impose the tastes, values, and ideas of a minority not merely on an economically consequential industry but on the vast majority of their fellow citizens—well, all right, moviegoers—as well.

For, to put the point simply, Breen was, if you will, the papal—or perhaps one should say the pap*ist*—Nuncio to Hollywood. He owed his job and his authority, and looked for most of his day-to-day decisions, to a power that preferred not to speak its name. It is the story of how Catholics came to operate a star chamber with arbitrary control over film content for something like three of the most crucial decades in the medium's history that is the most fascinating aspect of any account of screen censorship. It is also the aspect of that history that may have continuing cautionary value, since pressure-group politics in one way or another continue to control the crossroads where public policy and moral values meet.

This is not to imply that Catholics were first or always foremost in demanding screen censorship (or that the somewhat liberalized church of today continues on the old path). Starting as early as nickelodeon days, states and municipalities, acting under pressure from religious and reform groups of every kind, created literally hundreds of censorship boards to license the exhibition of movies. These entities were protected by a 1915 court ruling (not reversed until 1952) holding that movies were "common shows" like carnivals and thus not entitled to defense under the First Amendment. As a result, the studios were forced to cut and recut their products to conform to the whims of each locality's censors, and some films were banned outright one place or another. All in all, though, these boards were more nuisance than threat. However they were truncated, most movies finally played most places in some form or other.

In part because this system was so catch-as-catch-can, outrage over movie licentiousness grew among professional moralists during the 1920s, as the tastes of moviemakers and of a significant portion of their audience in an increasingly urbanized and secular culture became more sophisticated. In that period Protestants and Catholics at first joined equally in a chorus of disapproval that was not without its shrill anti-Semitic atonalities, since the movies were well known to be an industry in which Jews predominated. But as the twenties gave way to the thirties, and silent pictures gave way to sound, which promised greater "realism" and added the possibility of mischievous dialogue to imagery already deemed wicked enough, something akin to hysteria overtook the Catholic voices.

Hollywood sinfulness was thunderously denounced from the pulpit and in the pages of the church press. The threat of boycott was heavy in the air. The moguls, isolated by geography from the centers of Catholic power, distanced by their Hollywood provincialism, preoccupied by the conversion to sound, and frightened by the possible effects of the depression on their business, paid scant heed to this agitation. They also understood what history has since confirmed, that a racy reputation by no means assures a film box-office success. Sometimes it helps, sometimes it hurts, and often it is irrelevant compared to other factors (stars and story for example). Thus their challenges to conservative community standards tended to be more erratic than programmatic.

In other words, and no matter what some church zealots thought, the mainstream producers were not pornographers. As the vast majority of their works prove, they shared the basic middle-class morality of their public and quite earnestly propagated it to those who did not yet share in its blessings. The worst that can be said of them was that like most bourgeois papas they reserved the right to tell an off-color story now and then, especially if it was "cute." It may be, finally, that it was this firm sense of their own respectability that prevented them from taking the threat of censorship seriously until it was too late.

Will Hays, the perfect Wasp (small town, Presbyterian, Republican) they had appointed to head their trade associa-

tion and to clean up their image after several scandals involving movie stars in the early twenties, did not share their equa-
nimity. You could pretty much ignore the fragmented
Protestant community, but the monolithic structure of the
Catholic church gave it the ability to carry through on its boycott threats, and Hays repeatedly warned his constituency on
this point. Unfortunately he had no practical ideas for coun-
tering them. Equally unfortunately, someone else did.

He was Martin Quigley, a prominent Catholic layman
who also published an exhibitor's trade journal, the *Motion
Picture Herald.* In other words, his coreligionists were the
chief source of censorious agitation, his readers were the chief
victims of it, and he resolved to help both of them out, in the
process clearly hoping to become the grey eminence of movie
morality, not merely cleaning up movies but also excising
from them "things inimical to the Catholic Church," as he
rather casually—but chillingly—put it.

What he had in mind was a document, binding on all producers, which would specify what subjects movies could
never take up, what stylistic approaches to every topic would
be placed under careful review—in other words, he invented
the code under which the Breen office would eventually function. He obtained church approval to engage a Jesuit priest,
Father Daniel Lord, to draft this paper. Hays fell upon it eagerly when it was finished, and in 1930 the industry hastily
adopted it.

Whereupon, from the Catholic point of view, things immediately went from bad to worse. The moguls had understood the code as a public relations device, not as set of
commandments that would irresistibly rule their professional
lives. In the early thirties, with the depression cutting into
box-office revenues, they carelessly proceeded to threaten the
republic with such excitements as Jimmy Cagney's anarchical
Tommy Gun, Jean Harlow's naked nipples (visible for a
nanosecond in *Red-Headed Woman*), and—Mae West. The

double entendres of *She Done Him Wrong* are correctly credited with (temporarily) saving Paramount from bankruptcy and causing Quigley and Co. to put some muscle behind their code.

Her quaint little movie went into American release in 1933 simultaneously with the Vatican's release of the Most Reverend Amleto Giovanni Cicognani as its new apostolic delegate to the U.S. church. In his first public utterance on these shores, he declared that God and everyone beneath him in the hierarchy were calling Catholics "to a united and vigorous campaign for the purification of the cinema, which has become a deadly menace to morals." It may be that he was not responding to voices from on high. It is possible this was a put-up job, something his hosts asked him to say, for it helped Quigley and Co. to launch their next great idea, the Legion of Decency, which within a year was claiming that seven to nine million church members had solemnly pledged themselves not to attend movies the Legion's rating board (composed largely of middle-aged Catholic ladies) branded with the scarlet letter C (for condemned).

Here at last was a more than plausible boycott threat. To which its organizers kindly provided the solution—the concept of the seal of approval (a simple variation, of course, on the imprimatur the church had long awarded literature that met its standards) and a good Catholic soul to oversee its administration. Since Joe Breen already had a job in the Producers Association, thanks to Quigley, and was actively campaigning for this promotion, the new post went to him almost by default. And from the day he got it in 1934 until his retirement, his strategy for imposing his will on producers was to pretend a certain worldliness. Were it up to him, he would say, he'd let this or that bit of raciness go by. But the Legion . . . or, alternatively, the state boards (which were well stocked with his coreligionists . . . shrug. Upflung hands. Perhaps a sigh over the world's lack of sophistication.

It was a great dodge. It made him out a good fellow, an ally in the difficult task of applying a set of general rules to specific circumstances. To be sure, certain things (miscegenation, white slavery, nudity) were forthrightly banned. But much of the code required interpretation. What, for example, constituted "excessive and lustful kissing"? At what point did the presentation of adultery become censorably "attractive"? At what stage might "scenes of passion" cross an invisible line and "stimulate the lower and baser element"? There was as much room for argument in code law as there was in constitutional law, and Breen was clever at appearing not as the troubled producer's judge but as his *amicus curiae*. In fairness it must be said that occasionally, when the point at issue was social criticism and not sexual innuendo, he would sometimes stand with the producers against the conservative Hays or the church. For example, *Gentleman's Agreement*. He thought this pioneering study of anti-Semitism should be made. What he objected to was that its heroine was, heaven (or Darryl F. Zanuck) forfend, a divorcee. Still, his activities on the whole cannot be seen as anything but deadening to a free and (to my way of thinking) mentally healthy screen.

It is interesting how well Breen hid his tracks. Now and then someone like Edmund Wilson would quite casually refer to "the Catholic censorship" of movies—as if everyone understood *that*. But for purposes of public argument in the thirties and forties it was implicitly stipulated that the code administrators spoke for all decent-minded people. Even liberals who criticized their more absurd contortions were careful not to impute a narrow religious viewpoint to them.

Eventually, of course, Breen and conservative Catholicism undid themselves. After World War II, which had a vastly sophisticating effect on American morals and thought, Breen refused a code seal to a palpably decent, seriously made, seriously meant movie, Vittorio De Sica's *The Bicycle Thief*, because its child protagonist paused briefly to take a pee in the street and because the search for the stolen bike took the boy and his father through a brothel. Here, at last, was an unambiguously good movie on which liberal editorialists could make a strong case against the code. Emboldened by this response, many theaters played it without the seal and found that the sky did not fall. Breen looked even sillier when he refused a code seal to a mild little sex comedy, *The Moon Is Blue*. As Otto Preminger, its producer and director, pointed out, it was a quite moral comedy, in which a young woman successfully defended her virginity against wolfish assaults. Breen's refusal of the seal on the ground that the condition in question was mentioned out loud in the dialogue struck people as highly hypocritical, and despite lack of a seal and a C rating from the Legion it did well in release. (My date for this movie was a young Catholic woman, who was even more eager to see it than I was, and doubtless representative of a new churchly generation that was beginning not to step forward and take the Legion pledge when it was renewed in church each year.)

Together with the extension of the First Amendment to the movies (the historic argument was over another Italian movie, *The Miracle,* which had been banned in New York for "blasphemy"), and Cardinal Spellman making a laughingstock of himself by denouncing the rather innocent and jolly *Baby Doll* from his pulpit, the power of the church in the industry and with the public was damaged. Then, when the producers of movies like *Lolita* and *Who's Afraid of Virginia Woolf?* instituted what amounted to a voluntary rating system—they barred patrons under eighteen from their theaters and enforced the ban without seriously affecting profits—this phase of motion picture censorship began drawing to a close. Indeed, it was Catholics who recognized that moviemaking and moviegoing were no long remotely amenable to simple, single-standard morality, and who led the campaign for replacing the either-or seal system with the somewhat more flexible ratings system (which was what the Legion of Decency had been using, albeit with sterner standards, all along).

By that time Joe Breen had folded up his lace curtains and tottered off into retirement, doubtless feeling the sting of ingratitude. After all, he might have asked, movies had been more popular during his reign than ever before or since, so what harm had he done? Had he lived longer he might also have come to argue that his term of office closely coincided with what history now regards as the classic age of American cinema, a period of enormous creative energy (and prosperity) that remains historically unmatched. We can also add this truism to his defense: censorship often acts as a goad to creativity, imposing the need to find subtle and witty ways around its laws, which are sometimes preferable to head-on statements. When Nick Charles tosses Asta out of Nora's lower berth into the upper in their train compartment, we know what he has in mind. And, right under Breen's nose, Preston Sturges made a comedy about virgin birth, *The Miracle at Morgan's Creek,* that is infinitely more subtle and subversive—not to mention flat-out funnier— than *The Miracle.*

But all that is not entirely to the point. We can never know what might have been accomplished were censorship not in place. Being happy with some of what we have is not the same as being pleased about everything we missed— or about the summary excisions of significant material in earlier works. We can with even greater justification argue that the inability of the movies, when they were at the height of their influence, to deal with sexual issues forthrightly had the effect of imposing an adolescent mind-set about these matters on several generations. It seems to me that the influence of the Breen office was a factor in making the so-called sexual revolution more wrenching and confusing than it needed to have been. It might, indeed, have been no more than a sexual adjustment if our popular culture had not for decades been so gingerly, genteel, and duplicitous about this topic.

The situation has obviously improved in the two decades since the rating system has been in place. Films that are unambiguously ambiguous about the functioning of traditional morality, sexual and otherwise, do get made without censorious tampering. On the other hand, since 1968 the movie audience has been increasingly dominated by adolescents. The result is that fewer and fewer R-rated films, from which those under seventeen are (at least in theory) banned are produced, and, of course, movies threatened by an NC-17 rating (a genteelism for the old X) are always trimmed because newspapers and television will not carry advertising for films so rated. In the councils of the code office, horse trading of a kind that would be utterly familiar to Joe Breen continues unabated as producers haggle for more commercially desirable ratings.

The majority of American movies today (a little bit of irrelevant blunt language, the occasional insignificant flash of bare buns excepted) are generally bland, evasive, and "cute" about serious sexual matters—at least in comparison to what we were permitted to see in the sixties and early seventies, when movie people were eagerly testing the limits of the new code. I doubt, for example, that the brilliant opening of *Bonnie and Clyde* (Faye Dunaway gorgeously nude and playing with herself), which sets up the film's vital subtext, in which a life of crime is seen first as a substitute for and then as a stimulation to sexual adventure, could be released today. Meantime, Protestant fundamentalism speaks as threateningly as precode Catholicism ever did about the moral threat movies—and now television—is supposed to pose to youth. Indeed, given the modern media's ability to amplify controversy, nothing quite as extensive or hysterical as the campaign against *The Last Temptation of Christ* in 1988 or the uproar about Murphy Brown's out-of-wedlock baby has ever been seen in this country. Joe Breen may be gone, but the spirit that animated and supported him lives on. And retains a potential for mischief that the old boy might well have envied.

1990

Charles Laughton: No Room for Genius

Some years ago I was asked by **PBS** to cut down and slightly rearrange a rather rickety old **BBC** documentary called *The Epic that Never Was* in order to make it fit an American time slot. The program was about the adaptation of *I, Claudius,* the Robert Graves novel, which its producer, Alexander Korda, shut down, well after principal photography had begun, sometime in **1936**. In the documentary, various survivors of that disaster speculated about why Korda had taken this embarrassing action—something that almost never happens at this stage in a movie's life, no matter how much trouble is occurring on the set.

The inescapable implication of their testimony was that the canny producer, seeing that his star, Charles Laughton, and his director, the imperious Josef von Sternberg, simply could not work together, used an auto accident that temporarily incapacitated costar Merle Oberon (whom Korda would soon marry) as an excuse to collect his insurance money. This supposition was later confirmed by Simon Callow in his wise and hugely sympathetic biography of Laughton— "A Difficult Actor," as the subtitle identified him.

Callow stops short of calling this incident a tragedy, and so will I. But running the *I, Claudius* footage backward and forward in the editing room, I saw that what was in process of creation in those lavish sets in prewar England was something that almost certainly would have been one of the era's most memorable screen performances—and perhaps the definitive statement of his art by a very great screen actor.

Laughton at the moment had achieved, in a matter of four or five years, the peak of his powers, not to mention a vast international renown. His fame was no small accomplishment, considering his—to say the least—unprepossessing physical appearance and the limits it imposed on him. For, ironically, Charles Laughton was an actor who had all the equipment anyone needs to play the great tragic and heroic roles except the most basic one—romantic good looks.

That irony is compounded by the fact that during this period, as Laughton established himself as a world figure, his great contemporary, and the man who had in abundance what Laughton lacked—the handsome, dashing, and equally brilliant Laurence Olivier—was enduring a humiliating failure in the movies while the other great knights of his English theatrical generation—notably Gielgud and Richardson—were scarcely to be found anywhere on the screen. Today, of course, their reputations flourish while Laughton's is considerably discounted.

Was, indeed, at a discount when I encountered his *I, Claudius* footage. I had, of course, grown up on Charles Laughton. He was an inescapable presence in my moviegoing as a youngster—as the cranky *Canterville Ghost* (doubtless the first film I saw him in), as the cowardly schoolteacher finding the courage to oppose the Nazis occupying his French village in *This Land Is Mine* (a performance that grasped and moved

117

me at the time, though I could not say why at age ten, except that I had never seen anything quite like it), as the cold, manipulative, deeply menacing media mogul in *The Big Clock* (who was perhaps a version of Henry Luce, given that the author of the book on which the film is based, Kenneth Fearing, had worked, apparently unhappily, at Time Inc.). All this work had a quality the untutored always like in acting—boldness—and I became something of a fan.

Later, in the fifties, it became easy to get in direct touch with Laughton, who went around the country doing readings and, more famously, trouping with the First Drama Quartet in their staged reading of *Don Juan in Hell,* which he directed and starred in (with Charles Boyer, Cedric Hardwicke, and Agnes Moorehead). They played my college theater, and I was as wowed as anyone by the presence of all these movie stars on our provincial stage, so wowed that I remember nothing about the performance's details. The sheer glamour of the occasion swept me away.

But if Laughton was an inescapable presence in our lives, he was, by this time, a largely unexamined premise. Older people spoke affectionately about him but seemed to indulge him more than they appreciated him. Their line was that his hamminess was fun, but that we were under no obligation to take him seriously. By this time, too, all the talk from hip young show folks was of "the method," and they made actors like Laughton seem old hat, out of it. Laughton himself, in his interviews and other public appearances, seemed to accede quite cheerfully to his reputation for broadness, seemed to enjoy being a "character" in his own right rather than this or that "character" in a dramatic piece.

It was, I'm sure, something of a defensive ploy on his part. Why fight an impression so widely held? Indeed, knowing what we now know of the terrible insecurities that afflicted him on *I, Claudius,* whenever he undertook taxing and aspiring works, one begins to see that Laughton was, in these years, hiding in plain sight. Most of his later movie roles, whatever their charms, could not have challenged him profoundly or, more to the point, stirred his always lively fear of humiliating failure. The same could be said of his work in *Don Juan,* which, as I've indicated, had more the quality of a gracious personal appearance than of a demanding performance. The emphasis was all on text, not subtext, stuff these well-spoken veterans could declaim impressively without daring more dangerous country. One thinks of them picking up celebrity's small change in a dignified and, indeed, culturally commendable manner. One was obliged to appreciate this work, not to reckon with it.

But reckon one had to with *I, Claudius.* There was such range in the handful of finished sequences the documentary presented—shyness and slyness, intellect and childishness, and, finally, a moral force not untouched by vengefulness when the emperor's crown is finally offered to him. You don't often find these kinds of mood swings in star acting of that time—maybe of any time—and I wanted to see more of it and gain some sort of purchase on this curious career.

Happily, a variety of projects put me in touch with most of Laughton's achievements in the comparatively brief period during the 1930s when he created most of his great, sustained characterizations. What he accomplished—often against the odds set by bad scripts and indifferent direction—was both astonishing and utterly unique—a flaring assertion of talent, perhaps even of genius, that no one had expected of him and that his roles for the most part didn't demand.

Encountering his work when most of the movies themselves had diminished from inconsequentiality to, in many cases, risible irrelevance, my admiration for Laughton perversely grew. For over the several decades I've worked as a critic of a popular medium, my fascination with figures like Laughton and Alfred Hitchcock (for whom he worked twice), who invent public personae that duplicitously deepen the

119

general misunderstanding of what they're up to, encourage the broad audience to see them as genial entertainers, thus securing themselves the freedom to pursue more dangerous agendas unfettered, has also deepened.

This disguise is not one that such figures don of a sudden. It evolves over the years in response to changing perceptions of one's self and, indeed, others' perceptions of that self. Laughton, I imagine, came to Hollywood in the way most English actors of his time did—glad to get a little work that paid better than English movies or the West End theater, glad to spend a little time in the sun, not thinking American movies might become central to their careers, not particularly wanting that to happen. A restless, not to say driven, man, he probably imagined himself dropping in and out of town as good roles presented themselves, rather as Olivier would do once he conquered the medium. Certainly Laughton never embraced the other available option, joining the "British Colony," composed largely of character actors like Cedric Hardwicke and C. Aubrey Smith, making dull, steady livings by working reliably in the many adaptations of English literary classics, English history, that the studios thought constituted classy fare in the thirties and forties.

Laughton was not self-effacing enough for that kind of work. Jesse L. Lasky, the Paramount production chief who first signed him, could see that but didn't have many better ideas either. So rather than see him idle expensively on contract, the studio loaned him out to Universal to make *The Old Dark House,* an adaptation of a J. B. Priestley novel that was an attempt at modern-dress gothic. The understanding was that its rival must hold the picture back until Paramount had made and released what it was determined to promote as Laughton's debut film.

That turned out to be *Devil and the Deep*, in which he was awarded this remarkable—and telling—billing: "And introducing the eminent English character actor, Charles

Laughton." His eminence was none too happy with the project. To begin with, the screenplay was exotic drivel, with Laughton cast as a British submarine commander, Charles Sturm (no Drang in sight), patrolling the ramparts of empire from a remote base in West Africa, beset by a sexually restless wife, played by Tallulah Bankhead, during her only sustained, if feckless, assault on talking pictures, but actually rather good in this Marlene Dietrichish role. In it her roving eye keeps straying toward younger, comelier officers, settling briefly on Cary Grant before fixing itself firmly, disastrously on Gary Cooper, playing Sturm's second-in-command. The illicit lovers are, of course, found out, and the script maneuvers all the principals onto Sturm's boat, where he cracks up and sinks the thing. He goes down with his ship while the lovers go up with the rest of the escaping crew.

Worse than the silly scenario were the working conditions. Cooper, in the midst of a salary squabble with the studio, was uncharacteristically sulky and, despite his reputation as one of Hollywood's leading studs, impervious to Bankhead's determined advances. She, in turn, took an intense dislike to Laughton who, completing an unlikely triangle, was smitten by the gorgeous Cooper. Not that any overt homosexual advances were made, but Laughton, envying him his easy naturalism, would go to his grave proclaiming Cooper one of the best actors he had ever worked with.

In the movie's one memorable scene, a final confrontation with Cooper just before he pulls the sub's plug, Laughton has this poignant speech: "Must be a happy thing to look as you do. I suppose women love you. Must be a happy thing." As he speaks, he tugs and kneads his fleshy face, as if trying to reconform it to some imagined ideal of masculine beauty. It is a moment of near-sublime pathos—and a truly daring actor's choice, since it openly acknowledged, in his first important film, his dismay at the grotesque form in which his spirit was encased.

The Old Dark House offered opportunities for another kind of confession. This film now has the reputation of a camp classic, but that's perhaps only because it's hard to know how else to classify it—or possibly because we'd like to think it must be funny since it so utterly fails to be scary. Directed by James Whale after his success with *Frankenstein* but before he made his one authentic masterpiece (camp or otherwise), *Bride of Frankenstein* (which featured Elsa Lanchester, Laughton's wife, in her most memorable performance), it is also more or less the model for *The Rocky Horror Picture Show*, the midnight movie that became a rite of passage for recent adolescent generations.

The film offers two groups of motorists obliged to take refuge in, well, an old dark house on a stormy night. Its inhabitants are all to some degree insane, some of them murderously so. The trouble is that they are not really very threatening, and their guests cope with them in a fairly straightforward manner. Suspense—and surprises—are minimal and flatly presented. Laughton's Sir William Porterfield, a self-made midlands tycoon who retains a healthy awareness of his humble origins, is the most dynamic character present. He bustles in with a chorus girl on his arm and eager to organize the chaos he discovers. In the end he will lose his traveling companion to a figure played by Melvyn Douglas, whom we understand to have been damaged by his experiences in the Great War. True love and mutual regeneration are in the offing for these two as the picture ends.

But Sir William accepts this loss in a generous, worldly-wise, mildly surprising manner, for he is affected by a poignant class-consciousness, ultimately expressing the conviction that snubs from his social betters led to his beloved wife's early demise. He is touched that Douglas's swell can see beyond such matters, respond to the honest virtues of his chorine, and so blesses their match. One has to believe that an awareness of how far he had come from his own unpromising formative years—his parents were hotel keepers in Scarborough—was drawn on here. This was something we would often see in his work, frequently as implicit motivation for more monstrous behavior.

His next, very brief role for Paramount, in Cecil B. De-Mille's *The Sign of the Cross,* was more dangerously confessional, for he played an openly homosexual Nero. It is a particularly awful biblical nonspectacle, even by DeMille's standards, notable mainly for Claudette Colbert's once-notorious asses' milk bath, during which a couple of tantalizing glimpses of her nipples are afforded the carefully observant, at the end of which she, playing Laughton's empress, invites one of her attendants into the vast tub, with lesbian dalliance clearly in mind. (This was 1932, two years before Hollywood began to enforce seriously its new production code.) Laughton's Nero (complete with a puttied-on Roman nose) is both comically and dangerously wigged out on his own decadence. He has only three scenes, but their message is clear: he really doesn't give a hoot about the fate of the Christians, whom his courtiers are determined to persecute, as long as the annoying political issue they present doesn't interfere with his pleasures. Amidst the leaden pieties of the film, which was based on one of those turkey melodramas of the nineteenth-century stage that people of DeMille's generation nostalgically adored, Laughton's appearances as a man beset by the distractions of governance and the insistent demands of his own sexual nature provide the most DeMillian aspects of the work—given that the one thing that can sometimes still amuse us in the director's work is its loony sexual implications.

More to our present point, however, there's a boldness in this portrayal that is unexpected, particularly at that moment in screen history, when homosexuality, if it was hinted at all in a movie, was presented as harmlessly comedic, not as the root or the symptom—hard to tell which in this context—of something dangerous, almost psychopathic.

What's striking, then, about Laughton's first three American movies is that, weak as the films are, he managed to suggest not merely the full range of his gifts but, more important, to hint at the full range of his torments with considerable forthrightness. And in about a year's time to establish himself as a force to be reckoned with. To these performances he soon added his lovely, wordless piece, directed by Ernst Lubitsch, in the omnibus *If I Had a Million,* in which he plays a clerk who, having received word of the eponymous inheritance, makes his way from his desk through the hellish office where he's employed toward his awful boss's office, keeping an almost straight face on his good fortune until he enters and gives his chief tormentor a resounding, merrily rebellious raspberry.

Much more complex is his appearance as Dr. Moreau in *Island of Lost Souls,* based on the H. G. Wells fiction and twice remade but never improved upon. He was as mad a scientist as the horror genre ever offered, crossbreeding men and animals in his remote retreat with truly monstrous yet undeniably remarkable results. True to type, he's full of hubris about his work, which like Frankenstein and the others he regards as a nice challenge to God. But Laughton's performance in what should have been a conventionalized part—one that usually calls forth a good deal of shouting and eye-rolling—is beamish, self-amused, almost smug.

At one point he explains to Richard Arlen, an adventurer who has intruded on his space, what he's been up to. His creatures—half-man, half-animal—can talk, and Moreau cannot contain his pride: "That is my first great achievement—articulate speech controlled by the brain. That *was* an achievement." He is lolling nonchalant on a gurney in his laboratory (otherwise known as "the house of pain"), drawling out his words. "Oh," he adds, "it took a long time and infinite patience to make them talk." Then he points the toe of his well-polished shoe and studies it, his attitude rather like that of a clubman passing the afternoon in jokey idleness. "Someday I'll create a woman and it will be easier," he laughs—slyly, chillingly. It is one of those magically real moments that great actors sometimes instinctively achieve, where they break through the essential unreality of movies and deliver us, slightly stunned, to the realm of truly felt (and expressed) reality.

His next performance, back in England, in *The Private Life of Henry VIII*, next to Captain Bligh perhaps his most famous screen appearance and the one for which he won his only Academy Award, is perhaps more along what would come to seem Laughton's main line. Alexander Korda, whatever his gifts as a producer, was never much of a director, and cinematically the thing is stiff and stagy, without flow. But at the time that was not so important to audiences, and in a curious way it served Laughton. For as Callow says, this is a full-length portrait, not a head-and-shoulder one, and Korda's distanced camera allows us to take in fully the restless physical rambunctiousness of the king. It also permits us to see that this was a brave piece of work by the actor—almost satirically ballsy, a near-parody of the strutting, occasionally self-pitying, but always testosterone-driven heterosexual male. With his carelessness and occasional cruelties driven by almost boyish exuberance, he's like the CEO of a hot new start-up. These early passages, so vividly rendered, tend in memory to blot out the later ones, where the old king is observed in dotty decline, but they also serve to set up what was to come, providing the contrast that gives the end of this life its poignancy.

Yes, it's hammy. Several critics at the time called it that.

But it requires courage for an intelligent, knowing actor, which God knows Laughton was, to go over the top, banners waving, bugles blowing. It especially requires courage if you are a homosexual actor parodying the kind of careless maleness that has surely made your life a misery more than once.

Despite the success of this performance, Laughton did not linger over it or return to its tonalities. He was clearly intent, in this period, on not repeating himself. He went directly on to the repressed, repressive sadism of Elizabeth Barrett Browning's father in *The Barretts of Wimpole Street*, then to a broadly comic butler, won in a poker game and obliged to bring a touch of English civilization to the wild American West (he had a particularly glorious drunk scene) in *Ruggles of Red Gap*, finally to his great Inspector Javert in Richard Boleslavsky's haunting version of *Les Misérables*.

Boleslavsky had been a lancer in the Polish cavalry, one of Stanislavsky's most trusted disciples in the Moscow Art Theater, a hypnotic acting teacher, and one of the art's most seductive theoreticians (his unpretentious but inspiring little book, *Acting: The First Six Lessons*, remains in print). As much as anyone, he was responsible for establishing what came to be called "the method" in America. In the mid-thirties he was also establishing himself as one of Hollywood's most interesting and versatile directors, and if he had not died prematurely (in 1937) one suspects he might have achieved high status in the history of the medium. In any case, his *Les Miz*, broodingly photographed by the great Greg Toland, remains the standard by which all film and theatrical versions of the Victor Hugo classic ought to be judged. The same must be said for Laughton's Javert, so tightly wound, so aware of the monstrousness of his pursuit of the unhappy Jean Valjean, yet equally aware of how helplessly he is entrapped in his own obsession. The "ham" here is giving—no other word for it—a Stanislavskian performance, and I suppose it is precisely because this work is so controlled, so subtle, that it is passed

over by many commentators on Laughton's career. It just
doesn't have the flash of, say, his Captain Bligh, the role on
which so many impressionists would fasten, and the next
great performance in the Laughton canon.

As a film, *Mutiny on the Bounty* is everything *Les Misérables* is not—curiously sunny, clean, and tidy in the MGM
manner of the day. You don't for a moment believe that Bligh
and company have been on a voyage covering thousands of
miles and endless months at sea. Nor do many of the actors
portraying the ship's company persuade you that they are
horny-handed tars, press-ganged into His Majesty's service.
Only Laughton truly rivets our attention. The salient aspect
of his makeup here is heavy, beetling brows, said to have been
inspired by those of the director, Frank Lloyd, who came naturally by this feature and at one time hoped to play Bligh
himself. One almost thinks Laughton's characterization derived from those brows, for there is something sideways and
scuttling about it   rather like a cockroach surprised by light.
He refuses to squarely meet the eyes of the other actors (Clark
Gable, playing Fletcher Christian, the officer who finally leads
the mutiny, complained about the way Laughton kept screwing up his eyelines). Rarely has paranoia been physicalized so
vividly.

And rarely has intelligence been portrayed with such perverse power. Dustin Hoffman observed recently that the
really scary thing about Laughton's Bligh was that he was the
brightest man aboard the *Bounty,* maybe the smartest man in
any theater where the movie played, and he is not exaggerating by much. One feels the hopelessness in trying to outthink
or appease him; he's always a step ahead of everyone. Worse,
he believes any sign of human frailty on his part, any sympathetic acknowledgment of it in others, will be understood as
exploitable weakness, a chink in the armor of command that
could bring him to disaster.

There are hints in the script, performance, and historical

record that Bligh's nature may have been shaped by class resentments, that he was acutely aware that other officers, better connected, better born than he, are receiving preferments in the British navy, hints that his cruel repression of everyone under his command reflect his need to repress his own wayward, lower-class impulses. But you have to lean in very close to pick up these murmured undertones. What we have in *Mutiny on the Bounty*, especially in the long first act, which Laughton utterly dominates, is a meanness of spirit remarkable for its relentlessness. It bears none of the outward signs of madness, which is a way actors have of signaling that they are not responsible for the actions of their characters. It is, instead, a chillingly rational characterization. It is hard to think of any film performance that so boldly refuses to sue for the audience's favor. And coming from an actor so expert in finding something exculpatory in his monsters, it is the more astonishing. Eventually, when movie villainy is pursued with this intensity, we try to convince ourselves that it is a joke, begin to laugh nervously at it. We never laugh at Captain Bligh.

We do, perhaps, tend to forget the movie's second act in which, cast adrift with a handful of loyalists in a small boat, he navigates them across some 3,500 miles of ocean to a safe harbor and proves himself to be, as well, an inspired leader. Here we see the useful side of cold intelligence, deployed finally against a worthy enemy—irrational, unpredictable nature—begin to see that it is *human* nature he should never have been asked to contend with. Not that Laughton allows his Bligh to be softened by this ordeal. It reinforces his belief in his own righteousness, a belief that perhaps God himself was steadying the hand he kept on the small boat's tiller. At the end of the film, when some of the mutineers are tried for their crime, he is as unforgiving as ever.

It's no wonder that this became Laughton's signature performance. The sadness is that the movie that surrounds it is so lacking in energy so stodgy in its action. But that, of course, was Laughton's fate in general, so often obliged to fill in the empty spaces in empty enterprises.

For example, *Rembrandt,* his next film. He was back with Korda, both of them looking for a success to match *Henry VIII.* Again the project was carefully mounted, with a serious attempt to match the master's lighting, even though the film stock was black and white. Again the story line mainly concerned the protagonist's vexed relations with several women. And again Laughton's performance was admirable—in this case as restrained as his Henry had been rambunctious. Callow thinks it was autobiographical—the gifted and hugely aspiring artist besieged by distractions and misunderstandings—and that's plausible. Laughton learned to paint passably in order to play the part, and the scenes where Rembrandt is at his easel have a focus and energy rare in movie representations of the artistic life. (The experience also apparently led Laughton to begin amassing what would eventually become one of Hollywood's most tasteful art collections.)

Still, Laughton and Korda quarreled their way through production, and the actor was unhappy with some of his fellow players, notably Gertrude Lawrence, though his wife, Elsa Lanchester, in those days sometimes an add-on if you wanted to sign Laughton, was as good as she ever was, and remembered the film as one of her happiest collaborations with her husband. Yet whatever its occasional felicities, the film was more dutiful than inspired. Respectfully received by critics at the time, it was not the commercial success *Henry VIII* had been and perhaps added to Laughton's insecurities.

It is these, of course, that brought *I, Claudius* to ruin, though one can't help but think that if anyone other than von Sternberg had been at its helm it might have turned out differently. The director at this moment was a pathetic case. His relationship with Marlene Dietrich, whom he had discovered and whose early career he had obsessively shaped, was over. So was the vogue for the kind of movies they made—exotic romances deliriously mounted by a man with a real gift for wacky *mise-en-scène*. Unable to find work in Hollywood, the director went to ground in a London psychiatric hospital whither Dietrich directed Korda, promising to forgive a large fee he owed her for an earlier picture if he would employ her erstwhile Svengali. It was an idea Laughton endorsed. von Sternberg had befriended him when he suffered a brief but painful illness in Hollywood, demonstrating at that time warm sympathy for the actor's high ambitions.

But living rooms (and hospital rooms) are not movie sets. Bestriding those that Vincent Korda, the producer's gifted art director–brother, had created at the Denham studio outside London, von Sternberg went into dictatorial mode, treating Laughton with cold contempt. The director implied in his highly fictive autobiography that there was method in his madness. He imagined that Laughton was drawing on masochistic elements in his nature to inform his characterization and claimed he was merely helping him along. von Sternberg also wrote contemptuously of the actor as a child whom he, for one, was not about to further spoil. Besides, he wrote, actors were all empty vessels which, if they were wise, they allowed the director to fill with his genius. All his great successes, von Sternberg claimed, had occurred when his players acceded to this plan.

It is a ludicrous idea in general, and it was quite mad to apply it to Laughton. All *his* great successes had come in opposite circumstances, with directors at most murmuring support and attending to the technical details. More than ever he needed that kind of collaboration now, though it is difficult to determine why he was feeling particularly vulnerable, and even Callow is not very clear on this point. My own guess is that the actor was acutely aware of how fast and far he had traveled in a very short time. He was suddenly a star—but a star in a character actor's body. Which may have meant to him that prodigies of daring work were required to retain that status. Given the pace at which he had been driving himself, he may have been too drained to summon the energy this role required.

Its physical demands were large—Claudius was afflicted with a stammer and with a withered leg that caused him to limp grotesquely—and so were its emotional ones, for this was a deeply duplicitous man, hiding a brilliant intelligence beneath the manner of a fool. It was a rare challenge, but chilled by von Sternberg's contempt, Laughton found he could not even remember his lines, that his accent was slipping into strange territories. Thus beset, he felt he could not act the part fully, freely, intuitively. At one point he conceived the somewhat desperate notion that his model should be Edward VII (also a stammerer), and he took to playing a record of the monarch's recent abdication speech obsessively. That seemed close to *lèse-majesté* to Korda, who ordered his star to abandon the idea. Laughton also spent a lot of time wandering the sets, looking for inspiration in their architecture and also, doubtless, trying to avoid von Sternberg, who countered by ordering the stages kept lit, hoping that if inspiration should strike he could take quick advantage of it. Nothing, however, worked, and soon enough the director was back in hospital, where he lay when Oberon's auto accident gave Korda the excuse he needed to end everyone's agony.

Why Korda didn't simply hire a new director and keep going is a nice question, though it's possible the chronically underfinanced producer couldn't afford both to pay off von Sternberg and to hire a replacement. What's beyond question is the quality of Laughton's unfinished portrait. His Claudius was, most basically, a misfit in Imperial Rome, content to let his peers think him a mental defective while he tended his garden (actually a pig farm) and developed his dangerous intellect. A scene in which Laughton establishes this premise shows him amused by his own cleverness and slightly ashamed of it, too. Also shot was a sequence in which he is summoned to Rome to confront the mad Caligula (Emlyn Williams) and forced to abase himself in order that his life be spared. Again the self-knowledge is wonderful to behold. To be fully aware of your own cowardice, to offer no rationales for it ("someday I'll return, someday I'll have my revenge") is, paradoxically, one of the bravest choices an actor can make. Finally, there is the scene where the senate contemptuously, with much hilarity, offers the throne to this man they imagine to be a buffoon, and he arises to enumerate the terms on which he will accept it—first swallowing his stammer to charge his tormentors with corruption, then movingly to describe the rules under which he will reign, which can only be described as liberal and democratic.

How wonderfully unexpected this revelation is, especially in its lack of overt vengefulness. One gets the sense that Claudius, as emperor, will act not out of the need to redress personal grievances but out of the principles of rational governance that he evolved during his long exile. One also feels that perhaps Claudius is himself surprised by his own nobility. And possibly moved, heartened by the words that come to him uncalculated, under the pressure of the moment. From a hesitant beginning we see a man increasingly intoxicated by his own rhetoric, transformed perhaps by the act of speaking, at last, all that had been unspoken for so many years.

The abrupt juxtaposition of these fragments in the documentary, without plot to distract us, forms a powerful, microcosmic testimony to Laughton's gifts. Reviewing Laughton's work in the title role of Bertolt Brecht's *The Life of Galileo* on the New York stage a decade later, the critic Eric Bentley wrote that his "combination of physical grossness with intellectual finesse was theatrical in itself," and certainly that thought applies here. Obviously Laughton had played men of high intelligence before, and equally obviously he had never been able to disguise his physical being. But with Claudius's physical disabilities, and a strong hint that homosexuality (or perhaps it was bisexuality) had been closeted along with his intelligence, there is an unmatched richness—and poignancy—in this performance.

A sort of rude justice prevailed after the failure of this enterprise. Von Sternberg was shuffled to the fringe and in the three decades left to him made only a handful of pictures, some highly mannered, some routine, none successful critically or commercially. Mostly he spent the rest of his life railing at the industry for its failure to acknowledge his genius. Laughton, however, sailed on. Or seemed to. He went quickly into three minor English pictures, including Hitchcock's *Jamaica Inn*, the director's last (unhappy) London production before moving to America. Thereafter Laughton returned to America and to the last of his great lead roles, *The Hunchback of Notre Dame*, in which once again he offered the definitive interpretation of a classic Victor Hugo character—an enormously touching performance, not least for the stray-animal quality he brought to it—wary yet needy—and the open pathos he expressed about his looks—Captain Sturm writ large, perhaps. Or the hungering soul of Charles Laughton.

Physically it was his most taxing role, played beneath the heaviest makeup of his life. But this was not a hugely complex figure, and it was one to whom sympathy flowed very readily. After that, most of what Laughton did was still less demanding—possibly because he did not want to test his limits again, perhaps because the industry did not want him to for fear of a repetition of the *I, Claudius* mess. A lot of Laughton's film work in the forties and fifties was marginal—a Deanna Durbin movie, two Captain Kidds (the first in a distinctly low-rent production, the second opposite Abbott and Costello)—and quite a bit of it was broadly comedic versions of the public character that Laughton was becoming. There were some leads, of course, and I don't think I'm wrong in thinking that *This Land Is Mine* is the one that put him in something like full touch with his former grandeur. Directed by Jean Renoir, exiled by the war to Hollywood, the Dudley Nichols script now seems preachy and schematic, but Laughton's performance as an intelligent but sexually and politically timid man who finds the courage to admit his cowardice and then to transcend it in martyrdom, is neither. This is, if you will, *I, Claudius* (or anyway, certain aspects of that character) revisited, placed in a modern landscape.

But still, he had to face this truth: he was essentially back where he had started as far as the movies were concerned, back to being the eminent English character actor. It was time for reinvention, that is to say, for a return to the stage. After the war he worked intensively with Bertolt Brecht, shaping *The Life of Galileo* to specifications that suited his needs. Their production, staged first at the tiny Coronet Theater in Los Angeles, then in New York, has become something of a legend, though the play won a response more respectful than enthusiastic on Broadway. But it may have shown Laughton the way. To begin with, it was done in the playwright's famous presentational style, his intellectually inspiring attempt to break the "fourth wall" convention that had for so long ruled the theater, which was also a style well suited to Laughton's temperament. One has to believe it led him to look for other ways he might break with tradition and yet present himself in comfortably agreeable ways.

For instance, those reading tours, begun around this time. Appearing alone on a stage surrounded by a pile of books into which he seemingly casually dipped for texts he then read with great eloquence, he was exploring a new kind of theatricality. He received great acclaim for these performances, much of it touched by gratifying moral approval: the great man making difficult provincial tours to bring culture to the hungering masses. Whether or not this was acting is a nice question, but he was at least projecting an imaginative version of himself—the smart, funny, occasionally curmudgeonly, but often twinkling fat man who was a little bit in love with the sound of his own voice but employed it to advance his larger love, which was for language. One imagines him happy, basking in the gratitude of audiences flattered by his attention, and free to do as he pleased, without having to defend his vision of a role against the needs and opinions of directors, producers, fellow players.

These tours, in turn, inspired his work with the First Drama Quartet and, since they were self-staged, encouraged him to direct under the aegis of his producing partner, Paul Gregory. The most ambitious of these jobs—much larger in scope than the *Don Juan in Hell* chamber piece—was the theatrical event (it was never exactly a play) he carved from Stephen Vincent Benet's epic poem, *John Brown's Body*. Laughton, who had recently become an American citizen, brought passion and flair to the task, both in editing the text into something playable and in staging it in a manner that might loosely be termed Brechtian, though its politics were anything but those of the Marxist master. Later he would take over direction of something rather less grand, *The Caine Mutiny Court Martial,* helping Herman Wouk with the adaptation of his book's key sequence and staging it with potent simplicity, whatever one thought of the piece's curious morality. Finally (again with Gregory as producer), he directed his only movie, *The Night of the Hunter,* which is, like his directorial work in the theater, *sui generis,* and in some ways more interestingly so, since he was working here without the net that great—or at least self-consciously serious—writing can provide. It too challenges realistic convention—there is something distinctly expressionistic about many of his stagings for the camera—but rather cannily so. We are conscious of his mannerisms, but not so much that it interferes with our attendance on the creepy, suspenseful narrative.

So he was back, and on his own terms, and later in this period getting better movie work, too—*Hobson's Choice* and *Witness for the Prosecution,* in both of which he gave genially eccentric lead performances that fulfilled people's expectations without too much challenging them. Hobson, the shoemaker in David Lean's movie, and Sir Wilfrid Roberts, the defense counsel who takes on a difficult case despite ill health, are splendidly splenetic figures. Both see themselves as horrendously put upon, though in fact it is they who exploit others, and both are comical in a way that was new to Laughton. He was still in his fifties, but one could see a rich new territory opening up, something we could happily explore with him in older age.

Laughton, however, decided to undertake something much more dangerous, his 1959 Shakespeare season at Stratford-upon-Avon under Olivier's management. His confidence restored by the critical acclaim accorded his recent ventures, he must have felt that this represented a last chance to challenge his old rivals from the London stage, who had been building their reputations in the classics for years while he had been, as the purists saw it, frittering his gifts away. If this venture did not end all that badly, it did not end as well as Laughton might have hoped. His Bottom in *A Midsummer Night's Dream* was for the most part indulgently received—he was the first actor not to don an ass's head in the transformation scenes. His *King Lear,* a role to which he had aspired for decades, was more controversial. Some found it a revelation. Some found it too eccentric to bear. And critics aside, many of his coworkers at Stratford found him difficult to work with, rather withdrawn and, yes, insecure—perhaps in something like the way he had been on *I, Claudius,* though never incapacitatingly so. It was this experience that led Olivier to utter the words Callow drew on for his subtitle and for one of his book's epitaphs. "There's no room for genius in the theater, it's too much trouble. The only actor I ever knew who was a genius was Charles Laughton. Maybe that's why he was so difficult."

We should—perhaps belatedly—define that term a little more closely. Laughton was not "difficult" in the way so many actors are. He did not drink or dope, he was not chronically late for work, did not demand vast rewrites of his roles or openly challenge a director's authority. Indeed, we have the testimony of directors as diverse as Billy Wilder and Otto Preminger that he was delightful to work with—serious, full of ideas, open to their suggestions. Laughton, it would seem, was difficult in only one way—he perceived too many choices and had trouble making up his mind about which to play.

Now, alas, the larger choices open to him were narrowing. After Stratford, Laughton once again retreated. There was the distinctly minor *Under Ten Flags,* followed by his fairly reserved appearance in *Spartacus,* where again he played a figure not unlike Claudius, an intellectual of humane and liberal temperament trying to uphold those values in the Roman Senate. The irony here is that the vainglorious would-be dictator he is opposing (and the man with the much larger part) is Olivier. You may make what you will of the fact that it was Olivier who had fun playing the homosexual seducer of Tony Curtis while Laughton was asked to play an insatiable womanizer. You may make what you will of the fact that Olivier, well on the way to his lordship, could now safely slum in enterprises of this kind, secure in the knowledge that this would not harm his reputation as the world's greatest English-speaking actor, while Laughton could not. In the artfulness with which he conducted his career, Olivier was clearly Laughton's—everybody's—superior. But, of course, luck always favors the comely. And those who are clearheaded in their ambitions.

What luck Laughton had was now about to become incurably bad. He had turned sixty during the Stratford year, and though that's not old by our standards, it was by his. He had been at his trade from a very young age, had never been careful of his health, and had used himself relentlessly. Now he began to feel unwell, and eventually cancer was diagnosed. He refused to surrender to it, but he also must have known that there would be little time or energy for any more transformations. There was, however, just time for one more memorable performance. That he gave in the last months of his life in Preminger's all-star adaptation of Allen Drury's trashy best-seller about Washington politics, *Advise and Consent.*

Laughton's character is Seab Cooley, one of those senators from the then-solid South who have piled up seniority and parliamentary guile over decades in a safe seat. It was, at its simplest level, a role to which Laughton could apply all the guile he had acquired over the decades in many an unsafe seat. Moreover, there was an angle to his role that obviously amused him: Cooley was homophobic, and one of the film's several plot lines gives him the opportunity to vent that prejudice, which he does with great relish. That's the way of this performance. Cooley was many other things Laughton was not—a political reactionary, a shrewd defender of his own power, a clever manipulator in difficult situations. But he was also some things Laughton was—a man who relished broad theatrical gestures, a man who buried his most profound emotions beneath a colorful, simplifying image, a man of large talents and ambition who has been obliged to settle for a lesser role yet is determined to enjoy and exploit to the fullest what power it offers. To put the point simply, Laughton knew this character's strengths and weaknesses in his bones, and he threw himself into preparation for the role with uncommon intensity. He fastened on a real-life senator, John Stennis of Mississippi, not merely studying the man's accent and manner but actually asking the politician to read his movie lines into a tape recorder so he could hear, any time he needed to, his smallest regional nuances.

Yet in the end there is nothing studied about Laughton's

performance, Oozing a drawling, lazy charm, at once sinuous and transparently false, keeping the secret of how he will vote on the film's key issue—whether or not a dying president's nominee for secretary of state will or will not be confirmed—until the last minute and delighting in the fawning attention that brings him, his senator is wayward and unpredictable. You can't help loving his roguishness, you can't help but be slightly appalled by his demonic drives, and you can't help feeling that Laughton has once again created what he alone could create—a believable monster who was also a shrewd and subtle parody of a monster.

Did Laughton guess that this bold work, work that somehow dominates one's memory of this movie despite the fact that he has very few scenes in it, would be his valedictory? Did a sense of his impending death focus his mind most wonderfully? One thinks so. And that makes this signature performance even braver.

And entirely typical of him. For as we look back over this crowded career, one of the things that must strike us most forcefully is its ceaselessness. Despite the fact that he was sentenced to a lifetime's servitude within his own unattractive body, despite the many disappointments and occasional traumas he endured, despite the misunderstandings and misjudgment he created or was obliged to accept, Charles Laughton never slowed or stopped the effort to impose himself on the life of his times, never shied from making the bold, occasionally visionary effort, even when something more modest would have served him just as well.

There is something joyful in all his work, even when it is at its most serious, a pleasure in its own flamboyance that we can sense and respond to almost viscerally. We don't find that much in actors anymore. Everyone—performers, critics, the knowing audience—is so serious now about "the work." No one wants to be caught "acting." No one wants to admit that a sense of play is essential to successful play acting. And no one wants to stress the jagged contrasts—between strength and weakness, between self-awareness and utter heedlessness, between intelligence and stubbornness, between the droll and the deadly—that illuminate this career. That these are the products of a man who was often insecure, usually trying to hide the secrets of his life offstage, makes them the more remarkable.

Singular enough in its own time, this is a career that will not, cannot, be duplicated in our time, when a performer's emotional calculations must be made to seem much more finely calibrated than Laughton's ever were. In my eyes, though, he grows more treasurable the more he recedes from the world's view. For I'm convinced that if his like should recur, we would not be allowed to see him in the full glory that a less sophisticated but in some ways more culturally tolerant age permitted Charles Laughton.

1978

Laurence Olivier: The Master Builder

"Hollywood? Yes. Bit of fame. Good." Oh, rare—also shrewd—Ralph Richardson, who offered this response when his best acting friend, Laurence Olivier, asked him if he should accept Sam Goldwyn's offer to play Heathcliff in what turned out to be Everywoman's favorite screen romance, *Wuthering Heights*.

By that time—1938—Olivier was well established in the West End, and not merely as a dashing leading man in commercial comedies and melodramas. Some of the work on which ultimately the legend would depend had also been accomplished: the famous Romeo-Mercutio alternation with Gielgud in *Romeo and Juliet*, the controversially Freudianized *Hamlet*, the heroic *Coriolanus*. He had just finished playing Iago to "Ralphie's" *Othello*.

On the other hand, this conversation took place while the two were engaged in *Q Planes*, which was goofily typical of the work Olivier had up to then been able to get in the movies, both at home and in the United States. At that time in the movie world he was probably best known for the picture he didn't make, *Queen Christina,* from which Garbo had ordered him removed.

As we all know, Olivier accepted Goldwyn's offer, began to learn (as he later gracefully acknowledged) how to under-play for the camera under William Wyler's gruff Teutonic tutelage, and, quickly following *Wuthering Heights* with *Rebecca, Pride and Prejudice,* and *That Hamilton Woman* (a remarkable range of variations on his romantic theme), established his credentials as an authentic international dreamboat. The fact that his affair with Vivien Leigh was then at its height, and that *Gone with the Wind* (Everywoman's favorite screen epic) was simultaneously turning her into a figure equally fascinating to fandom, did him no harm either.

Bit of fame, indeed. Bit of luck, too. And Olivier, especially when he puttied his spirit with false humility (one of his least gratifying disguises—see his speech accepting his honorary Oscar in 1979), liked to stress that luck, along with talent and stamina, was essential to a successful acting career. Perhaps more so than even he admitted. For these pictures, this flamboyant passage in his life, did not, I think, express his true nature. The performances, particularly the crucial Heathcliff, were greater triumphs of acting, of false colors worn as if they were the true hues of his soul, than we have generally recognized.

For he was not really a romantic. He lacked the brooding core, the deep, dark, essentially unfathomable center, that forces this breed in upon themselves in endless investigation of their own enigma. Nor was he entirely comfortable in world-well-lost heroics, which is another aspect of the romantic temperament. He was, of course, a marvelously physical actor. Part of his theatrical legend (the American observer is, alas, almost completely dependent on rumor when discussing the most important aspect of Olivier's career) is based on the whirling energy he brought to his stage duels and fights, some sense of which we get from his Shakespearean movies. On stage, at a distance from the audience, movement and nobility of vocal expression could be used to create qualities that were not of the actor's essence. But in those movies in which he played more or less conventional leading roles, a certain weakness showed in close-up—not so much between his brow and his nostrils, where, taking his cue from his first acting teacher, he located the flaw in his handsomeness (hence all those false noses), but in the eyes, where wariness, even a curious timidity, sometimes lurked.

His greatest sustained screen performance, his cackling, scuttling, richly comic *Richard III,* owes its greatness, I think, to its lack of romantic overtone, its refusal to brood overlong on ill-use, or to propose that Richard's monstrousness is that of a deeply disappointed lover of the world, potentially redeemable if someone would just try a little tenderness on him. Similarly his *Henry V* avoids the poses of grandeur. He's a bustling, up-and-doing sort of monarch, narrowing the distance between himself and his troops (and between himself and his wartime audience, who did not need to be reminded that the exertions of plain people in battle are usually for the benefit of the swells). Even Olivier's movie *Hamlet,* following the Freudian pattern he had laid down earlier on the stage (he consulted with Freud's disciple-biographer Ernest Jones on his characterization), represents a deromanticizing impulse. After all, if you can "explain" Hamlet by resorting to the Oepidal theory, you rob him of romantic glamour. Noble mystery becomes a quotidian—indeed, if we are to believe classical psychoanalysis—universal problem. Understanding, familiarity of this sort, is, as we all know, the enemy of romance.

Olivier played life as he played his roles, in particular rejecting the romantic notion that great art is necessarily the product of great, intellectually unapproachable genius. Offstage he had, as Enid Bagnold, the novelist, put it, "a quality of invisibility." And he was himself contemptuous of self-proclaimed singularity. He liked to disclaim genius and to insist that his successes derived from hard work and honed craft, habits to which many coworkers attested. Peter Brook, the director whose seekings of the connection between performance and the infinite mark him as Olivier's opposite, wrote that "The dazzling virtuosity of his acting came from a painstakingly composed mosaic of tiny details, which when finally assembled could flash by in sequence with breathtaking speed, giving the illusion of glimmering thought."

Another way of putting all that is to say that Olivier was a prosodist, not a poet, a man who liked to work out a scheme for a performance, an "interpretation" which permitted him at all times to know consciously what he was doing, or trying to do. Tapping into the flow of his own personality was not for him, nor the inspiration of the moment. He could, in short, act the Byronic, but it was beyond him to be it. Not day in, day out. My dear chap—the noise, the confusion.

But how well the mantle of romance those first important film roles threw over him served unromantic Larry. He shrugged and shrugged, but he never quite shook it off. And a good thing, too. For the movie stardom that resulted from this essentially false first impression he made on the great world was what set him apart from his peers. It permitted him at least to begin what would turn out to be not merely one of the two or three most singular acting careers of our century but one of its most remarkable public lives, regardless of profession. Without Heathcliff and Max de Winter, Mr. Darcy and Lord Nelson, the alteration of theatrical classics and movies like *Q Planes* would probably have continued unabated—as it did for Richardson and Gielgud, for Michael Redgrave and Anthony Quayle and the other great Brits with whom he started out and to whose careers his, had it continued along its original lines, would logically have been compared. Doubtless he would have earned a good living and a good reputation with that not-quite-mass public that cares greatly for theatrical performance and forgives their legendary heroes' descents into movies that are not—so the higher fandom fondly believes—quite worthy of them. Eventually, of course, he would have had his knighthood. But not his peerage. For the fact is that none of Olivier's real peers, the other knights of the English theatrical realm, was ever what we have since learned to call "bankable." That is to say, none of them could have promised, with their presence, a reasonable box-office return on the Shakespeare films which Olivier—thanks to his Hollywood successes, circa 1939–1941—could when he sought backing for his *Henry V* and his *Hamlet* in the forties, his *Richard III* in the fifties.

His direction of these movies—very straightforward and welcoming, and demonstrating a capacity to manage complex production logistics efficiently—in turn enhanced his bankability in another realm. Besides being a distinguished actor and a great celebrity, he had now shown himself to be quite a practical manager where budgets and personnel and all that boring stuff were concerned. (He would later say, in fact, that his happiest professional moments came when he was directing movies.) All this suggested that—again unlike his peers—he might possess that rare blend of qualities necessary to lead a noncommercial theater. His stardom would broaden the audience when he appeared in one of the company's productions, his celebrity would generate interest in all its works, and his knowledgeability would help to ensure businesslike management of the enterprise. His first effort in this direction, as coleader of the Old Vic with Richardson immediately after World War II, ended abruptly and mysteriously. But there was Chichester and ultimately, of course, the National still to come. In all three venues he had the pick of the plums, the famous Oedipuff double bill, a premature Lear, a perfectly timed Othello, not to mention Chekhov and Strindberg and Ibsen and heaven knows what else one feels permanently deprived for not having witnessed. Talk about stamina! In a sense he revived the old tradition of the actor-manager. But now he was actor-manager to a nation—maybe even the world.

We fed off the international word of mouth his faraway performances generated, and the Shakespearean films seemed to guarantee the authenticity of what we heard. As did the tantalizing glimpses of Olivier that we caught in other films of the forties and fifties. His Hurstwood in Wyler's mostly mis-judged film version of *Sister Carrie* had a brave weakness about it—something confessional in it, one now thinks—and the dashing intellectuality of his "Gentleman Johnny" Bur-goyne in *The Devil's Disciple* was exquisitely executed. I even thought his work as the Prince of Carpathia ("the fox of the Balkans," as he is referred to in *The Prince and the Showgirl*) was a marvelously sly and very fully realized comic perfor-mance—the great man on working holiday but by no means taking the money and heading for the border.

There was, though, the beginning of a certain querulous-ness in critical and middlebrow response to that film. What was Sir Laurence doing? Directing Marilyn Monroe, working for the first time since his youth in so obviously a commercial enterprise? It didn't seem . . . well . . . fitting. The questions were almost immediately—if temporarily—stilled by his ap-pearance, first in London, then in New York and on film in *The Entertainer.* Yes, yes, it was commercial theater, and not even a terribly well-made play at that. But it contained a seri-ous, I-can-read message about the decline of empire. Implic-itly it contained another message as well. The willingness of the acknowledged leader of the older English theatrical gen-eration to appear in a work by John Osborne, the acknowl-edged leader of the next, was both an important endorsement and an important renewal.

Also, and here I do speak from personal knowledge of Olivier's performance in the play, it was a magnificent vehicle, something that permitted Olivier at last to unleash all his anti-heroic impulses, even (possibly) his preacher's son doubts about the appropriateness of a life spent upon the wicked stage. If you have only seen the movie version of the play, you have only seen the shadow of Olivier's greatness as Archie Rice, the broken-down (and breaking down) music hall comedian. Its mistaken obligations to realism and to montage interrupt the arc of Olivier's performance. Or maybe you just have to have had the living presence before you fully to appreciate this piece of work. In any case, seen within the simple yet effective stylizations of the original playscript it was breathtaking, the greatest performance I've ever seen on a stage. The mixture of fear and feeble bravado, the palpable contempt for self and context with which Olivier invested Archie, above all the brilliance with which he surfaces any performer's worst fear, which is loss of dominance over his audience, was riveting. It's the only play I've ever seen in which the *audience* ends up drenched in flopsweat.

It was something else as well. It was, in the sympathy he generated for this character without ever asking for it, a great statement of solidarity with everyone who dares to perform (no actor more obviously relished the company of players or worked harder not to prevent his titles and honors from distancing himself from them). It was also a great statement of contempt, on Olivier's part, for highfalutin definitions of the performer's art, for the breathless awe with which the innocently romantic often greeted him. This, he seemed to be saying, this is the essence of our occupation—this terror, endured in aid of this ephemera, in hopes of a moment's approving applause. Absurd, isn't it?

At the time, Olivier was heard to say that he had never been Hamlet, that he had always been Archie Rice at heart. People chuckled indulgently at his becoming modesty, and, of course, being a complex man, he did have more idealistic definitions of what he did. ("I believe in the theater," he said, in a nicely turned phrase in his maiden—and only—speech in the House of Lords. "I believe in it as the first glamorizer of thought.") But I took him seriously at the time, and I still do.

I was never to be in his presence again after that night at the Royale Theater on Broadway in the winter of 1958–1959. Like most people, I had to make do with the movies. But I must say that I loved much of what Olivier did in them. There was, for example, his marvelously seedy police detective in *Bunny Lake Is Missing.* There was his Mahdi in *Khartoum,* blacked up, whistling through the gap in his front teeth (which gap was taken by the faithful to be a sign that the historical Mahdi was a true prophet), which may be the wickedest portrayal of third-world lunacy we have yet had this side of Evelyn Waugh. There was his ponderously clever Soviet premier in *The Shoes of the Fisherman*—so very Russian. However silly their contexts, these were all marvelously observed performances, in which common types were given shrewd particularity by the actor. Indeed, as age and illness crept up on him, Olivier seemed more than a little grateful to shuck off the pretense of leading-manhood, to hide out under curious costumes and thick makeup. His lordship did not condescend to this work. He was what he loved best to be—an actor acting.

People fussed at him about it, wishing he would stand on his dignity instead of rolling around on the floor with the kids. Also they suspected a prolixity that verged on profligacy. Greatness is supposed to be hard to come by, doled out in small, widely separated doses. That Polaroid commercial, those not-so-hot American accents in the televised *Cat on a Hot Tin Roof* and in *The Betsy* and *Inchon,* that all-purpose middle European accent only slightly varied in projects as various as *Dracula, The Boys from Brazil,* and *The Jazz Singer.* But he charmed me in *A Little Romance* and scared me in *Marathon Man,* and Lord Marchmain's ferocious dottiness in

Brideshead Revisited, an old man's impersonation of old age demonstrated that he had not lost the capacity to let experience instruct him.

There was bravery in this, I think, or maybe just a shrewd sense of self-preservation. In the sixties and seventies he occasionally let it be known that he was so readily for hire because he felt a need to provide for his considerably younger wife, Joan Plowright, and their three children. But somehow he managed to survive the onslaught of illness that marked his last two decades, and somehow the kids finally grew up and went out on their own, and he had to admit, at last, that his slightly feeble excuse for busying himself with trivia was no longer available to him. Now at last he told the truth. He simply would not have known what to do with himself if he had stopped acting, might well have died before his time if he had embraced the invalid's idleness that was his for the asking. Indeed, in his autobiography he publicly thanked God for the movies, which enabled him to keep working after the energy required for stage work failed him. For all we know he thanked God for holographs, too, since one of those was used a couple of years before his death to project his image on stage in the London musical *Time*.

To those of us who believe that the best kind of heroism is to be found in the relentless practice of one's profession—how else do you continue learning, for God's sake?—he now became a genuinely heroic figure. And in his basic approach to work, which involved a rather cool and objective search for the mannerism or accent or physical detail that revealed the inner spirit of a character, there was something salutary. For it was the antithesis of the new romanticism—or should we call it merely the new egotism—of method acting. It is said that when they were making *Marathon Man* Dustin Hoffman kept himself awake for two days so that he could look—and above all feel—properly haggard for one of his scenes with Olivier. "You should learn to act, dear boy," his lordship murmured. "Then you wouldn't have to put yourself through this sort of thing."

There it is—the essence of what he stood for—craftsmanship, professionalism, practical intelligence, and the highest seriousness. That I define as not taking yourself, or your mission, or your reviews, *too* seriously—let other people do that for you if they are so disposed. This is especially important for actors, who must not let anything—especially self-importance—congeal their ability to do what they must always do, which is to retain the capacity to "play," in the most basic definition of the word. In his long maturity Olivier maintained that ability better than anyone—better than he had done in his youth, better than the carping critics of his lifesaving and, yes, life-enhancing "cameos" could see. We must, of course, be grateful that at least some of the great sustained performances—including half an Archie, which is better than none—are preserved on film and tape. But these other, smaller, perhaps more casual actor's moments, this little night music of his, are part of his legacy too, and they are by no means the least instructive part of what he leaves behind for those who follow in his . . . let's call it craft.

1989

Time Out: Or, Love in a Cold Climate

Don't cry for me, Green Bay Packers. The truth is I never left you.

No, never did. All through my wild days (to keep borrowing from the stupidest hit song this side of "Doggy in the Window"), my mad existence—and yours too during those many long years of also-running—I kept my promise.

Promise? Hmm. Might be getting into a little trouble here. Promise implies choice, the option of alternative loyalties considered and rationally denied in favor of something presumably more rewarding. If, though, you are born and raised in Wisconsin, the Packers are not a choice. They are a categorical imperative. Maybe even some sort of weird genetic imprint.

Please understand, I did my best to shake off this atavism. I grew up to be a movie critic. It is a trade that calls for an air of sophistication. Not to mention a sense of irony. Not to mention a certain cynicism. It is, in short, not work

151

ideally suited to a cheesehead. Not even to a cheesehead in denial.

Of course, it was not until comparatively recently that I found out I was a cheesehead. In my impressionable years, *tshotski* technology had not advanced to the point where moronic headgear, permitting its wearer to advertise his proud— not to say defiant—provinciality on national television, was readily available. National television itself was unavailable, except as one of *Popular Science*'s giddier predictions. We sometimes carried pennants to the game, and later tacked them up on our bedroom walls. Occasionally we wore plastic buttons bearing an inspirational legend on our lumberjack coats. Or green ribbons with a little gold football, or perhaps a tiny plastic football player in a Packer uniform in a stiff-arm pose, affixed to it.

A half-century ago we did not think of ourselves as anything grander—or goofier—than fans. And, as a Milwaukeean, I did not examine the premise that Green Bay itself was, as it remains, virtually *terra incognita* to me, a place I would eventually visit exactly twice in my life, with no lasting impression registered. It, or more properly the values its team seemed to personify, was strictly a country of the mind, which is naturally why it staked, and continues to claim, such a powerful and ineluctable allegiance.

In those far-off days, as they did until recently, the Packers played some of their home schedule in Milwaukee, which was, incidentally, the site of their 1944 triumph over the New York Giants in the NFL championship game. We are not talking County Stadium now. It was then, like a major league baseball franchise to fill it, a dream as remote as television to Milwaukeeans. No, we're talking State Fair Park in West Allis: covered wooden grandstand (built for harness racing) on one side of the field, temporary wooden bleachers on the other; Curly Lambeau in a natty topcoat (coaches duded out for games in those days) stalking the sidelines; and on the field those darkly glamorous figures, professional athletes.

There were giants among them, or so it seemed to innocent eyes: Clark Hinkle, the slashing fullback; Cecil Isbell, the cool passer and successor to the much admired Arnie Herber; Buckets Goldenberg, anchoring the line; and at left end an authentic legend, Don Hutson, tall, slender, fragile-seeming in pads that were famously lighter and less bulky than the other players wore, which left him freer to work his lithe magic on consistently befuddled opponents.

But they were suspect giants. Professional football in those days was a marginal and raffish enterprise, not all that far removed from its small-town beginnings (as the very existence of the Packers proved). Franchises moved around a lot (some things never change) but to avoid bankruptcy, not to make further gazillions. And sports conservatives like my father and my grandfather profoundly believed that football was an amateur's game, a college game. They did not think men should play it for money. They thought that having served their bright college years in bright college stadiums— marching bands, cheerleaders, pompoms, *faux* innocence— they should embrace their boring adult fates, become lawyers and doctors and businessmen, the way the NCAA propagandists were always claiming colleges athletes did. There was something morally ambivalent about clinging to this boyish thing—and being paid to do so, however humbly.

To be honest, dank State Fair Park, where in memory it is always drizzling, reinforced this view of things. The dazzling and modest Hutson aside, there seemed something not— well—clean-cut about pro football. On the other hand, one saw (or more often heard on **WTMJ**) the Packers meet and beat teams from large, often faraway places—the aforementioned Giants and the Bears, representing the nearest-by sink of iniquity, Chicago. Hey, in those days, by Green Bay and

Milwaukee standards, Cleveland and Detroit, Pittsburgh and Philadelphia (combined during the war into the Steagles) seemed big time. Once, before my wondering eyes, the Brooklyn Dodgers, briefly a football franchise, appeared in West Allis, led by a heavily publicized quarterback called Ace (talk about raffish!) Parker, and the Packers, led by Hutson, having a great day, taught them a thing or two about the game.

Thus do otherwise rational heads turn to cheese. For that's what it's all about, isn't it? Showing them smart guys up. This unconscious thought did not take conscious form for me until the Lombardi era. I was long gone from Wisconsin by then, living in New York, flirting (somewhat shamefully) with the Giants, in their way as in tune with their environment as the Packers were with theirs—neurotically striving, neurotically self-destructing in a peculiarly New York way. But sweeping left and sweeping right out of the swirling blizzards of youth, here came the Packers again, returned to hard-nosed primitivism by their almost parodically single-minded coach.

They were, as the sportswriters kept telling us, the last town team. They reminded people of the game's prehistoric roots—the Canton Bulldogs and the Decatur Staleys were recalled—and, by implication, of the relatively few years that separated all of us from a harder past, where the possibilities were much narrower. Even if Lombardi's teams had not been so—how shall we say?—basic, the weather they played in was.

Pre-television, before the meteorologists started calculating the wind-chill factor, the rest of the country was only dimly aware of the conditions in which, for at least half the season, we in the Midwest had always played football. I had myself played enough of it as a high school third-stringer to remember the shock of hitting the frozen tundra. Or the muddy tundra. Indeed, I spent most of my inept career in intimate communion with this native ground. I wouldn't say

that it built my character. But it shaped it—and not entirely
for the worse.

Now everyone could see it, almost feel it—the biting cold,
the freezing rain, the sleet, the snow, all that brutal stuff. It
awed these strangers. But it also made them snippy. Football,
like everything else, was entering the postmodern age—Astro-
turf, domed stadiums, expansion teams that played all season
in balmy temperatures—and these guys smacked of premod-
ern, not to say Paleolithic, times.

They didn't quite get it, the elsewhere fans. But we did,
proud to be winning, despite—no, because of—our club's lack
of chic. One of the other things I had learned at my parental
and grandparental knees was that sunbelt teams were morally
suspect. They were always throwing and catching the football
with their dry, warm hands. "Razzle-dazzle," my dad would
sniff, contemplating the far-off vagaries of, say, the Southwest
Conference. There was something not quite—I don't know—
manly, about those guys. And here were their inheritors, playing on plastic, under plastic.

Well, Lombardi came and went, the Packers sank into
mediocrity and worse, and I found myself eventually in hate-
ful Los Angeles, where the sun shines and the brain slowly rots
under its rays. I came to kind of like the Raiders, a blue-collar
team like the Packers (and avatar for Ron Wolf, the general
manager who rebuilt the Packers). I came to loathe the Rams,
who were the worst kind of losers—whiny losers, sort of like
Hollywood producers whose last picture had tanked. But
honestly, I didn't much care when they both went away. As for
the Packers, they weren't quite as dead to me as the Canton
Bulldogs—in season, I still turned first to the sports page on
Monday morning to see how they had done, sometimes when
they were alleged to pose a threat to some grander team, I
would surf in their direction on TV—but I assumed that they
and all they represented were doomed now to permanent ir-

155

relevance, permanent nostalgia, like most of the verities of my childhood.

But here they are once again, reborn like some sci-fi creature awakened from its long sleep under the ice cap, contending for the Super Bowl and demonstrating to sophisticated San Francisco and their "West Coast offense"—I imagine tight, pleased smiles on the faces of my personal patriarchy—and those expansion nonentities from Carolina something about true grit.

Never mind that the Packers themselves play a version of the West Coast offense; selective inattention is the mark of the true believer. Never mind that Bret Favre doesn't strike me as a Lombardi (or a Lambeau) kind of guy. His name and his style put one in mind of riverboat sharpsters—and, more to the point, of that raffish undercurrent that once ran beneath pro football. (Bret, say hello to Ace Parker. And surely you've heard of Johnny Blood?) He would have made Grandpa nuts. But he would have, I know, seemed dangerously glamorous to an eleven-year-old.

And the cheeseheads? Beyond Gramp's imagining. Or Dad's. Almost beyond mine, taught as I was to layer at least two sweaters over my provinciality, top it with some earmuffs, and run away to the big city as soon as possible. Now I'm not so sure. Maybe it's better to flaunt, and in the process self-satirize, your passions. As we edge toward the Super Bowl, I am sweetly reminded that at least I know where they're coming from, that love in a cold climate is bound to express itself in strange, wondrous, and curiously persistent ways.

1997

Satyajit Ray: Days and Nights in the Art Houses

In one of Alan Parker's best cartoons a couple of guys are standing in front of the Britain's National Film Theatre, looking at a poster advertising a Manttup Divad retrospective. "Oh super . . . the Indian Chappie?" one of them asks. The other (obviously management) replies: "No . . . er . . . Actually it's David Puttnam spelled backwards. . . . Seemed more foreign. . . . More in keeping with our usual programmes."

During the first quarter of 1992 that little comic sketch by the director, part of his 1970s–1980s cycle of drawings which send up the earnest pretensions of state-subsidized British film culture, kept popping into my mind. For I had been assigned to produce the film tribute to the greatest of "Indian Chappies," Satyajit Ray, for the 1992 Academy Award broadcast, on which he was to receive an honorary Oscar. Almost immediately I began to wish that his name was the backward spelling of some Anglo director. And to wish that, state subsidized or not, pretentious or not, there was something one could reasonably call a film culture in the United States.

For when I began telling people what I was working on, I discovered that it was only among my contemporaries—and, of course, the critics and film historians—that Ray was a recognizable name. And then only as a figure from our past. They, no more than I, had any sense of the size and strength of his body of work as it has developed in the last two decades or so. As for younger people, they had quite simply never heard of him.

This was a shock to me. But not as great as the dismay that came over me as I tried to get to work on my little montage, which instantly turned into the worst logistical nightmare I have endured in over two decades of making compilation films.

As far as I could determine, no American company held television rights (and therefore a viable print or tape) of any of Ray's films. For that matter, I could turn up no one who held American theatrical rights in any of his pictures. There were a few scattered, battered 16 mm prints of his films available in the audiovisual market, but most of them were near-unwatchable. One or two companies, though listing Ray titles for rental, informed me that complaints about the quality of their prints had caused them to stop circulating them. To put the point simply, there was simply no market for Ray's films in the United States, therefore no impetus to keep good copies of his work available for public exhibition. It is true that some archives, notably **MOMA**, had prints of some of Ray's best-known films, but as anyone who has ever tried to produce a television program that draws on these materials knows, archives live on a different calendar than TV does; you usually can't access the material you need in time to make your air date. Indeed, it sometimes seems to me that archivists aren't really interested in sharing their wealth with the outside world, it's strictly for scholarly private screenings. But that's another story.

Advised not to bother with Indian sources because in a poor nation film preservation is not a high priority and the state film bureaucracy is mysterious and impenetrable, I finally turned to Britain. There, at last, I was able to obtain airworthy prints. The reason for that, I believe, is simple and exemplary: it is because the National Film Theatre and the British Film Institute created and continue to sustain a small but commercially viable audience for movies that are not made in America and are not comedies or action films aimed at the only audience that seems to count these days—young, brain-damaged males.

The previous year Channel 4 in Britain had presented—in prime time, mind you—a retrospective that included almost all of Ray's best work. And the BBC also held significant titles that were invaluable to us. Both institutions were able to provide pristine one-inch tapes of the material we needed to produce our tribute to Ray. Had we needed it they could also have supplied us with documentaries about the director, which contained significant interviews with him as well as with documentaries that he had himself made, including his loving and thoughtful film about Rabindrinath Tagore, the Bengali writer (and Nobel Prize–winner) who was a friend of Ray's family and whose work was the source of three of Ray's most important films (*Charulata, The Home and the World, Three Daughters*).

Coping with the unexpected problems my project presented, I couldn't help but remember the days when Satyajit Ray, among other international filmmakers of his stature, first came to our attention. That was the 1950s, when almost every week something exciting was opening in the art houses. And not just in the major cities, either, but in places like Madison, Wisconsin, where I was going to college. Italian neorealism and the Ealing comedies from Britain had already opened our eyes to the alternative cinemas of other nations. And now here came Akira Kurosawa and Ingmar Bergman and the beginnings of the New Wave. Not to mention Brigitte Bardot.

There were actually long lines outside the one theater in Madison that specialized in foreign films. And the interest they stirred encouraged the weekend film series at the student union to program classics of the foreign film, everything from *Dr. Caligari* to *Children of Paradise*. And encouraged a group of us to form the first film society on a campus that, at that time, offered not a single course either in filmmaking or film history. (We funded ourselves largely with the profits derived from screenings of Leni Riefenstahl's *Olympiad* and, of course, *Ecstasy*). In the middle of the decade, when I moved to New York, I discovered there were three theaters within walking distance of my Greenwich Village apartment that played both new and old foreign films almost exclusively, with plenty more doing the same thing uptown.

I'm not going to claim that we were a generation of aesthetes. Going to these movies was, in some sense, morally bracing, a complex pleasure rather than a simple one like seeing American films. Struggling to comprehend exotic cultures, coming to grips—earnestly, soberly, talkatively—with new ways of seeing and with new filmic rhythms, set us apart, gave us a sense of being an elite. A dubious Bosley Crowther might advise his *New York Times* readers that *Pather Panchali* "should offer some subtle compensations to anyone who has the patience to sit through its almost two hours." But we knew Crowther was a hopeless case and made it into an art house hit; it played six months at one of those theaters near me in the Village, when it was replaced, with equal success, by *Aparajito*, the second film in the Apu trilogy.

I won't pretend I was always quick to understand the values of everything that was placed before us. Kurosawa, yes. Truffaut, yes. But Bergman, with the exception of *Wild*

Strawberries, eluded me at first. And, frankly, so did the story of Apu growing up. Or so I thought at the time. Reencountering the trilogy now, over three decades later, I was struck by how much of its seemingly artless imagery had stayed with me over the years. "Subtle compensations" indeed.

But I was a special and lucky case. My assignment forced this reengagement on me and gave me the wherewithal to obtain these Ray rarities from distant and disparate sources. Who, aside from a specialist—and I seriously doubt there are more than a half-dozen Ray experts in the United States—can see his work, let alone trace its development and preoccupations and contextualize them?

That's the general point I want to stress. When I started reviewing movies a quarter-century ago, I arrived on the job believing, based on my own formative moviegoing experiences, that such a creature as "the common viewer," kinsman to Virginia Woolf's "common reader," existed. It was my job to write for that by no means mythical individual. He or she was, I imagined, someone very like me, possessed of a good general knowledge of the movies, conversant with their history, and familiar not only with contemporary Hollywood pictures but with what was happening elsewhere in the world. I assumed, however, that this knowledge was not a specialized knowledge, that it coexisted with a similar knowledge of literature and (according to taste) at least some of the other arts, not to mention a certain political-psychological-sociological sophistication.

That person is, I think, disappearing—starving to death, actually, unable to find adequate sustenance in the United States these days. And I think the case of Satyajit Ray is very much to the point. The steady shrinkage of screens devoted to current foreign films and revivals is obvious. They exist, for the most part, in a few big cities and in a few major university towns. Compared to the old days, this truncated market can handle only a relatively few, very obviously appealing movies.

Something as vivid and lively as *La Femme Nikita* can still find a profitable audience there. On a more modest scale, so can films like *Europa, Europa* and *Raise the Red Lantern,* which have strong journalistic hooks that support substantial reviews and features about them in the national press. Finally there are the films, variously comic and inspirational—*Life Is Beautiful* and *The Full Monty* are recent examples—that are made abroad and therefore qualify as "art" releases but are, as much as any American studio product, commercial entertainments of the most sentimental sort. An artist going quietly about his proper business—building a large body of work around a set of sustaining themes—no longer has a chance in this context.

The small, knowledgeable distributors who used to work with these artists over a period of years (much as old-fashioned publishers and authors used to maintain long relationships) are no more. And the new distribution channels that once looked like such promising alternatives to the art houses—cable television, home video—are fundamentally uninterested in programming for a minority (and, what's worse, elitist) audience. It is simply not profitable enough. Besides, subtitles are hard to read on the small television screen.

As I learned a few years ago, when I taught a criticism course at the USC film school, young people today, even when they would like to, cannot replicate the experience the fifties generation enjoyed. Grousing about the fusty incomprehension of critics like Crowther, worrying as Dwight Macdonald taught us to about the tyranny of the middlebrows, we did not know, of course, how fortunate we were and could not see what was coming. But as I saw at USC, today's young people cannot gain convenient (or even inconvenient) access to their film heritage or to cinematic cosmopolitanism. They can't even obtain secondhand knowledge of these matters. You are holding in your hands [this piece was originally published in *Film Comment*] the only American film journal that attempts to address the common viewer reader, the only publication in the country that would contemplate publishing contemplations of Satyajit Ray. What the rest of the press concentrates on are grosses and gossip, much of the latter focused as much on the business of the movie business—what's doing well and what isn't at the box office, marketing issues, executive shifts—as it is on the romantic voyagings (and ego trippings) of the stars. To put the point another way, the brutally practical and materialistic climate of the day finds criticism, except insofar as it can be recruited to the marketing process, an irrelevance.

But I'm going to practice a little of it anyway, for working with Ray's work in some measure reanimated something like my youthful idealism about the movies and about the utility of the critical gesture, not as a way of passing ultimate judgments but as a way of stirring interest in, discussion of, yes, even passion for the movies in their infinite, and in this case, marvelously exotic variety.

I said earlier that coming upon the Apu trilogy anew I was struck by the lasting power of its quite simple imagery. But there were other things I could see about it now that were hidden from me thirty-five years ago. Viewing the three films back to back I was struck by their cumulative power. In everything but physical scale they constitute an epic. They range over two decades and embrace both village and city life in modern India and all of the most basic human emotions in the most tender and patient way. More important, I was now able to see that the films—especially the final one, *The World of Apu*—hinted at what I can now see as Satyajit Ray's great if always indirectly spoken theme.

That is the ineffectuality of the male in a colonial and postcolonial society. The trilogy begins with a portrait of Apu as an adorably curious, marvelously eager boy in an agricultural village. He remains undaunted by tragedies that surround him, which includes the death of his young sister. Even the passing of his father after the family moves to the city in *Aparajito* does not fatally daunt him. He acquires a teacher-mentor and eventually goes on to college. There, however, a certain languidness seems to overtake him, possibly, one senses, because there are so few opportunities for educated young men, and those that are available so often involve them in corruption (topics Ray would address more directly in the very lively series of films about urban commercial life that preoccupied him in the sixties—*The Middleman, The Adversary, Company, Ltd., Days and Nights in the Forest*).

In *The World of Apu* a certain fatalism has overtaken Ray's protagonist. He drifts into an arranged marriage to oblige a friend and his family, and though it is a happy one, his wife dies in childbirth and he surrenders to bitterness, abandoning his child to relatives, abandoning the novel to which he had been devoting himself. Though eventually he reunites with his son, even the trilogy's happy conclusion strikes an ambiguous note. One imagines Apu, chastened by the bitter experiences we have shared, now settling for a rather bland domesticity, for making a living rather than making a life of passionate commitment.

And so it seems to go with the men of Ray's films. In *The Chessplayers*, two nineteenth-century merchants devote themselves to their game while British troops march on their province to depose the indolent aesthete who rules it. Lost in their private preoccupations, they scarcely look up as the soldiers pass by. In *Charulata*, which Ray himself rightly regarded as his masterpiece, a man of inherited wealth devotes himself to what appears to be an essentially irrelevant newspaper while the film's eponymous protagonist, his bored wife, spends much of her time looking at the world through opera glasses and indulges in a flirtation with his young assistant. Her husband's inability to assert himself effectively in the world or in his own home is the fulcrum of a drama of disconnection. A similar drama is enacted in *The Home and the*

World. Again there is the bored wife and the ineffectual husband. This time the intruder is a revolutionary, boldly posturing but self-absorbed and ultimately corrupt. And the result is the same: passion blocked, virtually unexpressed, ultimately unconsummated.

I don't mean to imply that this is Ray's only way of stating his theme. Impotence is ragefully expressed in the city dramas. In his short, tightly woven television drama *Deliverance,* another preoccupied Brahmin exploits and ultimately is responsible for the death of an untouchable. In *Distant Thunder,* about the great famine that overtook parts of India during World War II, an entire population is victimized by mega-events. In the marvelous *Devi* he recounts the story of a rather ordinary woman who is incorrectly imagined to have healing powers and becomes, against her will, the center of a religious cult.

I also don't want to imply that Ray is always the delicately ironic realist. His father was the publisher of a children's magazine (which Ray later revived and edited), and some of his films (*The Adventures of Goopy and Bagha, The Golden Fortress*) are lovely fables. Nor, finally, do I wish to imply that all his films are masterpieces waiting to be discovered in the United States. Something like *Kanchenjungha* (his first color film) is about as exciting as reading a Bengali translation of a Henry James novella. Absorbing, finally hypnotic as most of Ray's work is, there are times when the Westerner does begin to snap his fingers impatiently. Ray can get lost—and lose us—in his patient exfoliations of his situations.

But that scarcely matters. What does matter is that this is a major body of work, embracing more than thirty gracefully executed films, the overriding theme of which—the psychological and cultural devastation of a society only recently freed from colonialism—is not without interest even to those people who are uninterested in cinema as such. What matters even more to me is that its felicities—there are no crude villains in Ray's work, no caricatured exploiters of the people (or heroes of the people, either)—and its subtle wisdom are unavailable to us in our present, devastated cultural climate. I wish I knew what do about this situation, beyond protesting it.

1992

Fellini: Send in the Clowns

In 1983, some thirty years after he made *I Vitelloni*, Federico Fellini was asked by Giovanni Grazzini, author of a marvelous book-length interview with the director, what first came to his mind when he recalled the film, "what image connects you to it?"

Fellini cited the sequence near the end of the film where the young loafers of the title are gathered along the waterfront of their provincial town. One of them, Leopoldo, has been pursuing an old actor-manager whose company has briefly come to rest there, trying to interest him in a play the youth has written. In this scene the actor finally makes it clear that his desire is not for the play but for its author. Shock and confusion on the writer's part; cynical derision from the old thespian.

Fellini: ". . . a grey winter sea and a low dense cloudy sky; my brother [Ricardo, one of the actors] his hand on his hat to keep the wind from carrying it away; Leopoldo Trieste's little scarf which blew into Moraldo's face; the noise of the surf, the cries of the sea gulls. . . . Then the giant face of Majeroni—

Achille Majeroni who played the part of the crazy old homosexual actor. . . ."

Yes, that looming face, unnaturally white, and the laughter issuing from it, mocking and in some way menacing. It is the image that, over the forty years since I saw it, remained my most vivid connection with it, too.

Coming upon this passage in Grazzini's book, I felt terribly pleased with myself. Imagine! My best memory of *I Vitelloni* coincides precisely with that of its creator. What an acute fellow I must be! As it happened, I was at the time reacquainting myself with Fellini's work, most of which I had not seen since its initial release, and catching up with some films I had missed entirely. Immersing myself in his work for a brief, intense period of time, I began to see that this sequence, and particularly the image of Majeroni, might represent an important and overlooked aspect of his sensibility.

Critics and film historians have tended to concentrate on Fellini's grander, more aspiring themes. Pirandello is sometimes evoked. Existentialism is mentioned. And, of course, "the silence of God." Fair enough—this is a very rich body of work. But what about show business?

Yes, show business, of all humble things. Or perhaps we should call it "low business"—that realm of clowns and magicians, chorus girls and lecherous impresarios, working the provinces, the less salubrious big-city music halls, on rare, lucky occasions the low-budget cinema, that from childhood on lured, tempted, and occasionally disgusted the great director. Show business, show people are the subject of Fellini's first directorial venture, *Variety Lights* (co-credited with Alberto Lattuada), and they are a crucial element in the last of his films to be released in the United States, *Intervista.* And whether he touches upon it only briefly or muses upon it at length, low business has never been absent for very long from the great filmography that links first feature with last.

Fellini is certainly an *auteur* in the classic definition of

the term. But he is also, and always, a showman as well, aware
that some significant part of his sensibility is rooted in the
cheap entertainments of his childhood, aware of the transformative powers even the most tinselly of these shows can exert
on the yearning imagination of a young boy or girl, yet also
aware of how one can be led astray by show biz, led into superficiality and silliness by the gush and rush of its people and
styles. If his attitude toward show people is always affectionate and indulgent, his attitude toward their enterprise is generally ambivalent. Yes, there is something redemptive in show
business. But there is, for Fellini, something dangerously distracting, too.

They are both there, that promise and that threat, in the
near-grotesque presentation of Majeroni. The promise to
Leopoldo is of escape—from provincial ennui and a climate of
petty ambition, which is bound to thwart his own more vault-
ing ambitions—though he doesn't know it yet. His innocent
eye does not (or will not) take in the threadbare quality of the
old ham's glamour. Nor does Leopoldo see that this figure
couldn't possibly give him the production he dreams of, even
if that promise were seriously meant. The threat to him, of
course, is escape's asking price, which is mainly but not entirely sexual. In the life proffered he would be trading one
kind of emptiness for another, possibly more bustling but not
more rewarding in a serious sense.

Now, Leopoldo is not Fellini's alter ego in *I Vitelloni*. A
character called Moraldo is. He is the only one of the vitelloni
who makes his escape from the provinces; we see him at the
end boarding a train, presumably for Rome, as Fellini did. We
know, from talk of a sequel Fellini wrote but never produced,
that, again like Fellini, Moraldo was to become a low-level
journalist in the capital, and we know from *Intervista* that it is
just such an early career that put Fellini in touch with the
movie world.

We also know, from all of Fellini's work, however personal

it is, that the director always maintained a certain distance from his own experience, an ability to objectify himself and his past, to perceive it from the journalist's stance, which permits one to see both sides of an issue or a situation and to mix satire—even a degree of cynicism—with whatever sentiment one brings to the remembrance of things past.

I am, I should say, very sympathetic to that stance. For I too am a provincial who found in journalism a way of escaping the dullness of my natural heritage and then found through journalism a way into show business (the television branch), about which—I don't believe I'm projecting too much—I feel an ambivalence similar to that which I find in Fellini's films. Transporting glamour and authentic tawdriness, genuine aspiration and depressing pretense, childish joys and a certain empty, even desperate, striving for effect, the wowing image, the big finish—these are the realities of "the business" (as we call it in America), and it is the exploration of these dualities that lie somewhere close to the heart of Fellini's vision.

His affection for show folks and for the sheer hubbub of their catch-as-catch-can existence is set forth most clearly perhaps in the utterly charming *Variety Lights,* which is also a tribute to the bravery with which small-timers confront the endless crises of life on the road. The story of a vaudeville troupe paddling perpetually through the provincial backwaters, it shows their fortunes briefly transformed by the addition to their company of a beautiful young woman, whose sexiness is enhanced by her apparent innocence of the effect it has on audiences as well as colleagues. In time, though, she learns, and just as her discoverer is building a new show and new hopes around her, she deserts the company for a much grander one. Fellini and Lattuada don't make much of this. Their last wry, shrugging images are of the little troupe bravely boarding a train, going back to the provinces, back to the only life they have known.

Some of this spirit infuses *Intervista* as well. It is basically

a memory piece, sweetly evoking the young Fellini's first contact with life in Cinecitta, the studio where he has made all his
films: an interview with a wildly temperamental actress, the
strangeness of seeing American Indians galloping across an
Italian landscape, the hilarity of a director attempting an operatic spectacle on the cheap, with his cardboard elephants
toppling over in the midst of a sequence. On one level it's a
lighthearted recollection of inconsequentiality, which is, of
course, one of the great lures of show business. Who wouldn't
prefer to be mixed up with this kind of magic-making instead
of sitting alone in a room with a typewriter, a blank piece of
paper, and your inchoate thoughts?

But on another level one can't help observing that
Cinecitta is a closed world, an asylum in which to find refuge
from the evils of a larger universe. Fellini entered it just as
World War II was beginning, when Italian fascism was at the
height of its power. That ability to provide a refuge from reality, its insistence on setting its own goofy agendas and mono-
maniacally pursuing them, no matter what is going on in the
world of great affairs, is one of the immemorial appeals of
show business.

Clowns, Fellini's documentary about circus funny men,
rich both in the history of their art and in the director's personal history, with special reference to his fascination with the
traditions of clowning, the evolution of its conventions, evokes
a similarly closed world. No matter what the condition of the
great world, clowns go on doing their innocent, highly traditional, highly self-referential thing. The film's best—anyway,
funniest—moment occurs when the director is seen settling
down to a very serious interview with a very serious journalist. Launching into a pretentious response to a pretentious
question about what the largest intentions of this work are, a
bucket falls unceremoniously on Fellini's head, after which
another one drops on his interrogator.

Thus does the director signal a couple of things to himself, to his audience. One message is very simple—remember our roots, don't take all this too seriously, don't interpret it too broadly or too metaphorically. Which is excellent advice. Except that the second thought cannot entirely be dismissed: there is something double-edged about clowns. They are both childish and grotesque, both cheerful and in some way threatening, like dream creatures made manifest. These humblest of show folks contain and present, in its starkest form, the most basic contradictions of show business, show people. Interesting that the most impressive sequence in *Clowns'* is a funeral procession, a not entirely humorous parody of mortality's last rites. Interesting that watching this film one inevitably recalls Majeroni, who within the generally neorealistic context of *I Vitelloni,* is presented through makeup, lighting, and angles in clownish terms. Interesting to think that clowns were "Felliniesque" centuries before that term was coined. In other words, these closed theatrical worlds are not entirely sealed off from the larger world. They too are touched with darkness. And it is a measure of Fellini's art that he insists on striking this note even when his ostensible mood is playful or nostalgic.

Take, for example, *And the Ship Sails On.* Again we are in a closed, highly conventionalized, and rather exotic theatrical world, that of an opera company, complete with a full roster of hangers-on (including critics and fans), who have chartered an ocean liner to transport them to the funeral of a legendary diva. Sailing across the Adriatic, they sail into World War I. They respond to it, as they do to all the "real" crises they encounter, by clinging to and asserting their art. They gather on the deck as their ship, incapacitated by an encounter with a Serbian battleship, begins to sink and bawl a defiant operatic chorus. Down below, as the water rises around him, a fan resolutely cranks through silent-film footage of the departed diva, an expression of moony devotion on his face. One of the company very operatically leaves the ship to join with a rebel boy in an assault on the battleship, which (again operatically) actually, astonishingly, succeeds. Once again one reflects on the armoring innocence of show people, on how their obsessive devotion to their own peculiar agendas protects them against the deadly importunings of the world and how much Fellini admires, albeit somewhat ironically, that capacity to maintain their bearings in a tumultuous world.

But . . . at the end of *And the Ship Sails On,* when we find its narrator sharing a lifeboat with a huge (and hugely, ambiguously, symbolic) rhinoceros and recounting the end of the tale, Fellini cuts backstage to his own set and crew filming the film. We see the camera, the lights, the mechanism by which the illusion of the little boat adrift on the broad rocking sea has been created. And another signal is sent. Fakery is fakery, fun is fun, but escapism, attractive and humane as show biz makes it seem, is still escapism. You can't live by it or through it.

And sweetly romantic as show business rootlessness can be made to seem by someone like Fellini, especially for audiences all too heavily rooted in routine, he has been at pains to suggest its downside. In one film quite early in his career, one quite late in it, he has stated his ambivalence about it dialectically. *La Strada,* which holds many riches, is also very starkly a tale of show business life at its most basic and most brutal. Zampano the strong man (Anthony Quinn) is essentially a survival artist—he works to eat, has no ambitions beyond those proposed to him by instinct and lust. He has bought Gelsomina (Giulietta Masina) to satisfy both and is frustrated because her spirit remains beyond his reach. It, in turn, is fully awakened by the tightrope walker (and holy fool) played by Richard Basehart, a dreamer who teaches her to see the world not as it is but as it might be. Those conflicts that were hinted at in *I Vitelloni* are here set forth in the most straightforward and ultimately tragic terms.

They are worked out with equal fullness, but in much

more approachable and genial terms, in *Ginger and Fred* some three decades later. Here Masina is paired with Marcello Mastroianni as a dance team who might once have felt completely at home in the *Variety Lights* company. Now retired, they are approached by a tacky but popular television show that specializes in providing its audiences with rare sights and acts it has requested. Will they return one last time to the stage? She wants to—their trouping days were the best of her life. He does not want to—they represent to him the vulgar and demeaning past. In other words, show business as redemption is placed in conflict with show business as a form of arrested development. In the end, though, they appear. The feathers of her boa shed and scatter all over the place as they do their turn. And he collapses on stage before it is over. It is, objectively, a disaster. But the audience loves it—loves their gameness, not to mention the memories they evoke. Their triumph is obviously an ambiguous one.

And Fellini? What, finally, is his attitude toward this subject to which he has so often returned, this subject which is ultimately self-reflexive? Who can possibly say for certain? But one cannot ignore the luminous, magical presence of Anita Ekberg in *La Dolce Vita*. Into the squalid world of the Via Veneto and *paparazzi* she descends (quite literally, since our first glimpse of her is alighting from an airplane), at once distant and yet seemingly approachable (like all movie stars). In the scheme of the film she functions as a goddess, a creature of mystery offering some unnamable prospect of redemption as she floats through the tormented, valueless world of Marcello (Mastroianni), who is, by all accounts, a revised version of *I Vitelloni*'s Moraldo. She is, I suspect, the ultimate idealization of the transformative power of—let's not call it show business, let's call it theatricality. Again, we know from many an interview that Fellini saw her in iconographic terms, visualizing her in the film erotically, but without carnality, as a dream made manifest. As infinite promise.

Nor can one ignore his other common-consent master-work, *8-1/2*. It too features a movie goddess (Claudia Cardinale) as a redemptive dream, and it is also a film too rich to be encompassed by any one-dimensional reading. But it is at its most obvious level the story of a blocked movie director, unable to imagine a film he has committed to making, the start date of which is immediately looming over him. The problem is that the medium, as he sees it, cannot contain his vision, and he cannot once again compromise with it, put on another show, however crowd-pleasing it may be. On the great set that has already been built for a film, he finally cancels the shoot. And then, out of the shadows, a magician appears. He's ready to work. Come on Maestro, let's go. Then the clowns appear, on parade. And Guido, the director, begins at last to direct their revels. Now, from all over the set, figures that we have met previously in Guido's dreams and reveries and on his professional rounds come ambling down the stairway of the set, ready to be directed, ordered, shaped into art. Among the voice-over lines we hear: "Life is a holiday; let us live it together."

And so, in a troubled film's final moments, a movie, a show, a very simple entertainment, far from the grand philosophical-psychological drama, the great "personal statement" Guido has all along been contemplating, finally begins. It is, perhaps, a conclusion that begs more questions than it answers—but then, most movie endings beg the questions the rest of the film raised. Yet it is also, as they say in show biz, a big finish—brassy, sentimental, full of good feelings, a marvelous anodyne to the psychological ditherings (stated, to be sure, with great panache and delicious irony) that have preceded it.

I must confess that when I first saw *La Dolce Vita* and *8-1/2* I did not care for them. Pauline Kael's famous put-down of the former as a "Come-Dressed-as-the-Sick-Soul-of-Europe-Party" and of the latter as very close to traditional "ladies magazine fiction," in which troubled genius discovers happiness by searching its own backyard, struck me as acute contrarianism. In some respects it still does. Fellini was never good with big ideas. Most showmen are not, despite their pretensions and the imputations of their gaga cult followers.

But going back to these movies now, after the intervention of the later, less breathlessly striving movies, the ironical spirit moving beneath those more heavily ambitious films becomes more obvious. It seems to me that Fellini sees the false pathos and the pretentiousness of Marcello's world-weary pose in *La Dolce Vita* quite clearly, especially in its earlier passages. And it is self-satire more than self-importance that sets the tone of *8-1/2*, a point to which Kael seems particularly blind. This spirit manifested itself unmistakably in the later, generally less celebrated, less chic films. In particular, *Intervista* gently mocks Fellini's former ambitions, putting them in an old man's wry perspective. And its portrayal of Mastroianni as a weary magician (he's discovered working in a commercial), Ekberg as a goddess gone to fat (she lives in seclusion, guarded by ferocious dogs), satirizes the director's former vision of them, perhaps their own former visions of themselves, but in a wry, kindly, acceptant way.

It also acknowledges, I think, the hopelessness of introspection, of Big Think. More simply, more realistically, it says what the end of *8-1/2* said more grandly, more theatrically. There, having manfully grappled with the Big Questions, Fellini falls back gratefully on the rituals of show business. At the end of his life he was still doing so, albeit more artlessly.

These rituals may not be so far from the rituals of Fellini's boyhood Catholicism in their capacity to soothe and comfort. There is, as he knew and we know, more to life than such rituals can possibly encompass. But it is a point he acknowledged in his work with increasing good humor, increasing regard for the comforts to be found in their simplicities and, perhaps, in the distracting busy work of realizing them, in his art. This is not nothing. It may in fact be everything, the best we can hope for in the post-Christian, postmodern, posteverything world. Or so one more and more thinks as, aging, one begins to stare into the void where old friends are beginning to disappear and the passionate agitations (and despairs) of youth reveal their paltriness. At a certain point in life there is only one thing one can reasonably ask: Yes, please, send in the clowns.

1993

Cinema Paradiso: The Rise and Fall of a Film Culture

The relevant statistics are very simple: in the 1990s the American share of the European film market has risen from something like 50 percent to something over 70 percent. Even in France, which at the moment has the Continent's most competitive movie industry, something very close to 60 percent of the films released there are American in origin, with indigenous products accounting for no more than 35 percent of the releases. These figures are, with only occasional exceptions, duplicated around the world.

When an industry representing a single nation, most especially a cultural industry, achieves market penetration of that sort—comparable to that of value-neutral products like Gillette razor blades—it causes alarm. Most obviously, in this case, it frightens people who make movies outside the United States as they face what appears to them, and is in fact, nearly irresistible competition. It also concerns the self-appointed but highly vocal guardians of national cultural purity everywhere, most especially in those countries, like France, which take particular—some might say arrogant—pride in the importance and singularity of their contributions to world civilization. You need only glance at the French press during the final round of the GATT treaty talks in 1993—the outrage that arose over the way American movies (and television and popular music) were dominating the local market, the passionate pleas for enhanced defenses against this invasion—to gauge the fear and loathing stirred by our "cultural imperialism." Indeed, you don't have to be a culture-proud French critic to understand, if not fully share, those emotions.

For the fact is that we Americans are affected by the overwhelming—not to say bullying—success of the popular culture we export to the world. I'm not talking about the huge contribution they make to the positive side of our balance of trade, which is nice for us but does not affect the way we think, feel, and dream the world. I'm talking about how catering to the world market affects the style and content of the movies that open every week at a theater near you. I'm also talking about how American dominance of the film trade affects what you don't see—perhaps I should say what you can no longer see—even in the art theaters that aren't particularly near to you, where, nowadays, the life of imported movies is typically nasty and short—though not, as a rule, brutish. Wan and wistful would be more like it.

It is the condition of this culture—the American film culture—the one I know and care the most about, that I want to address. But first we need briefly to consider the nostalgia—some of it false—that colors the arguments of the contemporary European film community against American film. Implicit in what it is saying is a notion that European film once enjoyed a golden age, both aesthetic and economic, which might somehow be restored through hard bargaining by their diplomats, harsh criticism of the interloping imperialists by their cultural commentators.

I don't think that's possible now or in the foreseeable future. I do think, however, that there was a brief historical moment, lasting no more than two decades, beginning sometime in the 1950s and ending sometime in the 1970s—we could argue for hours about how, precisely, to date this period—the passing of which all of us, Europeans and Americans alike, who value the unique expressive capacity of film must mourn. It was a period when, yes, the balance of trade with America tipped a little bit more favorably to foreign filmmakers. But more important, it was a period when the intellectual balance in this country swung decisively toward the foreign film, which was good for foreign producers' bank accounts but even better for our souls.

By this I mean that films then coming into the United States from France and Italy and Sweden and Japan and Spain and India and Britain utterly dominated the conversation among critics and the knowing audience, which definitely included young filmmakers not yet set in their ways. Everyone could see that the most basic grammar of film was being expanded in these films, and with it the range of subjects and ideas—which included the idea of film itself—that movies could address.

"Cinephilia," Susan Sontag calls this spirit in a recent article lamenting the decline of the movies, both as popular and high art, into their present near-decadent state. The term, she says, reflects "a conviction that cinema was an art unlike any other: quintessentially modern, distinctively accessible; poetic and mysterious and erotic and moral—all at the same time." It was, as she says, a religion, a crusade, and a worldview. It was also, I think, a way that culturally serious members of my generation, and those that immediately followed (among whom we must number such important and diverse filmmakers as Martin Scorsese, Woody Allen, and Steven Spielberg) defined themselves, set themselves apart from the somewhat

cinephobic intellectual and artistic communities that pre
ceded them.

Since some of our enthusiasm for the medium was based
on our first encounters with the great works of the past, our
passion partook too of a renaissance spirit, with this difference: most people living through renaissances are not aware
of their good fortune, while this one was quite clearly visible
to those of us reveling in its excitements. It seemed especially
glorious, perhaps, because American movies at that time were
in such a cautious phase—intellectually timid and stylistically
stodgy, the romantic elegance of the high silent era, the heedless verve of the talkies' first decade, and the dark mordancy
of the early postwar years now largely lost.

We must maintain our perspective about all this. Indeed,
as some of us look back on this period from the nineties, when
American domination of the world's popular culture has
reached unprecedented heights, it takes on its rather
poignant coloration precisely because it was so brief, precisely
because, despite the hopeful stirrings we felt, the movies,
viewed as an international economic enterprise, so quickly re-
verted to business as usual.

We were, I think, hopelessly naive. We just did not understand that the economic advantages that had accrued to
the American film industry over the years were in the long run
insuperable, that eventually they would guarantee its ability
to beat back any challenge, most particularly in its home market. I don't think we can sensibly discuss either our anom-
alous renaissance or the more typically brutal competitive
situation we see today without briefly examining how the
American industry achieved its historical hegemony.

We must begin by acknowledging that in the industry's
infancy the international playing field was quite level. Indeed,
I was surprised to learn from Victoria de Grazia's marvelously
thorough "Mass Culture and Sovereignty: The American Chal-

lenge to European Cinemas, 1920-1960," that in some of the years before World War I the French actually produced and exported more films than the Americans did, with the Italians, I gather, not too far behind. It is not hard to imagine why this free cinematic trade worked so well.

In those days films circulated more or less anonymously. They didn't carry credits, so audiences could not recognize their country of origin by the director's name or even by the names of their leading players, for the star system had not been invented. And remember, these were silent films, so language was not a giveaway either. Translate the intertitles into the local idiom and unless some famous landmark appeared in a shot it was nearly impossible to tell where a picture was made.

As a matter of fact, it seems that for a while no one cared. It was the miracle of moving images that people cared about—especially when they were deployed in the aid of gripping stories and spectacle. We all know, for instance, that in this century's early teens, Europeans pioneered the feature film while Americans hesitated over it. We know how Adolph Zukor, by importing a three-reel hand-colored *Passion Play*, a French adaptation of a German work, and by snapping up the American rights to Sarah Bernhardt's somewhat longer *Queen Elizabeth*, proved that Americans could and would sit still for movies of substantial duration. We know too that D. W. Griffith was inspired to make *The Birth of a Nation* by the example of *Quo Vadis?* and other Italian spectacles, because their length, splendor, and popularity threatened his status as the movies' first great narrative innovator. It is certainly possible to imagine that if great and terrible events had not intervened, the film industries of the United States and the major European nations might have retained rough economic parity, though I think that eventually the sheer size of its domestic market would eventually have given America a decisive economic advantage.

Be that as it may, the war virtually shut down production in the European nations. By the time it was over, the American industry had in effect reinvented itself, creating a model Europe could not hope to duplicate. For one thing, it was well along the way to becoming an oligopoly, with the production, distribution, and exhibition components of its handful of major companies vertically integrated. They all had the wherewithal to exploit offshore markets in ways their smaller, poorer competitors could not match. And whatever the quality of their films, the Europeans could not hope to penetrate the American market in the same way America was penetrating their markets. Nor could they, in their impoverished condition, hope to mount, more than occasionally, films with the luxurious sheen routinely applied to the American product once the studio system was fully functioning.

Perhaps most important, while the Europeans had been otherwise engaged, the Americans had developed the star system. It was during the war that the first generation of movie stars—Pickford, Chaplin, Fairbanks—was born in America, their huge salaries more than justified by the stability their reliable drawing power brought to a notoriously unstable business. It turned out, of course, that their iconic qualities were completely translatable in every corner of the globe—indeed, required no translation.

Almost everything I'm trying to say about the formative years of the motion picture industry can be encapsulated by the incident that serves as the prologue to *Movies and Money,* the excellent economic history of the medium by producer David Puttnam and Neil Watson. The place is Moscow. The time is Christmas Eve, 1925. Two films open that night. One is Sergei Eisenstein's national epic, *The Battleship Potemkin.* The other is an epic of quite a different sort—maybe we should call it an international epic—Douglas Fairbanks's *Robin Hood.* Both receive excellent reviews. But only one of them has what we have since learned to call "legs." Eisenstein's film plays for weeks to sparse crowds in a dozen theaters, then is withdrawn. Fairbanks's movie plays for months in better theaters, to packed houses.

The films are in one important way similar. Both are mounted on a no-expense-spared basis. It might even be argued that the Russian movie has certain advantages over its competitor, in that it is by a native son and takes up a recent event of shaping significance in the lives of his countrymen in a manner so electrifying that it would influence directors around the world for decades to come. The Fairbanks film, on the other hand, treats of a time, a place, and a myth remote from the Russian audience, and though it does so with great élan, no one argued then, and no one argues now, that it is a milestone in world cinematic history—though I must say, faced today with the choice confronting Muscovites seventy-four years ago, I think I'd probably opt for *Robin Hood*, too. Much less medicinal.

The difference between the two films comes down to two factors: *Robin Hood* had a great star at its center, a man of indefatigable charm and tireless—some said tiresome—energy. Moreover, even though he had cast himself up in Merrie Olde England, there was something distinctly, attractively American about Fairbanks. Here, as always, his character was populist, cheekily anti-elitist, genially subversive of authority, smart without being ideological or intellectual, and this movie, like all his movies, was romantic, dashing, humorous, optimistic, luxurious—and full of thrilling stunts that, like today's special effects, a lot of people wanted to see more than once, if only to try to figure out how they were done.

In *Life the Movie,* his study of the way modern, technologically driven popular culture has shaped our sensibilities, Neal Gabler writes that "In the movies the old was forever yielding to the new, the hypocrites of the past to the forthright new Americans of the future." That generalization obviously applies to the Fairbanks film with particular force. But the attitudes that its star and his film represented were reflected in hundreds, thousands of other American films as well. And their appeal, cutting across all class and national lines, explains, at least as well as the economic power of the American industry does, the dominance American films achieved in the world market in the 1920s and have retained ever since.

Gabler argues persuasively that the movies became "the ultimate weapon" in a culture war that began in the United States in the middle of the nineteenth century, well before the movies were invented. This war in effect pitted a fastidious elite, determined to impose, from the top down, something like the European organization of cultural activity on the masses, who preferred ruder, cruder more sensational experiences in everything from newspapers to religion. He also shows how the rise of the middle class and its middlebrow culture simultaneously "dumbed down" high culture and "spiffed up" low culture to create "the republic of entertainment," whose values, as Gabler's title suggests, have by now turned much of life, in both the public and private spheres, into a fantastic movielike narrative.

I think he is very largely correct and, more to our present point, I think what he is saying can be applied to the way the entire world's popular culture has developed in this century, with the influence of the intellectual and artistic elites marginalized everywhere. There are, however, some historical questions we ought to ask about the spirit in which the American movie business conducted itself in this cultural war.

Did Fairbanks and its other founders understand, before their international receipts told them so, how universal the attitudes and aspirations projected in their films were? No, of course not. When Fairbanks and his new bride, Mary Pickford, took a wedding trip to Europe in 1920 they were astonished at the crowds that greeted them—and several times they had reason to fear for life (or at least limb), so riotous were these outpourings, even in staid London and Oslo.

Did their successors and assigns, the merchants and craftsmen who presided over the classic and economically all-powerful Hollywood of the interwar years, fully comprehend the breadth of their films' reach? Yes, absolutely—they were proud of the way their movies represented American values overseas. Did they understand the depth of their influence on foreign audiences and calculate ways of enhancing that influence? The answer to that has to be no. Their foreign takings were economically significant to the American moguls—in those days about 20 percent of their grosses came from abroad—but they regarded that as found money, not, as their successors now do, as a vital, often determining, component of success.

Did they consciously tailor their films to please the international market? Perhaps occasionally. We know that Greta Garbo's star power derived from the fact that she was more popular with European audiences than she was with Americans. On the whole, however, the moguls were fiercely ethnocentric and, in any case, had trouble enough keeping abreast of the domestic audience's mood shifts. It is probably fair to say that they had no idea of how their movies were working on anyone, anywhere, anytime, had no sense of how that curious blend of reality and fantasy, which is the American movie, was, over time, reordering everyone's way of apprehending the world and their place in it.

Finally, did the Americans have any intention of driving their European competitors out of business? I think not. Driving them to the wall was good enough for the moguls. By this I mean—and again I rely on de Grazia—they sought every advantage they could in their foreign trade. Beginning in the 1920s, the American market was protected by tariffs on film imports and, perhaps more important, by the fact that the major studios controlled the major distribution systems and ran them on an exclusionary basis. Beyond that, an exception to the anti-trust laws permitted them to act as a cartel in their overseas dealings. They also had permanent and powerfully connected trade representatives in the major European capitals whose most basic technique was to threaten to cut off *all* American imports whenever a nation threatened to curtail some of them. Such was the appeal of American films that this brought exhibitors howling out of their theaters, outraged at this threat to their best profits.

I don't think we can entirely blame Hollywood for acting as it did in these years. It was in effect fighting fire with fire. For the European response to its invasion was essentially political. From the 1920s onward almost every European country with a substantial film industry tried to protect it with government subsidies and by raising tariffs on foreign movies—American offerings being, of course, the only ones they actually feared—and by imposing quotas, in a variety of forms, on the number of foreign films permitted to play on their screens. Meantime, the press and the artistic and intellectual community did all they could to encourage indigenous work, mostly by disparaging imported images.

In much of this activity there was an often obvious subcurrent of snobbery, even sometimes a panicky sense that the barbarians were about to breach the gates. And, indeed, there was a rudeness in the way America presented the case for its hell-for-leather democratic style. "It is easy to see why Hollywood movies attracted such opprobrium," Puttnam and Watson write. "They symbolized everything the European bourgeoisie found most threatening. . . . They championed the value of cash over culture. . . . They often championed the underdog, and they had developed largely outside the dominant social and cultural groups."

These defenses, both economic and cultural, were feeble, and the former in particular have often been deplored, not merely by parties at interest, like the Motion Picture Producers Association of America, but by free-market economists everywhere who have a special distaste for anything that interferes with the unimpeded flow of ideas. Largely for selfish reasons, I disagree—not with their general principle but with its application in this case. These subsidies and protections have, over many decades, proved vital to the survival of film industries that were essentially unable to defend themselves solely with their own resources. They were therefore vital to the production of many of world cinema's most influential and enduring masterpieces.

I am, of course, aware of the downside of these policies, most notably the hundreds, perhaps thousands, of really bad movies—quota quickies and the like—that were made to satisfy protectionist laws or were produced under subsidies. We in America never saw these films, and most people in their countries of origin avoided them as well. I am also aware that despite occasional short-lived successes, like those of Alexander Korda in England in the early thirties, the alternative strategy of trying to compete in the world mass market by imitating American genres or American spectacle rarely produced films that matched the real thing and were generally greeted with contempt everywhere (there were some notable exceptions, like some of the French *films noir* of the 1950s and the best Italian spaghetti westerns of the sixties, which revitalized the form).

What I am saying is that the largest successes of the European industries—the films that exerted an influence on filmmakers and cineastes the world over—came when they did what was most natural to them, which was to behave like a traditional producing arts organization—like an opera company, say, or a national theater, encouraging individual film artists to work in the old-fashioned way, expressing personal visions as they had been shaped by the national cultures in which they were born and raised. These films, many of them landmarks of film history, could not and would not have been made without some sort of official subvention.

German expressionism, the epic cinema of the Soviet Union, the romantic humanism of the French—these movements did attract a profitable minority audience internationally. More important, they exerted an influence on American filmmakers. Serious directors studied them and occasionally borrowed techniques from them. King Vidor, the greatest of American silent-filmmakers, openly acknowledged the example set for him by Eisenstein and the other great Russians, and the influence of German expressionism on his sensibility is highly visible in *The Crowd*. In the long run, though, the largest effect European films had on American directors was the example of authorship they offered. Well before the *auteur* theory was promulgated, many American filmmakers learned to envy the relative autonomy of their leading foreign counterparts, their ability to assert openly their particular ways of seeing on the screen. Another way of saying that is that since the houses in which these directors worked were so rickety, there were no domineering house styles they had to overcome. In time, when the power of the American studios, based on their long-term contractual relations with filmmakers, declined, American directors would assert their claim to this right of authorship.

Mainly, however, in the years between the wars the European industry functioned as a sort of farm system for Hollywood. European actors, like their directorial counterparts, worked in movies in part because they offered the hope that the Americans would eventually take notice, or perhaps take pity, and permit them to project their gifts onto more and larger screens. Having established themselves in their native lands, they were either swept up by offers from Hollywood that they couldn't refuse or, once Hitler came to power, fled there with some hope that their reputations had preceded them. Not all of them prospered hugely or long. But it is probably true that many film artists owed something of their later careers to the often deplored protectionist measures deployed on behalf of their native film industries. For if these did little to stem the tide of American releases in the period between the wars, they did at least permit the likes of Fritz Lang, Alfred Hitchcock, and Jean Renoir among the directors, Marlene Dietrich, Charles Boyer, and Laurence Olivier among the stars—to name just a few at the top of the emigré list—to develop their talents and their international renown more or less coherently in familiar, emotionally and artistically sustaining surroundings.

World War II did not have quite the same effect on worldwide film production that the first great war did. Fragile as they were, the European industries were, indeed, industries now. They had substantial employee and investor bases. They could not simply be shut down for the duration. On the Continent, of course, the Nazis were eager to create what amounted to a European cinematic union, relying in particular on their Italian allies and the conquered French to help them supply theaters everywhere they ruled. Joseph Goebbels, the German propaganda minister, particularly loved the Hollywood manner and encouraged the production of slick—well, anyway, slick-ish—escapist fare. It's eerie to see how closely many German-made wartime films match the peppy, romantically patriotic mood of so many American movies of that time. To the mass media, all wars are alike—no matter which side they enlist on.

One irony of this period should perhaps be noted. During the war, one industry, that of Great Britain, perhaps did better with its exports to the United States than it ever had before. Pictures like *In Which We Serve, One of Our Aircraft Is Missing, This Happy Breed,* Olivier's *Henry V,* and, immediately after the war, *Stairway to Heaven* (to call Michael Powell's film by its American title), buoyed by America's sense of solidarity with its closest ally, actually achieved something like mass-market distribution here. This proved to be a mixed blessing in that the British industry, basing its hopes on the American market, expanded too rapidly, too expensively and—its lovely little Ealing comedies and the occasional *Hamlet* or *The Red Shoes* aside—suffered postwar reverses that more or less permanently affected its confidence.

Perhaps the Brits could be said to have paid a typical pioneer's price for opening new territories—a lot of hard work and hardships which prepared the way for others to follow. But some of us have reason to be grateful to them. For opening our eyes. The first foreign film I ever saw was Powell's *One of Our Aircraft Is Missing,* probably when I was nine or ten years old during the war. Its foreignness didn't register on me, though its understated suspensefulness did. But the foreignness of pictures like *I Know Where I'm Going!* and the terrific trio of *films noir* made by Carol Reed (*Odd Man Out, The Fallen Idol, The Third Man*), not to mention those splendid little studies of English eccentricity out of Ealing (*Tight Little Island, Kind Hearts and Coronets, The Man in the White Suit*), did register most happily on me, on everyone who came of age culturally in the immediate postwar years. We didn't have to deal with subtitles, only with differently accented English. We didn't have to deal with disconcertingly exotic customs or realities harshly different from our own. I'm tempted to call it a typically British introduction to the wider world—thoughtful, reasonable, civilized.

It came not a moment too soon. For something interesting, perhaps even unprecedented, was beginning to happen all over that world. It's clear now, I think, that with the end of the war a flood of pent-up creative energy was suddenly released in film communities everywhere. One could see it almost immediately in Italy, where filmmakers released from bondage to the fascist state and its "white telephone" movies bestartled us with the neorealism (*Open City, The Bicycle Thief*) that sometimes shaded over into something like magic realism (*Miracle in Milan*). Not since the very earliest days of the cinema had directors used the streets for their settings, the lives of ordinary people for their subjects, with this intensity. It struck people with revelatory force and opened us up to other kinds of exoticism. Within the first postwar decade we would confront, at the movies, the violence of Kurosawa's medieval Japan, the dour lusts of Bergman's Sweden, the social confusions of Ray's India. Meanwhile, in Paris, around the office of *Cahiers du Cinéma,* the New Wave was beginning to form.

Let's pause over that for a moment, for this is where "cinephilia" found its voice and its theoretical foundation. Curiously, the first thing to animate the young cineastes at *Cahiers* was the release in France and everywhere on the Continent that the Nazis had oppressed for a half-decade, of all the American movies that could not be shown there during those years. Looked at from a narrow economic perspective, you could see them as victims, for before the war ended the American industry was planning a bold strategy to regain its lost European markets and was certainly aided in so doing by the military and civilian authorities charged with furthering the Continent's recovery.

Basically, it would seem, it simply planned to overwhelm the European market with all the American movies it had been for so long denied. This obviously represented something like unfair competition. But what did that matter to François Truffaut, Jean-Luc Godard, Jacques Rivette, and Eric Rohmer? This flood of film struck them with an energizing force these pictures could not have achieved had they appeared over several years on a routine release pattern. In the torrent they spotted the work of directors like Hitchcock, Howard Hawks, and Raoul Walsh, among many others who had been dismissed as mere entertainers in the United States, and their enthusiastic commentaries would eventually prove instrumental in rescuing the reputations of these artists.

Moreover, their openness to all kinds of cinematic experience set a critical example for much of the world.

More important to them, they began to contemplate nothing less than a revolutionary reform of French cinema. They didn't necessarily want it to imitate American styles and subject matter (though the cross-references in films they eventually made, ranging from *Bob le flambeur* to *Contempt* are countless) but rather to embrace its populist spirit. French movies, in their view, were too devoted to literary subject matter, stiffened with bourgeois cultural aspirations—*le cinéma de papa* they called it. They found a model to inform their work in their cinema's prewar history—Jean Renoir—but more significantly their attitudes—and by the mid-fifties their films—both shaped and reflected the way all of us began to approach movies. I don't know if I had heard of *Cahiers du Cinéma* in those days, but what it stood for was somehow seeping into American movie culture—and rising up out of it as well. Another way of saying this is that, local issues aside, the Parisian cinephiles were beginning to articulate ideas and attitudes that were less coherently held by the first postwar generation the world over.

When I left college in 1956 and moved to New York, some of my cinematic provincialism had already been rubbed off me. By the time I arrived in Manhattan I had seen that young Swedish couple making love nude among the reeds in *One Summer of Happiness*. I had committed to memory the divine contours of Brigitte Bardot's oft-brandished bottom. Indeed, most historians believe that the huge popular success of *And God Created Woman* was the largest factor in opening the American market to films from abroad. Let me put this as dryly as I can: we must never underestimate how much the insinuating power of the movies derives from their eroticism.

In short, I was hip. But I was not entirely prepared for the riches I found in New York. There were three theaters within walking distance of my Greenwich Village apartment playing both new and old foreign films almost exclusively, with plenty more doing the same thing just a subway ride away. I'm not going to claim that we were a generation of aesthetes. Going to these movies in those days was in some sense morally bracing, a complex pleasure rather than a simple one like seeing an American film. But struggling to comprehend exotic cultures, trying to catch the beat of new filmic rhythms, soberly talking all this through, earnestly weighing, judging, opining was also a wonderfully heady experience. If you will forgive the oxymoron, we felt we were part of a democratically self-selected elite that was in some way reshaping the culture.

And you know what? We were. In the period between 1950 and the early seventies the number of theaters playing "art" films in the United States rose from one hundred to over seven hundred. By 1958 the number of films imported from abroad actually exceeded the number produced in the United States, a situation that would persist for another decade. By 1964 Hollywood, which had troubles that far exceeded those posed by foreign competition (the loss of its theater chains to anti-trust action, the loss of its mass audience to television, the loss of corporate autonomy to independent, star-driven production), was asking Congress to do for it what governments abroad had done for their movie producers—grant them subsidies. By 1974 Hollywood's hometown paper, the *Los Angeles Times*, was calling for a tariff to protect American producers against imported films.

I didn't know or care about any of this at the time. Neither did anyone else I knew. We continued to go to American movies, of course, despite the fact that a hugely creative period—the era of *film noir*, of socially conscious realism, of often mordant social criticism—was largely cut off by the introduction of CinemaScope in 1953 and its demand for elephantine spectacle. But we continued to hope for the best from American movies and were sometimes rewarded by something like *The Street Smell of Success*. I want to stress that we were not, most of us, self-consciously elitist. I thought then, and I think now, that a truly healthy movie culture is one in which some kind of balance is maintained between populism—which is where the roots of the medium are—and elitism—which is where its artistic future is usually predicted to be. It's when people like Godard start saying things like, "Films are made for one or maybe two people" that we are in the deepest imaginable trouble.

But still. . . . What we cinephiles talked about most earnestly, most excitedly, through the late fifties and well into the seventies was *The 400 Blows* and *Breathless* and *Jules and Jim* and *Hiroshima, Mon Amour*. Also *The Seventh Seal* and *Wild Strawberries*. Also *Rashomon* and *Throne of Blood*. Also *La Dolce Vita* and *8-1/2* and *L'Avventura*. Also *The Loneliness of the Long-Distance Runner* and *Billy Liar* and *Room at the Top*. And, eventually, *Loves of a Blonde* and *Closely Watched Trains*.

What a miraculous list that is! What a range of styles and subject matter it encompasses! How easily it could be extended into the hundreds. And, I cannot resist adding, how many of these films—notably, ironically those created by the New Wave, otherwise so rebellious against tradition—owed their existence to state subsidies and protections. Especially in the later years of this period it's also appropriate to observe that many of our most acclaimed imports owed their existence to investments by major American studios, which now judged that those seven hundred art houses constituted a real market, their patrons something like a profitably exploitable film culture. This was not big business for the studios, but it was some business at a time when many feared that there might soon be no business at all for them.

Not that the health of this market was solely dependent on the studios. There was in those days a small army of knowledgeable independent distributors, many of whom had been in the import trade for years, many of whom established relationships with foreign film artists which extended faithfully over many years. These relationships were imitated by audiences. I mean, we went to "the new Fellini" or "the new Bergman," whatever our friends or the critics might have said about them. It was one of the obligations we owed to the art.

Journalism too began to feel that obligation. As Hollywood films approached the nadir of their popularity in the late sixties, when weekly ticket sales dropped below twenty million, down from the ninety million they had enjoyed in the late forties, magazines and newspapers began, ironically, to expand and upgrade their coverage of movies. There was a feeling that old-line critics like Bosley Crowther, for several decades the *New York Times*'s lead reviewer, were just not capable of coping with the Godardian jump cut.

I was one of those sensibilities, hired by *Life*, to review pretty much whatever I cared to review in its pages. We had the largest weekly circulation in America, but compared to television it was small, and advertisers were beginning to desert us. Like the movies themselves, *Life* was trying to reposition itself in a realm somewhere between the elite and the mass. Its review section was a sop to the community that was now tentatively tasting foreign films in the same spirit they were sampling foreign cuisines. All right, call us middlebrows if you must. I've never been afraid of the word.

But call us also a community—a community capable of sustaining, through our interest, coherent artistic careers for the great filmmakers of the world. That community began to break up sometime in the seventies. The reasons for this are many, but perhaps the most important one is that Hollywood recovered from its long swoon. It was reclaiming our interest with movies like *Bonnie and Clyde* (which owed much to the New Wave) and *The Godfather* pictures and *Chinatown*, though I think that was a minor factor in its resurgence.

There were several much bigger things that changed the

commercial equations for Hollywood. The biggest of them was that it had by this time learned to stop worrying and love television. Producing for it and licensing its films to it for extraordinary fees, the studios found the economic stability they had been seeking since the loss of their theater chains. Hollywood also accepted the fact that, domestically speaking, it was now what we have since learned to call "a niche player." Its niche was essentially composed of young males, roughly fifteen to twenty-four, whose interests largely controlled the choice of venues where the great American dating game was played out. They became, these youngsters, the last reliable audience for movies in the United States, and what they wanted was testosterone-driven action. By the eighties, surveys were telling us that four of five older Americans did not go to the movies—ever. They were at home with their tellies and their fears of crime in the streets.

By this time, too, Hollywood noticed that what played so well for brain-damaged American teenagers was also going down very well overseas. Some trace this recognition to *Jaws*, others to *Star Wars*, but that's unimportant. What is important is that what *The Economist* recently called "the generic blockbuster" plays as well in Pisa as it does in Peoria. "Such films," as the magazine observed, "are driven by special effects that can be appreciated by people with minimal grasp of English rather than by dialogue and plot. They eschew fine-grained cultural observation for generic subjects that anybody can identify with, regardless of national origin." All through the postwar period American producers had contented themselves with making about 30 percent of their grosses abroad. Now that figure began to creep up to 50 percent. In many cases it was more than that; I know of films that doubled, tripled, even quadrupled their domestic take overseas.

William Friedkin, the director, put it this way: "It was like when McDonald's got a foothold, the taste for good food

197

just disappeared." But that wasn't quite the right analogy, for the rise of the fast-food chains in America was accompanied by a rising interest in gourmet foods among upscale consumers. The trouble in movies was that all the restaurants, plain and fancy, were essentially under the control of the same few managements, who were simply uninterested in the modest profits generated by their specialty operations.

Naturally the studios began making more and more would-be blockbusters, creating the generally moronic climate pervading today's multiplex. Naturally this bad coinage drove out the good everywhere it was introduced. Even in the United States, when a studio makes a good, serious, but by no means esoteric movie—something like *L.A. Confidential* or *Without Limits*—its marketing department does not know how to sell it, and it fails. In fairness, I suppose we must acknowledge that unimaginably rich America does support an independent film movement and that it, in turn, is providing a place for younger filmmakers—ranging from Stanley Tucci (*Big Night*) to Bryan Singer (*The Usual Suspects*) to develop their talents. Still, their audiences remain minuscule, and one has no confidence that when they enter the commercial mainstream they will be able to preserve their singularity.

Meantime the number of screens playing imports here is now perhaps 2 percent of the total. "We are kept on reservations like the Cherokee or the Navajo," the French director Bertrand Tavernier said not too long ago. Foreign films do sometimes escape the reservation, but only if they are publicizably shocking (like *Trainspotting*) or raise political issues that are of general, as opposed to specialized, journalistic interest (like films from mainland China, which always have to struggle against totalitarian restraints if they are to be seen in the West or from Iran, whose culture is now essentially closed to us). Every once in a while, of course, some film from abroad that serves the romantic, comedic, feel-good needs of the middlebrow audience that Hollywood now largely ignores or no longer knows how to charm — something like *Four Weddings and a Funeral, Like Water for Chocolate,* or *Life Is Beautiful*—breaks out. But we are rather obviously not talking Bergman or Godard here, are we?

Overseas the always fragile indigenous industries are reduced to panic not merely by the loss of the American market but by their inability to compete with the Americans at home. They can't get the playdates, and so they can't get the audience they require. What we are now witnessing at the movies is a culmination of trends that we have observed beginning in the deeper reaches of the movie past, in the 1920s, trends that have rightly concerned foreign filmmakers, governments, and cultural commentators almost from the beginning of the medium. I do not believe it is possible to legislate against them. For I think we are witnessing, all over the world, the ultimate triumph of Neal Gabler's Republic of Entertainment. Or should we call it finally by its rightful name — the Tyranny of Entertainment.

It was inevitable, of course, that the revered figures of the worldwide cinematic renaissance that began in the fifties should age, fall ill, retire, and die. It was inevitable that some of them, before their time, should succumb to loopy ideological distractions, as Godard did. That's not the problem. The problem is that sometime about a quarter of a century ago it became impossible for their would-be successors to build the kind of coherent careers these artists enjoyed. Sontag justifiably wonders if the likes of Krzyszt of Zanussi, Theo Angelopolous, Béla Tarr, and Aleksandr Sokurov, all directors working at a level that once would have made them names to be reckoned with in the international film world, but are presently marginalized figures, can persist, let alone prosper, in today's film world. No one anywhere can conveniently see their work unless he haunts the film festivals. Only a very few viewers can develop an intelligent sense of their themes, their development as artists—and who is left for them to talk to?

For they are caught up, as we all are, in a machine that is best described as a viciously reciprocating engine. Without major artistic figures around which its interests may coalesce, the old cinephile community becomes distracted, wanders off. Without such a community to address, without the faithful audience it once promised, serious filmmakers cannot build steadily functioning careers, steadily developing bodies of work. Certainly the most important of all artists' rights—the right to fail—is denied them.

Meantime the independent distributors, vital to the health of the cinephile community, falter and fail. Journalism loses interest—just try and get substantial space for a serious, subtitled movie today—and devotes itself more and more to industry economic gossip—last week's grosses, next week's executive shuffle. In the film schools, in the college community in general, there is no interest in the movie past, which for most students today seems to end with, yes, *Star Wars*; nothing worthwhile for them to love and link with as they contemplate their futures. Were they to make *Star Wars* today, they would not know, as George Lucas did, to look to Kurosawa's *The Hidden Fortress* for ideas and inspiration. Nor would they help subsidize one of the Japanese master's late works, *Kagemusha,* as Lucas and Martin Scorsese did out of gratitude and lifelong admiration.

Perhaps out of generational loyalty I sentimentalize the lost cinematic community of my formative years. Possibly in offering these generalizations I exaggerate the consequences of its demise. Yet it seems to me the dismal figures don't profoundly lie. And the evidence of decline, of irrecoverable loss, is placed before us every week on the screen. In what we see. In what we no longer see.

1998

Sam Fuller: Movie Bozo

White-maned, white-suited, his omnipresent cigar cocked at a jaunty angle, Sam Fuller, encountered in Parisian exile, briefly stilled the stream of consciousness that usually rushed unchecked across his gravelbed larynx. He was searching for something he rarely offered in his movies—a neat summarizing idea. "That's it," he finally offered. "A director takes a song, a lyric, and makes a symphony of it. Does that make sense to you?"

Generally speaking, sure. But not in Sam's case—unless you thought of him as a sort of Charles Ives, drawing on the vernacular only to subvert it with a big, blatting, unforgettable off-key note: the brave soldier who, having fired the last shot of the Civil War, contemptuously spreads his battlefield picnic on a fallen foe's body only to discover it still twitching with life; the beautiful blonde hooker whose wig falls off in a tussle with her John, revealing a perfectly bald pate; the western hero who coolly plugs his lover when the bad guy tries to use her as a shield in a gunfight.

No *High Noon*ish hesitations for him, no code-of-the-

West niceties. Or for his creator. Sam didn't strain for (and could never fully explain) these bold, indelibly transgressive images. They just came naturally to an uninhibited spirit shaped by youthful service to tabloids and pulp fiction and hard, decorated soldiering with the First Infantry in World War II.

Haute Hollywood patronized him—low budgets, no Oscars, no life-achievement awards—and the dominant middle-brow critics of his high time, the fifties and early sixties, prissily dismissed him. His career in those days largely depended on Hollywood's old roughneck, lowbrow fringe, with the occasional subvention from someone like Darryl Zanuck, who probably saw in Sam some of the smash-and-grab spirit of his early Warner Bros. days. To them he was simply a guy who could deliver exploitable subject matter and violent (though rarely headlong) action, and didn't care about, or maybe even notice, what else he might be up to.

To everyone else, though, he was a man rummaging the junk heap of American culture, beguiled by the kind of gaudy trash in which they believed the movies should no longer traffic. Or maybe it was worse than that. Maybe it was really a dung heap he was pawing through. In which case, if you were a serious artiste, it was possibly okay to explore it. If eventually you deplored it. Or tacked on a little liberal uplift at the end of the picture. But you weren't ever supposed to be as exuberantly unjudgmental about the vulgarly obsessed creatures scuttling across it as Sam was.

His was, as Manny Farber, just about the only contemporary critic who understood Sam, once put it, "termite art," gnawing away at conventional boundaries, heedless of—likely ignorant of—conventional good taste, which was the province of "white elephant art" (and the Academy Awards). Another way of putting that point is that Sam's people never tried to evade the brutal logic of events—or fate. They accepted whatever cards destiny dealt them in a variety of ways, ranging from the calm to the hysterical, but never, ever with self-pity. Or with anything smacking of piety, liberalish or otherwise.

For me, his key scene is one that stands at the emotional center of *Pickup on South Street,* which is one of the few Fuller films that still gets played occasionally in respectable venues like AMC. That's the one in which Richard Widmark plays a cop-hating pickpocket who dips into a purse on a subway and comes up with a roll of microfilm that Communist spies are passing from hand to hand. This brings the FBI into his life and brings his paranoia to a snarling boil. It also brings the reds to the door of a character played by Thelma Ritter, who is for once not required to play the funny voice of reason commenting on the misbehavior of her social betters. Here she is a profoundly weary woman who sells ties on the street and may or may not have observed something about the missing microfilm. But she's not going to cooperate with the goons threatening her. This is not because she is particularly patriotic. It's because in her exhaustion she just doesn't give a shit about all the things that set other people into passionate motion. She counts the ways she has been worn down by life and then tells her interrogators to go ahead and kill her if that's what they want to do. Eventually—this being a Sam Fuller film—they oblige her.

The scene is wonderfully played by Ritter, who probably never had another passage in which she was for so long the focus of the camera's undivided attention. Certainly she never had one in which her character's history and feelings were so fully exposed. It is also—except for the fact that he didn't usually write monologues—a characteristic Fuller scene. He was good with crane and tracking shots when he had the budget for them, but he was at heart a rather claustrophobic director. He liked dark, tight spaces, like the shabby room Ritter inhabits, liked their oppressiveness, their lack of options. He also liked marginal loners, pushed to the far edge of polite society. And he liked stark, melodramatic choices of the kind Ritter confronts here.

These qualities naturally counted against him when he was at his most fecund in the fifties and sixties. He seemed old-fashioned in his insistence on celebrating the mulishness of the lower orders, in his failure to provide the increasingly middle-class, middlebrow movie audience with bourgeois heroes standing around in their grey flannel suits trying to make fastidious moral choices in a world where the stakes were rarely deadly.

In this connection I think there is an apt comparison to be made between Fuller's *Shock Corridor* and Elia Kazan's *Gentleman's Agreement*. Both are about journalists going underground in order to experience, in the fullest emotional sense, an important story. In the latter film, as everyone knows, Gregory Peck's magazine writer assumes a Jewish identity in order to feel the full impact of anti-Semitism. About the worst thing that happens to him is that he gets turned away from a fancy restricted hotel. In Fuller's movie a reporter gets himself committed to an insane asylum in order to investigate conditions there. Among other things, he witnesses (another of those astonishing Fullerian reversals) a black man driven so nuts by racism that he becomes in his mind a Ku Klux Klansman, spouting the most hatefully racist speeches. Eventually the reporter himself is driven insane by the experience.

Yes, the thing is improbably, crudely melodramatic. But it does follow out the logic of the deception fully and powerfully. To have achieved the same effect, *Gentleman's Agreement*, which brought Kazan an Oscar, but which he has since virtually disowned because of its politeness, would have had to show Peck's character beaten to death (or nearly so) by neo-Nazis.

It's the same way with *Run of the Arrow*, the film that

contains that bestartling picnic scene. The would-be diner is Rod Steiger, playing a Confederate soldier so lost to the Lost Cause that he joins the Indians opposing the Yankee army that is trying to pacify them in the postwar West. You could call it "Run of the Logic" I suppose, for nothing occurs in his life to make him change his mind about his old enemies. He remains what he was when we first met him—a violent hater. Sam shows how that emotion twists and stunts him, as single-minded passions tend to do to many of his characters, but he will not grant him, or us bleeding hearts in the audience, a pleasing last-minute redemption. People like this don't re-form, can't be talked out of their madness. And what Sam is saying to us is, "Don't go there." Because if you do, you won't come back.

Let me return to some of the other images I mentioned earlier. Take, for instance, that bald hooker (played by Constance Towers). Her condition is the (highly) visible symbol of a profoundly wounded nature, which thwarts her ambition to find respectability. What we learn as *The Naked Kiss* develops is that she was sexually abused as a child, a theme that was (peculiar as it may seem now) utterly untouched in the movies, anywhere in popular culture, at the time the film was released in 1964. Inevitably, this being a Fuller film, she must seek revenge. Inevitably this leads to an end that does not provide her, or us watching, with anything we would recognize as emotional release.

Consider, as well, the woman shot by that implacable gunman at the end of *Forty Guns*. She is played by Barbara Stanwyck, and she is not exactly the local schoolmarm. She is, in fact, a cattle baroness, and she is introduced in the film's brilliantly arresting title sequence riding at the head of the eponymous troop of gunslingers who enforce her will on this range. We soon come to understand that they are also her studs, summoned to sexual service whenever the whim strikes her, which is probably every night. Hey, if you're a baroness, act like a baroness. Home on this range was a lot more interesting than it was in *The Big Valley*.

Be that as it may, it turns out that Barry Sullivan, as an itinerant lawman trying to bring her psychokiller brother to justice, is man enough to replace all of her enforcer-studs. Their relationship is what passes for love in Fuller's world. But he also is what he is—a man with an obsession. So when her vile brother uses Stanwyck as a shield in the climactic confrontation with Sullivan, the latter does not hesitate even for a nanosecond to plug her in order to get a clear shot at him. Sam meant her to die, but that was too much for the studio. They made him shoot a piece in which it was revealed that he only winged her. But, the staging of what preceded it makes the director's bleak intention perfectly clear.

Like a lot of hard guys, Sam was sentimental about kids and animals, and there were vague implications here and there in his work, as more than one critic has observed, that the United States of America might ultimately come out okay. The ideals behind it were sound and maybe capable of eventually straightening out the many kinks its general population suffered. But that was not an idea that became manifest in his films until quite late in Sam's career. For most of it, he was suspect in all the best places as a vulgar sensationalist. Gavin Millar put it this way in the cautious entry he wrote for Richard Roud's *Cinema: A Critical Dictionary*: "There are defenders . . . who believe he deploys these weapons knowingly and with irony. There are others, his equally passionate detractors, who feel that the crudity, illiteracy and melodrama is . . . a true measure of his sensibility." Roud himself could not resist adding that he counted himself among the latter, was indeed "repelled" by Sam's work.

I think this dichotomy is essentially a false one. I don't for a minute think Sam was an ironist. On the other hand, I don't think he was an illiterate. I think he was, in the profoundest sense, a "movie bozo," to borrow Jeanine Basinger's (quite intentionally ironic) phrase. With it she meant, I think, to identify those of us who are committed to film's unique, essentially non- and often anti-literary way of telling stories, telling lives, working on an audience, and are often enough put down by those whose standards are shaped by aesthetics borrowed from the traditional arts. In this us-against-them context, Sam Fuller is one of the great test cases.

By this I mean he was committed, as few were or are, to a full exploration of the medium's inherent melodramatic logic. Almost all movies take us into emotional realms we usually do not explore in life, therefore to confrontations we are usually able to avoid in reality. The idea is always logically to force seemingly normal people, folks with whom we can easily identify, into situations that are illogically deadly—and then see what happens to them. Most movies, having taken them there, let them off the hook, permitting the audience to escape with their heroic-romantic illusions intact. Sam's tendency was to imperil not-so-nice people and then *not* let them off the hook, thereby testing the limits of our commitment to movie logic.

This strikes me as an honorable and courageous thing to do. But also for him the only possible thing to do. For if you are a fatalist about human destiny, how can you do anything but embrace the inherent logic of your medium—no matter how often others evade or elide it? This is something our most interesting filmmakers (Scorsese, Tarentino, the Coen Brothers) have increasingly tried to do in recent years, which is why Sam Fuller's stock has risen among them and among serious cinephiles, too. We have belatedly come to relish the shock of the transgressive, to enjoy seeing the deadly, implicit logic of screen narrative fully manifested before our eyes.

We also like seeing—at this comparatively late date in the history of the medium—someone ignore the conventions—the last-minute rescue or change of heart—by which we are usually released from that logic and sent home happy. It is not important to us that Sam's way of achieving the transgressive effect was usually not subtle. Oh no, one thinks, he's not really going to . . . oh my God, he is. And then we laugh. At the sheer, sometimes childlike bravado of the thing. At the truth that transcends "realism."

In our movie bozo souls we are not "repelled" by Sam's signature sequences but rather revel in their perversity, in the way they liberate us from the sentimental conventions of decades of moviegoing. The question of how "knowing" Sam was when he conceived and realized one of these sequences is rendered irrelevant by the value of the act, the terrible honesty of it.

When I think of his career, another of Sam's great images occurs to me—the soldier's helmet, a bullet hole drilled in its center, that we see under the opening titles of (logically enough) *The Steel Helmet.* We imagine it to be just a piece of battlefield detritus, but then it begins to move and we see that there is a man, Sergeant Zack (played by that Fuller favorite, blunt Gene Evans), underneath—a hard-bitten, hard-used survivor, a crazy glitter in his eyes, who is going to live to fight another day, die another day.

Oh yes, die. No body of American film work is more touched by the certainty of mortality than Sam Fuller's, none is more conscious of the absurdity of goals, ideologies, perhaps even of action itself, given that overwhelming reality. The narrative arcs of his movies so often turn into closed circles, with people ending up pretty much back where they began, and often enough dying somewhere near their starting point. That certainly is true of *The Steel Helmet,* in which a patrol, a veritable UN of racial types, wanders inconclusively through the fog and darkness of the Korean War, as much as anything trying to figure out what—beyond their own survival—their mission might be.

Zack, their leader, was Sam in a sense—scarred but

scrambling, tough but gallant, capable of gruff sentiment—and just a little bit mad. For the director, like his protagonist, had no shrewdness, no skill at temporizing talk or pretentious promises—coin of the new, post-sixties Hollywood realm—and he was forced further and further afield to keep working.

But that unquenchable spirit of his kept him going and brought him back from near oblivion in 1980 to make a reasonably big-budget, studio-backed movie about his beloved *Big Red One.* It's a movie that—even in the reedited version the studio released—makes you feel the terror and loneliness of modern warfare—the individual caught in the vast machinery of death, the uncertainty of small-unit camaraderie, ever threatened by the random hits of mortality's mortar fire. It is also a movie that ends terribly at a concentration camp, with Lee Marvin's sergeant, a knowing but not cynical veteran of World War I—a guy as hard as any Gene Evans ever played for Sam—rescuing a child, who dies as Marvin gives him a victory ride on his shoulders. Much as Sam believed in the justness of this war and the comradely virtues displayed by ordinary men called upon to fight in it (as he was), he could not end his film on a note of unambiguous triumph, could not avoid this acknowledgment of fate's cruelty.

Typically of this career, his next movie, *White Dog,* was deemed unreleasable, though it is as powerful a condemnation of racism as anyone has ever made. The problem, of course, was its title creature, an animal that had been conditioned to attack black people. The movie is about its successful retraining—one of those uncharacteristically optimistic notes I mentioned earlier—but the idea that basic instincts could be tampered with, made to serve vile ends, was for many unthinkable. We need to believe that the snarling beasts of unreason have long since been put to sleep, that whatever issues still plague us are soluble with a nice little chat—or maybe another law designed to enforce good behavior.

I suppose what I've been saying here is that Sam's glory

lay in the fact that he never believed the taint of something like original sin could be erased from human endeavor, that we might occasionally achieve a grace note or two in life but never the amazement of total grace.

How deeply he considered such matters I can't say—nobody, I think, can say. For he reveled in his identity as a man who simply went ahead and made movies in a heedless, hell-for-leather way. Which implies, I think, an instinctive understanding that movies, especially the best American movies, are not about being "true to life," which is the basic bad rap critics have been laying on them for pretty close to a hundred years now. They are most profoundly about being untrue to our publicly expressed ideas about life—and about being true to our secret life, to that pulpy place where our darkest whimsies, our maddest impulses, both deadly and romantic, live. What one finally loved best about Sam was the ease with which he lived and worked in that place, the sense he conveyed through his outrageous imagery that finally there was no other place worth talking about.

He was a paradox—a populist who was never widely popular. And probably never will be. But in his later years European admirers like Godard and Wim Wenders took to casting him in their films, while the Americans who learned from him—the Scorseses and Tarentinos—began to cast him as an artistic hero. Sam, the deadly innocent, the sweet-souled subversive, beamed upon them, for he sensed that in their admiration lay the beginnings of the small corner of immortality that will be always, uniquely his. Some of us will remember him as a filmmaker whose time came too late for his profit, but not too late to honor its prophet—one of the few, true American originals.

1998

Richard Brooks: Tales Out of School

I knew Richard Brooks before I knew him. In 1952, when I was a young man thinking about becoming a journalist, he made a movie called *Deadline, USA*. It was about a crusading newspaper editor, played by Humphrey Bogart, fighting to save his failing paper and at the same time trying to finish an investigative story about mob murder and corruption. I loved that picture on first sight, and I still love it, with that special affection you hold for the books and plays and movies that get into your head and change your mind—or maybe I should say change the way your mind works—in your impressionable years. I won't say it sealed my professional future. But in some way it influenced it.

Later, when we became friends, I began to see far more clearly how much of Richard was in that movie. Despite its blustery melodrama, the realism of the way it looked rang different, rang truer than most movies of its moment. It was a quality that marked the man and marked so many of his movies, from *The Blackboard Jungle* to *In Cold Blood,* which is his visual masterpiece.

And there was the sound of the movie. It was a sound peculiar to his generation of writers, tough yet literate, gruff yet unafraid of idealistic sentiment. It was the sound of people who received the most important part of their education from experience and from the public library, not from film school, people who had written some journalism (Richard worked briefly on a paper in Philadelphia and had been a radio news writer), admired Hemingway and possibly the *Black Mask* school of detective-story writers.

Then there was the character of the editor, played by Bogart, who was a version of Richard—gallant, dangerous, sweet, principled, touched by loneliness and by a certain old-fashioned reserve about his deepest emotions—except, of course, his always roiling anger at temporizers, compromisers, liars, and egomaniacs. About them, Richard never had any problem expressing his outraged feelings.

Finally, there was this little scene in *Deadline* that is, to me, the heart of the picture and was, though I didn't know it at the time, the true expression of Richard's heart. In it an old immigrant lady suddenly appears in the city room, bearing the evidence Bogart's character needs to complete his big story. He asks her why she brought the material to the paper, not to the police. She tells him, very simply, that when she first came to this country she learned that cops were not to be trusted, but that she had learned to trust this good, grey newspaper because it had never lied to her, because it used words honestly and carefully.

Richard told me later that he based this character on his own mother. In 1990, when he accepted the first Writers Guild–Directors Guild Preston Sturges Award for his life's work in those two crafts, he thanked just three people, all of whom encouraged that love of words that lay at the center of his talent—his mother who revered education, the school-

teacher who taught him to read and write, and a nameless
stranger he encountered in a railroad yard when he was hobo-
ing around the country. When Richard identified himself to
this fellow as a writer, he gently inquired into Richard's credentials. Had he read Tolstoy, Dostoevsky, Dickens? Richard
had to admit he had not. His interlocutor—one of those auto-
didacts who used to be easily found in the American working
class (the man was a train dispatcher), insisted that you could
not be a great writer unless you were first a great reader. "For
every word you write, you should read a thousand," he said.
Or words to that effect.

That's why most of Richard's movies were adaptations of
important books and plays. He wanted us to be great readers,
too. And it made no difference to him whether what we read
were images or words. He liked to say that every aspect of
moviemaking—setting up a shot, or helping an actor find a
character, or editing a scene—was a form of writing. But
when he wrote, when he was actually putting words on a page,
he never used them idly. He used them ferociously, to express
his ideas.

Or maybe I should say his idea. For it seems to me
that everything he did stemmed from just one basic notion,
which revolved around an old-fashioned definition of honor.
Racism, capital punishment, religious or sexual exploitation—these dishonored those who practiced them and the society that tolerated them. He was always willing to interrupt
the flow of his images in order to make sure we clearly heard
what he was trying to say. This sometimes distracted people
and prevented them from appreciating what a marvelous creator of images he was. It harmed his reputation among critics,
too.

Including sometimes this critic. I remember urging him,
after I'd seen an early cut of *Looking for Mr. Goodbar,* to excise
some of the wordy psychologizing that explained his heroine's
untoward behavior. All of that, I said, he had made clear by

213

implication. But he wouldn't hear of it. He wanted to make sure the slow readers got the point, too.

This disagreement did not, however, interfere with our friendship, which built warily over the years. I first met Richard after I had written a delighted review of *The Professionals* in 1966, my first year as a critic. Richard sent me a graceful telegram, thanking me for the notice. It's something most moviemakers don't do. But Richard was never one to stand on ceremony or abide by convention. Somehow we got together a little later, and the next thing I knew I was playing tennis with him and his gang when I started spending some time in Los Angeles. It was then that I learned something crucial about Richard. Gene Kelly and I were the weakest players in that fast and furious game. But that made no difference to Richard. We loved what we were doing—or, this being tennis, what we were trying so hard to do—and we did the best we could, and that was all Richard ever asked of anyone—in tennis, in movies, in life.

A couple decades later my late wife Carol and I moved to Los Angeles. I ran into Richard at some ceremonial luncheon, and the three of us began a friendship that will remain one of the ornaments of my life. I loved the rough courtliness of his way with Carol. She loved the angry passion of the lion in winter. And we both loved sitting in his kitchen, listening to the greatest of all his narratives—the narrative of his life.

He wore his hair in a brush cut, a convenient style imposed upon him in the Marine Corps during World War II, which he saw no reason to alter. Generally he wore sweat suits because they too required minimal upkeep. His meals were simple—often a chili of his own concoction. He was partial—in his late years too partial—to aquavit.

On those long, lovely nights his words flowed differently than they did from the screen. He was a hypnotic storyteller, a master of the telling pause, the rising and falling inflection.

Best of all, he let the stories make their own points, in their own ways. There was no overt editorializing.

He talked a lot about his early writing days. Before the war he had drifted to Los Angeles and got a job at NBC that required him to write (and recite on the air) a short story five days a week. To maintain his pace he was sometimes obliged to borrow from the masters, of course, especially tales with a surprise dramatic twist, but he learned to disguise his sources with inventions of his own. This plagiarism was in his mind benign—the stuff was all in the public domain, and he was both learning from and teaching from it.

The experience got him his first movie job—as a humble junior writer at that humblest of studios, Universal. You can find his credit on the old *Don Winslow of the Navy* serial and on the insanely exotic Maria Montez–Jon Hall feature, *Cobra Woman*. Trying to work up something a little more educational for Montez and Hall to do, he proposed a story about the construction of the Suez Canal. A studio executive wanted Riffs in the story. Richard patiently explained that they lived in Sigmund Romberg's part of Africa. The man remained adamant, and Richard ended the discussion by enlisting in the Marine Corps.

He had a good war, supervising production of a film about the battle of the Marianas, which he wrote and narrated. Not himself a combat cameraman, he was delegated by some of them to request that they be allowed to carry sidearms into battle. Haltingly, Corporal Brooks approached their commander, General Howland ("Howlin' Mad") Smith, with the idea. The general harshly rejected it. He told Richard he wanted nothing to distract the photographers from their primary mission, which as he saw it, was as a goad to bravery. He said he didn't even care if there was film in their cameras. "There are," he said, "no cowards in front of a camera." It was, for Richard, another lesson in the power of the medium toward which he was drifting, but to which he was not yet fully committed.

For the moment he had more pressing errands. Putting his film together at the Quantico marine base, he found he had time to work on a novel. He wrote it with the quickness he had learned in his last civilian jobs, sent it off to Harper & Brothers, and soon had a letter from Edward Aswell, the editor who had pasted Thomas Wolfe's last two novels together, asking him if they might meet to discuss the manuscript. Richard got a weekend pass and reported to Aswell's house in suburban Connecticut. The editor was complimentary but had some suggestions for the final chapters. Richard said he'd be glad to try them but wondered what the practical point of the exercise was. "Didn't anyone tell you?" Aswell asked. "You're on our spring list." Richard always said he remembered nothing about the rest of the weekend. Aswell's words blotted everything from his consciousness. At thirty-two he had at last become what he had always wanted to be—a writer in the traditional form he revered.

The book was called *The Brick Foxhole,* and it was about the brutal murder of a homosexual marine by a sadistic sergeant. In the movie adaptation (with which Richard had nothing to do) the victim became a Jew, and *Crossfire* became a pioneering portrayal of anti-Semitism on the screen. This was all right with Richard, who was Jewish, though he rarely mentioned that fact and seemed to have had no religious training. "Everybody's got troubles," he remembered thinking at the time, meaning all minorities, of course, and troubles of that sort—the troubles of the put-upon—were—or were about to be—his business.

There are two more tales he liked to tell about his first book (there was a second, *The Producer,* with its title character largely based on his postwar mentor, Mark Hellinger). Sinclair Lewis welcomed the novel with a highly appreciative review, and when Richard wrote him a thank-you note, Lewis replied with an invitation to meet next time he was in New York. They did—at the old Astor Bar on Broadway. Richard told him that someday he intended to film what he regarded as Lewis's best novel, *Elmer Gantry.* Lewis replied that if he did, his adaptation should not be too slavish. "Make it into a movie," the novelist said. Richard always said that freed him when, some fifteen years later he turned the novel into what may be his best—certainly one of his most rambunctious— films.

Meantime, back at Quantico another marine approached Richard as he was reading one night in the library. The man had read *The Brick Foxhole* and asked if it was going to be made into a movie. Richard said he didn't know. Well, said this man, he was an actor in civilian life, and he was deter- mined to play the killer in the film. "I know everything about that guy," he said. Richard said, well, fine, and good luck to you. The actor's name was Robert Ryan, and *Crossfire* was the film that reestablished his career after a wartime hiatus. Much later, Richard's *The Professionals* offered this fine actor and fine man one of the few memorable roles of his final years.

Richard adored John Huston, who was writing for Hellinger—uncredited—at the same time Richard was. He may have patterned himself a little bit after Huston, but I suspect there was a natural affinity between them—literate men's men that they were, and dramatic speakers, and adven- turers. Huston invited him to cowrite *Key Largo,* taking him along to the eponymous island for mood's sake, then, accord- ing to Richard, parking himself on the dock with a fishing pole while Richard toiled at his portable, rewriting until his friend grudgingly approved the day's scene. Knowing Richard's am- bition to direct, Huston also brought him onto his set so he could learn how to manage a production. The cinematogra- pher was the distinguished Karl Freund, who one day pressed a couple of reels of 16 mm film on Richard. Freund too knew of Richard's directorial aspirations, and said he thought these shorts, which he had directed in Germany, would aid in his education. Richard ran them that night and discovered they were pornographic. The next day he returned them to the cameraman, complimented him on their lighting, but wondered what lesson he should take from them. "Get to the fucking point," Freund replied. "To this day, when I line up a shot," Richard would say when he recounted the anecdote, "those words come back to me."

It would be a few years before he became a director. Under contract at MGM, he was repeatedly promised his shot. He thought, for example, that he might direct his screenplay for *Any Number Can Play*. But Louis B. Mayer said an untried craftsman couldn't possibly handle a powerful star like Clark Gable. Maybe next time, Mayer said. So Richard cowrote *Mystery Street* and, since that was a low-budget item, thought he might be given a chance to direct it. But no, "Mr. Mayer" (as Richard always called him) was giving Ricardo Montalban his first starring role in that film. He would need an experienced director to help him. Maybe next time, the mogul said again.

Richard was more than ever determined to hold Mayer to that half-promise and somehow managed to get a copy of his unfinished script for *Crisis* to Cary Grant. He then put himself in the actor's way at the racetrack and pitched himself as director. Grant, who had and would help others to make this leap, said that if the rest of the script was as good as what he'd seen, he would support Richard's ambition. "I guess what you don't know about directing I probably do," said the actor.

He was required to offer one more bit of support. During the first week's shooting, Richard was walking beside a camera dollying toward the star, his hand resting on the instrument. Somehow he managed to get his foot under the dolly's wheels. He suppressed his cry of pain, but of course the operator reported a bump in the shot. And people noticed the blood oozing out of Richard's shoe. Grant hurried over and began urging a quick trip to a nearby emergency room. No, said Richard, if I leave the set they'll have some other director down here in a minute. Well, said Grant, then they'll have to find another actor, too. Richard reported to the hospital, where no broken bones were found, and he soon returned with his foot bound in heavy bandages and carrying a cane. There are mock humorous stills of Grant preparing to take a swing at Richard's aching foot with that cane.

I've put these stories down here because, of course, I want to save them. Richard never wrote them out, despite many urgings, because the finality of an autobiographical summing up was unbearable to him. He never drew down his very substantial Writers Guild and Directors Guild pensions for the same reason. To the end of his days—and he was nearing eighty when he died—he maintained the fiction that he was going to make at least one more movie. As late as 1987 he mortgaged his house in order to take an option on an Elmore Leonard novel that caught his eye.

I've also committed these stories to print because, as you may have noticed, this tale of one man's halting, comical, outraged, aspiring, and ultimately inspiring journey through the twentieth century contains no villains. There was a certain cognitive dissonance in this, because Richard was almost parodistically paranoid about letting his work out into the world of fools and knaves. Studio executives were never allowed to read his scripts at leisure. He would come in, read them aloud, then bear the manuscript away, saved from their Xerox machines and the threat they posed to his intellectual property. Actors had to accept parts in his films largely on faith and perhaps the perusal of one or two key scenes. On set they were doled out the day's pages but never got to study the entire script.

Yet for all these dark suspicions, and for all its richness in hilarious people who did dumb things and said stupid things, Richard's life story was mainly about men and women who solved a problem for him, eased his path, defended him against his enemies, or simply graced his spirit with a kindly word or an understanding gesture. Sometimes these people, surprisingly enough, turned out to be studio executives—including the one he caught trying to sneak a premature peek at one of his movies and who was last seen being chased down a studio street by a roaring Richard. Even "Mr. Mayer," that legendary ogre, was treated kindly in this narrative; Richard was very sympathetic in recounting encounters with him after he had been pushed from power at the studio he had built and was wandering about Hollywood, lost and unattended, pretending to be involved in new enterprises.

The same was true of Truman Capote. He had chosen Richard from many competitors to direct the movie version of *In Cold Blood* because once, long ago, he had observed Richard to be the only person present standing up to John Huston at a London dinner party when Huston went on a drunken tear, verbally assaulting everyone at the table. Then, as they went into production, he leagued with Richard to fight the studio which had wanted to hire major stars for the film and shoot it in color. Later, when Capote was exiled from polite society by his literary indiscretions and his descent into drugs and drink, Richard stood by him—keeping in touch, offering loans. It was the payback he felt a man who had long since proved to him his loyalty and bravery deserved.

I'm sure Capote's fate, like Mayer's, had a special poignancy for Richard in his old age, clinging as he did to the belief that he would himself come back from the failures of his last two pictures, from his increasing—but not total—isolation from a Hollywood that had changed immeasurably over his lifetime.

Mind you, there was nothing pathetic in the way he carried himself. He was still in touch with young actors, writers, directors, full of intemperate advice. And with studio people, too. And he could still gather his forces and successfully pitch an idea. They still sought him out, too—almost to the end his agent was reporting offers to him. One time, having secured a development deal for a story that had occurred to him—it was about a female star trying to make a comeback after a Capote-like (or Judy Garland–like) fall—he enlisted my help with the treatment. I had a wonderful—and highly educational—time working on the project with him at weekly meetings. Eventually we produced the treatment, but when it was time to turn it into a script he dispensed with my services. "Are you crazy?" he inquired. "I can't *write* with anyone." He had, it seemed, just needed a congenial sounding board while he worked out the story, someone to assuage his old man's loneliness.

That was fine with me, and the truth was that I couldn't quite imagine the practical ways we, given our disparately prickly natures, might accomplish the hard work of making a detailed shooting script out of an outline's generalities. Yet I also felt Richard had reached a point where he could not *not* write with a partner—someone to keep him focused. Thereafter when I inquired about our project he always changed the subject. Eventually he switched to another idea—about Hollywood child prostitutes and an organization that was trying to save them.

A year or two later I got enough financing to shoot a group of interviews with directors of his generation, aiming toward a series of television profiles, and naturally I included Richard. He died, however, before I got backing to complete the series, and it was in 1994 that I finally started putting together the program about him. It was not easy. A lot of his films, frankly, don't wear well. *Elmer Gantry* does, because of its strong performances, because of its passionate assault on false fundamentalist piety, as relevant today as it was in Lewis's day, because of the spectacular fire sequence with which it concludes, a brilliant directorial *tour de force*. So does *The Professionals* with its celebration of old-fashioned male dutifulness and gallantry. So does the idealism of *Deadline, USA,* however cornily it is sometimes expressed.

We also discovered in one of Richard's most obscure efforts, *The Last Hunt,* a very powerful portrait of frontier psychopathy (from Robert Taylor, of all unlikely sources). It was about the slaughter of the buffalo herds of the Great Plains in the nineteenth century, and Richard made it into a very prescient appeal for the preservation of wilderness and its creatures well before the topic became fashionable. In almost all of Richard's work we also found potent sequences: the great Paul Newman–Elizabeth Taylor fight scene in his adaptation (beset by a still censorious production code) of *Cat on a Hot Tin Roof*; the poignant recollection of his blighted childhood by Robert Blake in *In Cold Blood*; Gene Hackman's wonderful, pacifistic, monologic reminiscence of the battle of San Juan Hill in *Bite the Bullet.*

Most of these moments were in fact monologues—Richard in effect facing the camera and artlessly telling whatever truth he had in mind. But his earnestness sometimes disarmed him. However powerful his educational impulses, great, greatly complex works like *The Brothers Karamazov* and *Lord Jim* were beyond him—in the first case embarrassingly so, in the latter more narrowly (he made it into a pretty fair, overlong adventure yarn with yet another poignant monologue about the paper-thin distance between courage and cowardice by Peter O'Toole in the title role). In other cases, like *Blackboard Jungle,* with its pioneering rock score and its occasionally touching portrayal of liberal idealism frustrated by the intractability of racism, he backed away from the grimmest implications of his story in order to leave us hope for improvement. It seems simplistic now. Something similar happens in his adaptation of *In Cold Blood.* We know now that Capote was in love with one of the killers whose story he told, and that he intended his book as an implicit plea against capital punishment. Richard—sharing this belief on principle—forced up this point in his adaptation. But especially after his extraordinarily powerful recreation of the murders for which the killers are executed, one recoils from it. Visually he had already contradicted himself, shown us a motiveless malignity from the consequences of which, in the end, we do not want to see anyone discharged.

It was, I think, a misfortune that Richard was at the height of his powers during the 1950s, when serious American filmmaking was often defined by the sobriety with which it addressed social and psychological issues, made us "think." It encouraged, rewarded Richard's generous, hopeful, educative impulses while suppressing what was darker in his nature, more in tune with our—his own—desperations and absurdities. It was also a time when the new wide-screen processes, supposed to overwhelm the tiny black-and-white images of television, encouraged epic filmmaking, which was not Richard's best vein, and also encouraged the adaptation of the kind of sweeping fictional "classics" which, again, appealed to the teacher in him but tended to overawe his rambunctious side.

It was weird, knowing him as I came to know him, to reencounter these films of his and find them so often embracing the saving lie instead of the bitter truth. It is hard, having been his friend, and remembering how well the critics and the industry once received his work, seeing the cinephiles now discounting Richard's work as they focus their attention on, say, Douglas Sirk's gloriously loopy romances or Budd Boetticher's classically austere westerns, or Sam Fuller's surreal transgressions.

The latter, especially, form a salient contrast to Richard's work, especially since the two men—who knew and liked each other in their early days—were in so many respects similar. Both were proudly *writer*-directors who had been significantly shaped by youthful poverty, journalistic and B-movie apprenticeships, and World War II soldiering. Both were roughneck *littérateurs,* both had a healthy suspicion of the Hollywood power structure that sometimes shaded over into slightly unhealthy paranoia, both presented themselves as tough guys, yet both were greatly beloved by their faithful casts and crews, responding to their underlying sweetness of spirit and the fierce loyalty they demonstrated to their coworkers. Most important, both knew in their bones the irrationality and violence of American life, the ways in which they could suddenly burst through the thin membrane of civility we stretch over it, and both wanted to say something cautionary about our recklessness. The difference was that Richard retained the old-fashioned belief that rationality could, would eventually answer irrationality. All we had to do was think things through. His best movies are about men doing just that and then pulling back from whatever abyss tempts them. Sam's are about going over the edge, often enough about not even noticing there is an edge until it's too late.

Put it another way: Sam was a premature postmodernist; Richard was a liberal whose work looks naive to the postliberal age. So he, who for all his leonine independence always worked at the center of the system, is now marginalized while Sam, who was essentially a fringe operator, now seems much more central to movie history, to current history. This is an irony. But it is not for me a bitter one.

For having said all that, having made the critical gestures that I, given my nature, cannot avoid, I am obliged to temper them. I think that in some quite profound way Richard was always true to himself in his work. For there was another theme to the personal history he so entrancingly entrusted to the friends of his late life. In that story the young wanderer—the immigrants' son, the newspaperman, the radio writer, the onetime marine, the sometime novelist—finds a home. It was an unlikely home. It was one with which he conducted a lover's quarrel for something like a half-century. It was, of all unlikely places, the movie business.

It was perhaps the only thing he idealized. "I love the movies," Richard said. "I love making them and preparing for them and getting them done." More than that, he said he loved the people who made them. "And it's people who make movies—not buildings, not logos." From this passion he took a kind of consolation for whatever failures might occur to him. "They're going to break your heart a hundred times, over and over again as you . . . make a movie. But if you love your job it's going to come out okay." Maybe, I think he was saying, not so okay with the critics, not so okay at the box office, not so okay with posterity. But okay with you, the moviemaker, if you've done your best, fought the good fight as you define it, with good friends at your side. What more can a man do?

One of Richard's last public acts, in the midst of a bitter writers' strike, was to journey out—limping from the bad hip that kept him in constant pain, the operation for which brought him to his deathbed—to make a gallant, hilarious, inspirational speech to his beleaguered fellow craftsmen. What he was saying, directly through his open expression of love for movie people, indirectly by his act of solidarity with his young inheritors, was that you could function sanely in this lunatic business only if you shared with your community a certain idealism, the desire that often dares not speak its name in Hollywood, to build something that informs and delights and gives some shape and meaning, however ephemeral, to our experience, our sense of the world.

Will one fail that ideal more often than one realizes it? Naturally. But looking back on my first contact with Richard—that review of mine—I think he was responding to what was not merely a flattering notice, but to some subtext in that piece that indicated to him that, though I was a reviewer, the class enemy, I shared his idealistic love for this exasperating, entrancing, ultimately obsessing, ultimately defeating medium. In any case, he honored me and my wife with his fiercely loyal friendship, by making us, as he did so many others, the repositories of his experience, the meanings he extracted from them, and, best of all, his romantic sense of a fast-disappearing past.

In the course of this friendship he taught me this lesson: that it does not really make that much difference whether the work you do is finally judged to be "great," particularly if "greatness" is decreed by critics who know nothing—not in their bones, anyway—of the confusions, improvisations, and compromises that go into making that most communal of expressions, a movie. What really matters is what greatness of spirit—that compound of honor, passion, decent impulse, and, yes, eccentricity and awareness of your own flaws—you bring to that work, that process, that mess.

One of my favorite passages in all of American literature occurs in Willa Cather's *A Lost Lady.* In it a young man encounters an aging western pioneer just before he dies. The old man, without really trying, just by being what he is, passes on to the younger man a sense of a tradition that will sustain him: "The taste and smell and song of it, the visions these men had seen in the air and followed—these he had caught in a kind of afterglow in their own faces—and this would always be his." So it was with Richard and his old-fashioned ways, his old-fashioned morality. I loved him and, as the years gather more oppressively around me, I find myself thinking of him often and thanking him for this infinitely treasurable gift.

1992

Real Reality Bites

When he was at the height of his fame, some eighty years ago, D. W. Griffith was occasionally wont to muse about how much larger still the public's regard for him might be if only the world were more sensibly organized. It was, for example, a matter of bitter irony to him that, though there was a "thinking class" of "picture fans" who understood and appreciated the primacy of the director in the creative process of filmmaking, this elite's opinions were generally drowned out by the clamor of the star worshipers, that mass of simpletons who mistakenly focused their yearning adoration on those creatures who were actually but the instruments of the director's genius-struck will. He saw no hope for immediate reform of this defect but posited an evolutionary possibility. He had observed that, even as he spoke, the military leader had been replaced in the American pantheon by the captain of industry; might it not be possible in, say, fifty or a hundred years, that the industrialist in his turn would be replaced in the popular dream of glory by the creative artist? He rather thought so. In which case, he implied, the movie director, that crucial

227

figure in the process of turning the medium into a self-conscious art, would at last receive his just desserts from the audience.

The moral of this story is simple: be careful what you want, you may end up with the Auteur Theory. And Larry Lazar. Larry is the anti-hero of what seems to me the most acute novel yet published about contemporary moviemaking, Josh Greenfeld's *The Return of Mr. Hollywood,* which is the first fiction, as far as I know, to offer the "artist" not as the victim of mogul manipulation but as the manipulator of his ostensible superiors, not to mention the media, his collaborators (especially them), and such comely young women bearing scripts that "need work" as cross his path. If Sammy Glick had been born a generation or two later, gone to college, and done the outside reading, he would have been Larry Lazar.

The difference between these two comically rendered monsters of the untrammeled ego is only one of style. Poor Sammy, operating in Hollywood toward the end of what a Marxist might call its period of primitive accumulation, had no choice but to appear as he was, a grubby little grabber (with a certain hustler's charm) clambering his way upward in a world where money and power, as visibly deployed as possible, were the only means of measuring one's success.

They remain, of course, an excellent test of how one's doing—and not just in Hollywood, either. But the arrival of Griffith's millennium—in which a large public (that likes to think of itself as knowing) hungers for artist-heroes and possesses an easily understandable critical theory to help locate them in the jostling crowd of near-anonymous figures who claim some credit for a movie—offers the shrewd operative an attractive alternative to Sammy's vulgar push-and-shove. This consists of the presentation of the auteurial self in a rather delicately nuanced light: a loyal opponent of the system, wryly aware of its shortcomings yet bravely continuing to use it in what appears to be an artistically conscientious, morally independent way. This figure must not permit himself to be observed truckling to studio authority, but neither must he permit himself to pass over into the grandiose mode (therein lies self-destruction) or into the posture of the full-scale revolutionary (therein lies madness).

But I can't say this as well as Larry Lazar himself does in the delicious parody of an AFI "Dialogue on Film" with which Greenfeld prefaces his novel. "It's very tricky being an artist in the system," he begins his address to the students. "Especially if you're a personal filmmaker like me. I want to be successful. But I don't want to be successful if it means doing what they want me to do and not having any control. I'm an artist and I can't work that way. . . . I deal with real reality. I don't make dumb films about cops and killers and globs in space and somebody possessed by demons. . . . But then nobody asked me to be an artist, to be a director who makes personal statements. What do the studios know or care about my personal statements anyway? . . . They want to use my art to make their commerce and I want to use their commerce to make my art. So long as I have a hit every once in a while the system will let me continue to function as a personal filmmaker making personal statements."

There—except for the false modesty ("It's not that I'm a Joyce or a Proust or a Thomas Mann . . .")—you have it all, the archetypal credo of the model modern major motion picture director. And as hype it is glorious—except for its having only a tangential relationship to the "real reality" of how a Larry Lazar actually operates. It is, of course, Greenfeld's business to explore and explain that reality—often hilariously, always intelligently, and, finally, rather touchingly.

The Return of Mr. Hollywood concerns a week of high vulnerability in Larry's life. Or, anyway, a week in which, were he a person of normal susceptibilities, he would have been in such a condition. For it is Greenfeld's sly device to discover Larry in that state of anxious limbo where, perforce, most directors spend most of their time these days—between pictures. To this he quickly adds a focusing personal crisis—the sudden death of Larry's mother—which forces him to return to his New York roots for the funeral and to a confrontation with representatives of his past and the shaping memories they awaken. Conventionally, one expects from a novel based on premises of this kind that its protagonist will be forced by his passage through dire straits to reexamine himself and perhaps reform himself. Instead what we get in *Mr. Hollywood* is an exquisite working model of a defense mechanism, perfectly designed for and sited in our culture, humming merrily, imperviously along, immune to all criticism, all appeals.

To see the awesome symmetry of this construct it is necessary to pull apart the main elements of Greenfeld's tale— professional style and personal history—in order to examine how perfectly machined, to hairline tolerances, is their join. Begin, as he does, with Larry in Lotus land. His last picture, *Herbie and Milty,* has just opened in a fashion that is typical for "personal statements" that somehow fail to touch a universal chord. In New York, L.A., and the other urban centers where a sizable segment of the public understands and appreciates the difference between artists who are fighting the good fight "within the system," and hacks for hire, reviews have been respectful, business respectable. Elsewhere, in those venues where the word *"auteur"* looks like a typographical error, it is "toilet time." Which means that Larry's next project, *Remember, Remember,* just now rolling out of the studio's mimeograph department, is in danger.

It is, like all of Larry's personal statements, "funny and moving and tender and it dealt with real reality." Or, as the studio's production chief says, "Fucking your ex-girlfriend's daughter is a nice theme. . . . An audience can relate to it." Moreover, the boss is aware of the prestige that accrues to him and his enterprise these days when it stands behind the work of a self-proclaimed artist like Larry. Indeed, so impressed is

he with Larry's reputation that he can scarcely bring himself
to make a suggestion or offer a criticism of the work in
progress. "If they just put 'He made *Herbie and Milty*' on my
tombstone I will die happy," he asserts before gently proposing that maybe, just maybe *Remember, Remember* could be—
how to put this?—a little, well, funnier? He is also aware, alas,
that the bottom line on Larry's vision—the grosses—is just a
little blurry. He will require time to dither.

The moral line on these allegedly personal statements
is also blurry. For the fact is that Larry has required a
screenwriter-collaborator to make all of them up until *Remember, Remember,* and if neither the studio boss nor the critics have noticed that little detail, Larry has. And it has been
gnawing at him. To the point that he has expropriated an idea
of his *Herbie and Milty* collaborator (and an old friend) and
passed it off as entirely his own: "Until now I had only heard
of the word 'inspiration.' . . . But it's a whole piece and it
practically wrote itself," he blithely proclaims. Nor is this the
end of his sins. For in order to work on this script, to follow
"inspiration's" dictates, he has abandoned, as we later learn,
collaborative work with another friend without having actually written a word but having pocketed two-thirds of the development money. Worse, such is the nature of their deal, his
pal cannot show the script he has completed to the studio
that paid for it or to anyone else without Larry's approval,
which of course he will not grant. In the end the only satisfaction available to the exploited scrivener is to try to impose a
little real reality on Larry—this is to say, punch him out.

Much good it does him. For by this time we are aware of
what makes Larry run. And it is not, primarily, something as
simple as material gain. It is total self-delusion, entirely without hypocrisy. He really believes he is writing when he is steal-
ing, writing when bouncing half-formed ideas or hair-trigger
responses in the general direction of someone hunched over a
word processor. And who, other than one of these—a grape

picker, as Larry describes the movie writer—is going to know that this is not exactly an artistic function? Not a studio executive. Not an actor. Not the girl from the studio press department who rides out to the airport in the limousine to make sure it meets the plane Larry is on. Not his relatives in the Bronx, pleased that their boy has made good in show biz. In their innocence they have no choice but to accept Larry on his own inflated terms.

Indeed, it is in their interest to accede to them. They make him seem more glamorous and their proximity to him more glamorous. Real reality? Isolated in the cocoon of his fantasy, he couldn't find it if he wanted to—because no one would be the least bit interested in helping him look for it. For he is now, as the rabbi intones at his mother's funeral, "a show business great. A giant. Like Eddie Cantor. George Jessel. Jack Benny. David Begelman." As such, of course, he was consolation and reward for his mother's struggles, for "Sally loved show business. This above all she loved; show business. . . . And who of us does not love show business?"

Who, indeed? And who would not make of his heart's desire something yet more wondrous than it is? Who would not elevate its clever craftsmen, even its humble journeymen, to the status of conscious artists? Honoring them, we honor our own good taste. And turn what was once idle recreation into critical function. How sweet it is!

And not least for the recipients of our self-interested beneficence. For as the real realities crowd in on him in the course of his mournful duties in New York, Larry handles them with ease—by turning them into movie sequences. They either remind him of movies past or they suggest to him shots he might incorporate in movies future. When either indigestion or psychosomatic troubles present themselves to him as a heart attack in the Holland Tunnel, his first thought is that the staging leaves a lot to be desired. You could never get a camera crane in here. A bridge would be a much better

setting, with Manhattan's lights glowing in the background.
Larry Lazar, with a little help from almost all of us, has radically redefined art; it is a tool not for intensifying one's response to life but for dissociating oneself from it.

We begin to sense something else, too, as his childhood is
forced back into his consciousness: as the only child of an economically marginal Jewish family he was, inevitably, the center of their hopes, therefore of their attention. It was surely a
mixed blessing—Mom as comic ogre and all that. But equally
as surely, the need to be at the center of things, to be indulged,
catered to, fussed over, was permanently implanted. And that,
of course, is precisely what the director-as-*auteur* becomes
when a fine-feathered theory becomes a vulgar Hollywood
habit of mind: "the baby-as-king," as Mike Nichols once described the treatment accorded directors on today's movie lo-
cations.

I don't mean to suggest that authentic *auteurs* do not
exist in the United States of America. People with tempera-
ments as varied as Stanley Kubrick, Martin Scorsese, Woody
Allen, and the Coen Brothers consistently make movies on
which their tastes and talents are indelibly stamped. But
some of these directors don't even take the possessory credit
("A Larry Lazar Film"), and none of them seems to feel the
need to make large claims for himself as a visionary or a rebel.
They apparently think that *auteur* is an honorific, not a job
description, a title to be awarded by others (or by history),
based on consistent performance, as it has been to the likes of
Hawks, Hitchcock, Lubitsch, Lang, John Ford, most of whose
careers were fully shaped (or, in the case of Lubitsch, entirely
over) before the term was invented, and who thus could not
have claimed it had they wanted to. Let me put the point very
simply: if a director runs around calling himself an *auteur,* you
can be pretty sure he isn't one.

I suppose we can't blame our real-life Larry Lazars for
using the notion of authorship to appeal over the heads of

their bosses when they're in trouble—or merely when they wish to impress the impressionable and get a little ego gratification. It is not a matter that comes up in the novel, but in the "real reality" of today's Hollywood, studios are afraid to impose their judgments on directors who have achieved any sort of standing with the public, lest the latter rush to the press with claims that their visions are being tampered with, knowing that by now there is an automatic presumption that they are the victims, the producers their vulgar exploiters.

This is, of course, a scorched-earth strategy. Once a film is reedited by the studio and word of that gets out (see, for instance, what happened to Sergio Leone's masterpiece, *Once Upon a Time in America,* or the *Heaven's Gate* mess), reviewers and moviegoers inevitably regard whatever is released as damaged goods, and just as inevitably it fails at the box office. Since we usually can't see the director's original cut, we actually have no way of judging the merits of the argument, even though logic should tell us that in the lunatic world of movies the possibility that the studio could occasionally be right, or that both parties may be wrong, should not be discounted.

Logic, of course, has very little to do with the movie business, and, in any case, we all fight with what weapons come to hand when we feel threatened or merely insecure. But it is very useful of Josh Greenfeld to show us, in this coolly knowing, amusingly spiteful book—doubtless at least partially a *roman à clef* (Larry's filmography and physical attributes bear more than a passing resemblance to those of Paul Mazursky, with whom Greenfeld wrote *Harry and Tonto*)—how what amounts to a critical conceit has been turned into a careerist's ploy.

More important, perhaps, *The Return of Mr. Hollywood* causes us to reflect on how radically the nature of the studios, bosses has changed over the years. Looking back to the days when the major production companies were managed by the legendary moguls—the Mayers, Cohns, and Jack Warners—

we think of them as father figures of a crudely comical, capri
ciously scary kind, ruling over their studio families with avari-
cious and, if you were a contract starlet, endlessly wandering
hands. What Josh Greenfeld implies is that studio bosses have
in recent times undergone what amounts to a sex-change operation. Those fearsome Jewish father figures of yore have, in
effect, turned into Jewish mothers. Where once they terrified,
they now indulge. Where once they threw the tantrums, they
now try to placate the iron whims of others. We live now in an
age of aesthetic as well as political correctness, and this is not
necessarily a change for the better: not for the industry, not
for its products, not for the public, and most certainly not for
the Larry Lazars of this world.

1984

Advantage, Andy

When Andy Sarris played tennis—this was back in the seventies—he would usually take up a position a few feet in from
the baseline, not generally regarded as an ideal place, strate-
gically speaking, to cover the court, but one that worked un-
cannily well for him. Somehow he seemed to reach just about
everything hit in his direction by moving just an efficient step
or two forward or back, left or right. His contact with the ball
was not elegant—more of a swat than a stroke, if I correctly
recall those long-ago doubles matches—but his shots were
smart and deft, and often enough winners. Anyway, he made
you scramble to return them while he projected a serene, un-
ruffled, almost genial air, unless, of course, he and his partner
(usually his wife, the lithesome Molly Haskell) fell into mut-
tered critical dispute over who should have been covering a
ball that somehow skipped between them.

There was, I thought at the time, an analogy between
Sarris the tennis player and Sarris the film critic. His stance
on the court was not entirely unlike his stance as our leading
practitioner of autuerism: firmly committed to a carefully

chosen position which he defended with a nice blend of passion, good nature, and individuality—above all, the latter.

I continue to think there is probably a kernel of truth in
this observation: tennis and criticism are both games that test
and reveal the character of those who play them, tennis probably more clearly than reviewing, since it offers no opportunity to cover your mistakes of perception and judgment with
a nice diversionary phrase. But I don't want to trap Andy (or
myself) in so limited and limiting an analogy. He deserves better than that. Anyone who has stayed the course as long as he
has does, particularly if he or she has maintained surpassing
grace under the pressure of unrelenting controversy for so
many years.

It was, in fact, as a controversialist that I first heard of
Andy. Before I became a movie reviewer he had written his famous article, "Notes on the Auteur Theory in 1962," in *Film
Culture,* a magazine then totally unknown to me. Like a lot of
people (as Andy would ruefully admit), what I knew of it was
Pauline Kael's famous assault on it, written in 1963 but discovered by me in 1965, when she included it in her first collection of essays, which for my sins I reviewed favorably in the
New York Times Book Review. She was even then a devastating
polemicist, with a special gift for making anyone who disagreed with her look not just wrong but foolish. The portrait
of Andy that emerged from her piece was a sort of idiot savant
desperately hammering together a theoretical structure—in
my mind's eye (or maybe hers) it looked something like the
Our Gang clubhouse—to shelter what she implicitly identified
as an arrested passion for old Hollywood crap.

She shared the same passion, of course. Everyone who
writes about the movies—with the possible exception of John
Simon—inevitably does. That was especially true in those
days, when the movies everyone—well, anyway, the better
critics and knowing audiences—cared for most and remembered best were always getting pulled over by the middlebrow

culture cops and failing their sobriety tests. We were all groping for words—a new critical vocabulary, if you will—that
could be used to capture and define on the page this self-
evident, but until then sternly denied, reality of the movies
and our relationship to them.

Kael and Sarris were unquestionably the leaders in this
effort. You didn't have to choose between them at first
(though even in those early days Pauline was busy recruiting
that little cell of not entirely secret agents that eventually
came to be known as the Paulettes). But you did find yourself
drifting toward one camp or the other.

At first I leaned toward her, partly because I met her before I met Andy, and there was something curiously compelling—even (I hate to say it) inspiring—about this almost
demonically possessed little woman: partly because in those
days—before the meanness, hysteria, and power-tripping took
over completely—she wrote so entertainingly; partly because
I was coming at movie reviewing from the same direction she
was—that is to say, from an essentially literary-political-
moralizing direction—and did not fully apprehend the possibilities of other approaches, of which auteurism, with its
stress on the manner in which directorial personalities asserted themselves on screen through visual metaphors, was by
far the most interesting. (It was also, because of the unusual
stress it placed on critical vocabularity as it attempted to
translate these metaphors into words, by far the easiest to
make fun of.)

My understanding of what Andy and his coreligionists
were up to dawned rather slowly, and only after I met him.
This was sometime in the fall of 1966, at one of the founding
meetings of the National Society of Film Critics. It was
greatly aided by the fact that I immediately found him such a
likable guy—especially in this slightly lunatic context.

We had come together, about a dozen of us who wrote for
magazines, because at the time the only significant associa-

tion of movie reviewers was the New York Film Critics Circle, which then confined its membership to writers working for the city's daily papers. They were a stodgy crowd, unresponsive to new ways of making and seeing movies—this was, after all, the ascendant age of Bergman and Fellini, Truffaut and Godard—and generally exemplars of what Andy at one of our early meetings dubbed "creeping Crowtherism," after the hopeless Bosley, who had been the *New York Times*'s lead reviewer for almost three decades. His—their—idea of a good movie was the old Hollywood's idea of a good movie: something with a sobering social message, or maybe a careful literary adaptation.

On the whole, we were right about our competitors. They were not very good critics, so it was probably useful to raise an alternative organizational voice against them. On the other hand, I'm not certain that we were made of stuff all that hipper and finer. We were surely more actively aware that movies had suddenly become a hot topic in the better New York intellectual circles where there was much talk (a lot of it rather patronizing, I thought) about this "new" art form. Personal experience—invitations to appear on public broadcasting panel shows, not to mention academic and church basement forums—had taught many of us that it was possible to earn more than a living out of this work, that some sort of a public career could now be made as a movie reviewer. Our group activities—publishing an annual anthology of our writings, issuing statements on issues of concern to the film community (mainly involving censorship questions), very marginally added to such social esteem and intellectual authority as we were suddenly enjoying. But, frankly, the first thing we thought of doing was giving awards like the big guys did: throwing a party, rubbing up against movie stars, having some fun, for godsake.

Alas, in those early years we kept giving our prizes to Ingmar Bergman and his gloomy, faraway ilk, a habit that tended to dampen our festivities. But no matter. Our names got in the paper, people—especially movie people—started to reckon with us a little bit, and our modest fame grew a trifle more. This was, I think, particularly gratifying to Kael. She had been the prime mover in the foundation of the society, cheerily making common cause with reviewers she fundamentally held in contempt, because she wanted to enhance the status of her occupation (profession, with its implication of definable standards of competence, is too grand a word for movie reviewers), and believed that in numbers there must be power. This was to some degree understandable. She had been wandering the fringes for decades, writing film notes for the theaters she managed, broadcasting on nonprofit radio, contributing to obscure magazines. Belatedly—she was in her mid-forties at the time—she was beginning to gain national attention, writing for a variety of national magazines before settling down at the *New Yorker,* and she was determined to enjoy it to the fullest. Andy's history, though he was a decade younger than Pauline, was not dissimilar. Indeed, of the society's twelve founding members, he and Pauline were the only ones who were at that time fully committed, professionally and emotionally, to movies as a topic.

The rest of us were just passing through. Or so we thought. Some of us were slumming novelists. Others—me among them—had journalistic agendas more "serious" than opining about movies for the rest of their lives. In other words, this was for most of us a part-time, and, we guessed, short-term occupation, a way of piecing out our incomes and looking sort of "with it," as the saying used to go. What did we care about the long-run status of movie critics? In the long run most of us imagined we would be doing something else.

Andy, of course, knew otherwise, knew that he, at least, was a lifer. Given his background and his commitment to film, I'm sure he enjoyed the modest celebrity now being thrust upon us as much as anyone. But he had taken a message quite

240

the opposite of Kael's from his previous experience. He was a self-described "cultist"—I think purist is a better word—of the cinema and had no desire to transcend that status, may even have thought that to do so would be to betray his calling—and his better nature. He had observed, he would later write, that most of the people who had previously made names for themselves in this field were widely perceived in much the way most of National Society's membership perceived themselves, that is to say, as "being too good to be reviewing movies." In contrast, people coming out of the little film journals, as he had, "were not considered much good for anything else."

This was fine with him. And liberating. For as he would also reflect, "the cultist does not require the justification of a career to pursue his passion, and the careerist does." He understood perfectly well that the mainstream press, which at the time was either hiring movie reviewers for the first time or trying to raise its standards in this realm, were not about to engage him except on an occasional basis, simply because he was so dauntingly, scarily knowledgeable about his subject. Besides, this being the sixties, when all American institutions were generally supposed to be in a pre-revolutionary condition of some sort, editors—and their trendier readers— wanted a kind of literary performance that was outside his range: an edge of out-with-the-old malice, a sense that the medium was in crisis like everything else and that virtually every movie could be seen as an event with a potential either to deepen or redeem that crisis.

Surprised and delighted to find himself making a decent living doing what, given his ardor, he would have done—and often enough had done—for no fee at all, he was serenely content with his lot. Indeed, he once swore me to secrecy on this point: editors must never know, he said, that most of us would write without recompense, so pressing was our need to express ourselves on this topic to which we were so deeply committed.

I'm not certain that I entirely agreed with him about that, though, on the other hand, here I am, writing about Andy for free, just because I care about the subject, so surely I knew what he was talking about. In any case, there's not the slightest doubt that my good feelings about him began at those early meetings of the society, where he presented himself as a serious man, deeply engaged in his work but utterly without pretense or guile.

In the group's squabbles, of which there were many, he would speak his piece in a high-pitched rush of words, intelligence, and, I thought, a kind of innocence—anyway a lack of calculation—attractively combined. He was like an adolescent who had just discovered ideas and his own skill with them. His capacity to excite himself with his own thoughts, combined with his obliviousness to the way that excitement might be perceived in a crowd very concerned with the weight, measure, and ironic assay of its own words, was wonderfully refreshing. He did not love arguments—seemed to me rather abashed when he found himself drawn into them, and entirely lacked Kael's killer instincts—but he did not shrink from them either. For he understood that his passionate intellect was bound to get him into troubles that the rest of his rather sweet nature would have preferred to avoid. And that he had no choice but to accept this contradictory and often discomfiting state of affairs.

His lively sense of his own marginality led him to a sense that the whole critical enterprise was a marginal one. He had to embrace it because, it seemed, that was his fate (he is a Greek, after all). But he did not believe that group action was likely to elevate his status or that of movie criticism in general, even imagining that this ragtag squadron was up to such a task. Certainly he did not imagine that we were going to effect a revolutionary reformation of the entire motion picture industry.

Kael, I think, did—and maybe one or two others among

us as well. At this time—remember, we're still in the sixties—she was always insisting that the studio system was on the verge of collapse and just needed a few strategic pushes to make it tumble into a heap. She advanced at the time a notion that the leading filmmakers might organize themselves into some sort of cooperative which could find creative bliss outside the industry as it was presently constituted.

This loopy notion grew out of Kael's essentially Manichean—should one say Marxist?—view of the way the system worked. Though she often struck the poses of a populist, she was ever a nervous one. The movie audience was, in her view, basically guileless, therefore defenseless against exploitation by a soulless and "rotten" industry. Worse, because it was bereft of moral and aesthetic vision, that industry, as she saw it, corrupted not only the audience but all whom it employed. Or almost all. For within it there toiled a few artists of exemplary integrity, lonely rebels pursuing their singular visions against desperate odds, in the process rendering themselves virtually unemployable. When they were occasionally allowed to work, their films, their visions, were almost always subjected to cuts and revisions by the vile studios. Many of these filmmakers—not all of whom were quite what she believed them to be—she personally befriended and tried to keep on the path of righteousness. All of them she was quick to defend, and to urge us as a group to defend, when they claimed irreconcilable artistic differences with their employers.

They were only a few, these favorites. With those who stood outside her charmed circle she was usually brutal. And not only in print. In our early hubris we took to inviting directors to join us in off-the-record dialogues, which took place on Sunday evenings in the Algonquin Hotel dining room, which was not open for business that night but which, without cooking smells to cover it, always smelled of cat piss. The idea was to suggest that the relationship between critics and creators need not always be a hostile one, that perhaps we could make common cause against the Philistines.

In theory this was admirable. In practice it usually deteriorated into a cat fight. Or should I say a pissing contest? And it was usually Kael, one of whose favorite epitaphs for her unfavorite moviemakers was "whore," who started it. I don't recall her actually using that word in these sessions, but sooner or later she would, under the guise of free and open discussion, launch into a vicious assault on our guest. We were used to it, of course—we had all, at one time or another, been the victims of these near-sociopathic outbursts—but they shocked people who had come expecting a polite exchange of ideas. David Lean was so distressed by his evening with the critics that he would claim (with considerable melodramatic license) that it prevented him from making a film for fourteen years. John Frankenheimer, bless his heart, gave back as good as he got. Others fell somewhat befuddled between these two extremes, but the tone Kael kept setting subverted the purpose of these gatherings and we soon abandoned them.

Andy, perhaps needless to say, always did his best to keep these dialogues on a courteous track. That was his nature, however blustery he might grow in advancing or defending his own positions. It was also a signal of his indifference to Kael's reformist zeal. The system's products had, after all, provided him with much pleasure over the years, and it had supported many careers that were in his view entirely admirable. Even if revolutionary overhaul were a practical possibility—which, of course, it was not—he was clearly not certain that it was such a great idea. Or that the National Society of Film Critics could provide the cadre to carry its banners.

In this period I began to see why Kael's animus against him, and Andy's answering passion, were both so deep. If he was right, if coherent and worthy authorial careers could be created and sustained in the motion picture industry as it had for so long been constituted, then her strictures and her calls for radical reform were pointless. If, on the other hand, she was right, then his heroes must partake of the system's corruption, which would render their careers (and his enthusiasms) suspect.

Beyond that, it stood to reason that if the industry was as bad off as she insisted, it required not just a Savonarola—a slot she was happily filling—but an intellectual czar, a job for which she was self-nominated. Her favorite critical locution, that imperious "we" in which she attempted to sweep all readers up into her response to a film, thereby banishing argument by implying that none could possibly exist, was the tip-off. So were her confident imputations of shabby motives to filmmakers, which sometimes had mere gossip for backing, often enough not even that—just wild surmises. She also liked to pull stupid and pretentious quotations from press releases, a form in which no one is at his best, and use them against filmmakers.

Taking nothing away from her gifts—she was usually very good on performance, for example, with a talent for characterizing an actor's work in vividly evocative, often implicitly sexual, ways—she remained, I've always thought, a critic for people who didn't go very much to the movies but knew what they thought of the medium—also not very much—yet loved to overhear falsely knowing conversations about them. This crowd had no need for a defined critical position; they had neither the time nor the inclination to track or question Kael's outrageously overstated, baroquely rationalized prejudices for and against various moviemakers. Just as they ignored her when she was in her Madame DeFarge mode, they failed to observe her highly personal, hugely eccentric enthusiasms. They didn't notice, for example, her peculiar devotion to her journeyman pal, Irvin Kershner, didn't recall for long her dippy assertion that being present at the New York Film Festival debut of *Last Tango in Paris* was like being there for the premiere of Stravinsky's *Rites of Spring*.

What did they care about the difference between a momentary sensation and a watershed event in the history of modernism? It was enough for them to enjoy the *spritz*, the performance, and move on to their next diversion.

It is not entirely fair or agreeable to keep measuring Andy's performance against this one, and I apologize for it. On the other hand, one of the unexamined premises of careless writing about film these days is the notion that this woman was "the greatest film critic who ever wrote." I want to suggest that there are other possibilities. I also want to suggest that for that weird notion to be even remotely plausible, Kael would have had to build a body of work out of a premise somewhat more complex (and rationally definable) than the "sexiness" of the medium—though it was useful of her to acknowledge publicly that formerly dirty little secret—to build her pieces on something of more lasting interest than how a movie succeeded or failed in turning her on.

In truth, Andy was much more fullhearted about movies, a much more mature lover, if you will, in that he was far more patient with the object of his affections, infinitely more forgiving of mistakes, especially if they were committed by an artist he had admired over the years. Nor was his regard affected by gossip or speculative innuendo, real or imagined personal slights. This cool but scarcely dispassionate manner was a projection of his serene historicism. His work always implied that the movies would survive the latest stinker (and the latest putative masterpiece, too) and that society and culture—along with the ordinary moviegoer—would probably do the same. He was maybe an evolutionist, but only as far as individual careers, not the medium itself, were concerned. He was definitely not a revolutionist. Indeed, one of our points of contact was that we were both anti-Stalinist liberals, therefore naturally suspicious of the kind of revolutionary posturing that was so much a part of sixties cultural rhetoric.

Given that premise, we deplored other kinds of democratic centralism. There never was, and never would be, an Andrew's sisterhood comparable to the Paulettes. There's an irony here. Of all contemporary critics, Andy is most committed to what we might loosely term an ideology, a defined body of principles which inform the bulk of his judgments, but that was his thing, and he had no desire to make it your thing. There are only two reviews of books of mine that I treasure, not because they were generally favorable but because their writer seemed to understand not just their texts but the subtexts. That writer was in both instances Andy, and in the case of the second volume he forgave a couple of rather snappish attacks on his own writing to pursue what he felt were more important matters. Such generosity, I'm here to tell you, is not all that common among our—um—colleagues.

Andy called his WBAI radio program and his column in the *Village Voice* "Films in Focus," and that said it all. He had a gift for contextualizing movies, placing them accurately in the long run of a director's or actor's career or a genre's development. I have nearly always learned something I needed to know—indeed, should have known—from Andy's reviews. I also learned from him that the least important thing a good critic has to offer is his opinion of the work at hand. Andy was not shy about expressing them. And I was not shy about disagreeing with them. But that never interfered with our friendship. Or my respect for him. For early on I began to see, from his example and my own instincts, that broad judgment— thumbs up, thumbs down—was less interesting than the process of arriving at it, the range of reference you brought to it, the sense of how film culture interacted with general culture to produce the work under discussion.

I also began to see, as he ranged across the past in his writing, how tyrannical the here-and-now was in considering movies. By this I mean that Andy, more than any other critic, made you see that however carelessly and crassly the movies as an economic institution had been managed, however shabbily (or, equally damaging, however indulgently) it had treated some of its talent, something we could call art and some people we might call artists had emerged from all the previous crises the medium had endured, all the chaos that must attend creation in an industrialized context.

He specifically argued against applying the idea of progress to the movies, insisting that the cinema rises and falls "in relation to the artists involved," that is to say, on the basis of individual achievement, not on the basis of industrial conditions or climate of opinion at any given moment. These may or may not influence a true film artist in a variety of ways, but they are incapable of distracting him from his fundamental obsessions. The obvious corollary to this argument is that there are no golden ages in the history of this (or any other) expressive form. And no ages of brass or lead either. There are only filmmakers, struggling harder or less hard, depending on their mood and the atmosphere of the moment, to place their visions before us.

Andy was naturally aware that some people's careers had been at various times inhibited by the working conditions in Hollywood. He was equally aware of the havoc that shifts in fashion—which are not made unilaterally in Hollywood, for which critics and the general public also bear responsibility—can wreak on individual artists. But in the long run of history the work abides and ultimately makes its value (or lack of value) clear to the discerning observer. "Formal excellence and visual wit are seldom appreciated at first glance as are the topical sensations of the hour," he wrote.

That was in *The American Cinema,* which Andy published in 1968. Bravely published, I might say, given the reception given (not by Kael alone) to his previous essays in auteurism. Bravely published, I might add, given the arguments he must have known it would engender. The issue was not so much seeing film history exclusively through directorial careers. By this time, I think, most of us were consciously or unconsciously doing so. It was a great convenience—a thread through the morass—and it was in the largest sense just. Directors did have their preoccupations and their stylistic signatures. These did very often prevail over studio manner or genre conventions, and you could perceive what they were over the long run of their work. And make critical judgments about them on that basis. In a sense we all became—probably had been from the start, if we were at all serious about movies—autuerists. Even Pauline. Even, eventually, the jokiest TV reviewer, cramming his opinions into a minute toward the end of the local news.

No, the problem was those damned rankings of his. For three decades now I've been having half-serious, half-satirical conversations with colleagues over whether this or that old favorite should be up- (or down-) graded from, say, "Lightly Likable" to "The Far Side of Paradise." Whether, in fact, some of the guys in "Less than Meets the Eye" belonged in "Strained Seriousness," or vice versa. By me, Preston Sturges is a "Pantheon" director and Orson Welles is a "Fringe Benefit." Or not. Depends on when you ask me. Same with Josef von Sternberg, that master of "Expressive Esoterica." And Fritz Lang, whose seriousness sometimes seems pretty strained to me.

But finally all that is beside the point. Andy has himself revised his opinions, if not his book, making his peace in later articles with the likes of Billy Wilder and John Huston, whom he had underestimated. And the book continues to reside, tattered and battered, on my reference shelf, within arm's length of the word processor. For the essays on the major figures Andy considers are gems. After all these years they continue to stir fresh thought—something the old pieces of only the best critics accomplish—as well as admiration for the aptness of the examples chosen to illuminate a director's style, appreciation for the forthrightness of his arguments—you always know where the writer is coming from—and pleasure in the mannerly confidence of their judgments. When he speaks ill of a body of work, Andy does so without malice and with an earnest effort to find its saving graces. When he speaks well of a career, he does so with seductive generosity. In either case he leaves you room for principled argument.

If I were to categorize movie reviewing in Sarrisian terms I guess I'd call it "expressive ephemera." Given the power of any film to command mass attention on its initial release, and the rise in recent times of venues where, however erratically, these works can be kept alive endlessly, one has to know that even the worst movie is going to persist and influence people in ways that the best, most thoughtful, review of it never will. Given this hard reality, a critic's only hope of creating something of lasting usability is somehow to evade the tyranny of the purely topical, to put movies not merely into "focus" but into long-range perspective.

I speak with strong feelings on this matter, for my work frequently obliges me to consult old reviews, and it is nearly always a chastening experience. The carelessness and superficiality of the judgments, the refusal to look for, let alone find, thematic or generic resonances in the movies, the preoccupation with side issues (if I read one more stupid word about violence in the movies I think I'm likely to resort to it myself) is deeply depressing. And that says nothing of the clumsy expression, the motiveless malignity of much reviewing. In this sere country, it is Sarris—and a few others, most of them not regular reviewers—who provide the oases. Or perhaps one should say some high ground from which one can calmly survey the landscape of the past.

I don't suppose any critic consciously sets out to provide such services. We are, like the actors and directors we write about, bound by the limits of our nature and our sensibilities. And by what products are on offer when we are writing. But we can certainly learn to aspire beyond those limits. And learn to conduct ourselves, as Andy has, with decency and discretion and a respect for the feelings of our subjects. "Movie Love," to borrow a phrase, is okay; it is, I guess, within the realm of more or less normal human experience. But like all passions it needs to be tempered when we speak of it in public by kindness and irony. And in this particular case, by the knowledge that history, to which movies like everything else we make are eventually subject, is a dispassionate judge. It doesn't care what the maker's motive was, or what his circumstances were at the time, or even what he thought his message might be. Auden's famous lines about history ultimately forgiving Paul Claudel his political sins because he wrote so well, definitely apply. So does something Alfred Hitchcock of The Pantheon once said to me. An artist, he remarked, would be a fool to wonder whether the apples he was painting were sweet or sour: "Who cares? It's his style, his manner of painting them—that's where the emotion comes from." All of Andy's criticism, it seems to me, was aimed at that kind of judgment, the anatomizing of manner, not morals.

I began with an image of Andy at play. Let me close with another one. Some years ago he and I were both invited to an extraordinarily grand New York party, given in honor of a new book's prominent author. Its site was one of those endless apartments in The Dakota, every room of which could have been used as a set for a glamorous movie about big-city swells. They were out in force: movie stars, television personalities, media powers. Arriving alone, I was overwhelmed by the dazzle and wandered about, slightly panic-stricken, looking for someone closer to my own station in life. Eventually I penetrated the kitchen, where a bar was set up and canapés were being served. There, thank God, was Andy. He was seated at a table. He was reading the *New York Post,* which, newspaper junkie that he is, he had prudently brought with him. Oblivious to the hubbub swirling about him, he was patiently awaiting the arrival of his wife, who is much better at these occasions than he is—or I am. What were they to him, these preening, chattering celebrities and wannabes? He knew who he was, which was perhaps more than he had dared dream he might be when he started out to do what he wanted to do, but not less than he had dared hope to be either. This is a huge advantage for anyone, but it is especially so for a critic. It purifies his gestures of ambition, frees them of strategic considerations, and permits him simply to state his case—for whatever modest good it may do his soul, whatever quite unpredictable and certainly unprogrammatic good it may do in the world.

1997

The Star on the Stairs

Quick. Name three Miss Americas.

Sure. Easy. Vanessa Williams. Bess Meyerson. And . . .
and . . . you know, what's-her-name. The one who's married to
what's-his-name. Mary Ann . . . er . . . Mobley.

Very good.

But think about it a minute. You remember Mobley because for a long time she helped her husband, Gary Collins,
host the televised broadcast of the Miss America Pageant fi-
nals every September, thereby reminding you of her career's
only unambiguous triumph.

You remember Meyerson partly because she was the first
Jew to crack what essentially remains a bastion of white-
bread Americana, partly because she managed to have some
kind of public career—on game shows and in New York politics—mostly, alas, because of her fall into rather pathetic
scandal (shoplifting) late in a life that was perhaps shortened
by that sad, bad publicity.

And you're technically wrong about Vanessa Williams.
She won all right, but her name is stricken from the records

because after she was crowned it was discovered that she had posed for dirty pictures. She's sort of the Shoeless Joe Jackson of beauty contests, though in her cast the omitted items of clothing were somewhat more crucial to the preservation of *amour propre*—her's and the pageant's. Unlike the disgraced ballplayer, she has gone on to a fairly respectable—and, in its way, rather heartening—career as a recording artist, Broadway replacement, and occasional movie player.

All right, let's try a harder question. Name last year's winner of the *Palme d'Or* at the Cannes Film Festival.

I know. I know. It's impossible.

Let's try something a little easier. Name the winner of the Academy Award for best picture five years ago. Okay, two years ago.

Give up again? Me too. Even though as a film critic I'm supposed to be able to remember such things—at least for a little while.

But there you are. Even though the Oscars are unquestionably the most famous awards people bestow on one another, the subject of an annual media feeding-frenzy, and reputedly, the world's most-watched television program, the winners somehow start escaping from memory not long after the producers of the major prizewinners stop buying display ads trumpeting their victories.

These examples of fame's flightiness are not chosen idly. They are occasioned by reading *Hype and Glory,* William Goldman's vastly amusing account of the remarkable year in which, for his sins, he served as a juror at the Cannes festival and as a judge at the Atlantic City revels. (The Oscars get in there because Goldman, a prodigiously prolific screenwriter, often intrudes thoughts about the movies in general, the Academy Awards specifically—he has himself won two—for illustrative purposes.)

Goldman's book achieves pride of place in this review not merely for its shrewdness and entertainment value, but because the institutions with which he involved himself are microcosms in which the rest of us can observe certain crucial aspects of the modern history of hype.

Let's take them up in the order of their foundation. The Miss America Pageant, as it is now called, had precious little pageantry about it when it was staged for the first time in 1921. It was just another beauty contest, supposed to get a little ink for Atlantic City, a resort then catering mainly to the sweltering masses of nearby Philadelphia, but hoping to go national. The girls paraded about in swimsuits and were awarded prizes solely on the basis of looks as determined by a jury of local boosters. Nothing was said about such matters as talent, energy, communication, or poise, all qualities venireman Goldman was told he must look out for on the instructional tape he was sent after he was impaneled. Certainly "Olympic Ability"—the most befuddling of the attributes the pageant claimed to seek—was not on anyone's mind in the beginning.

In other words, this peculiarly American institution—it attracts eighty thousand contestants to its local, preliminary rounds—began as "ballyhoo," a fine old word, borrowed from circus argot, which was much used by press agents and newsmen in what I like to think of as publicity's Age of Innocence. The term has a genial ring to it, signaling that what is done in its name need not be taken too seriously (even when fraud was involved, as often was the case in those days) and signaling, as well, that nothing so grand as "public relations," which aims at larger, long-term effects, was taking place.

No one, in short, was thinking big about Miss America in its early days. It was, to borrow the title of Candice Jacobson Furthman's useful and well-illustrated compilation of great (or at least amusing) moments in the genre, a *Publicity Stunt!* And by no means the most imaginative of them. This was, after all, the great age of wing-walking and flagpole sitting. All over America human flies were scaling skyscraper walls, promoting this or that product. To be sure, the evil geniuses of corporate PR, Ivy Lee (model for John Dos Passos's J. Ward Morehouse in the *U.S.A. trilogy*) and Edward Bernays were beginning their careers, but people were much more intrigued by the promotions of the half-forgotten Harry Reichenbach, up out of sideshows and magic acts. He it was who slipped a lion in a hotel room there to terrorize a bellboy serving an alleged African explorer, the ensuing hubbub serving to publicize a Tarzan picture; planted reports that silent star Clara Kimball Young had been kidnaped by Mexican bandits; had a young woman in the audience at a showing of *Trilby* pretend to be mesmerized by an on-screen hypnotist. Once, to help his client Francis X. Bushman get a raise, he and the actor strolled Broadway dribbling pennies out of their pockets, attracting a large crowd, which followed them to the movie company's offices. Executives there, observing the size of Bushman's following, wrote a new contract for him—or so legend claims.

The point of these classic exercises in ballyhoo is precisely their pointedness. They were created to have an immediate practical effect on the commercial prospects of a specific product, production, or personality and then to evanesce, leaving behind nothing more than a cheshire cat grin. So it was with the Miss America contest when it began. Modest form—the more or less arbitrary selection of the prettiest among a number of pretty girls drawn from every state in the land—matched modest function—getting a picture or two and a short piece in which Atlantic City was mentioned, into the newspapers. No attempt was made to suggest that the winner was a paradigm of American virtues and values. Nor were successful contestants rewarded with scholarships, implying that the brief humiliation of appearing in public half-naked, in high heels, was redeemed by a greater good, the encouragement of individual intellectual development and the enlargement of a socially responsive educated class. It was all very simple and straightforward—unconfusing.

The same might be said of the Cannes Film Festival. It too was conceived (in 1946) as a way to publicize a resort town—and, not incidentally, book some underutilized hotel space in the pleasant month before the Riviera's summer season commenced. As for the Academy Awards, they began, ironically enough, purer in heart than any major prize-giving this side of the Nobels. To be sure, the establishment of an awards program was among the stated purposes of the Academy of Motion Picture Arts and Sciences when it was founded in 1927, but it was well down the list. The larger purposes of the Academy were promoting harmony among the various movie crafts (this included attempting to solve labor disputes), helping to set and disseminate technical standards at a moment when the arrival of sound and color was addling everyone, and serving as a dignified front for a raffish industry that had been from its beginnings an irresistible target for aesthetes and moralists. Being show folk, the Academy members surely hoped the awards they established within a year of their organization's founding would gather some nice publicity, but mostly the annual ceremony was a family affair—a reason for what people used to call "the movie colony" to get together for a self-congratulatory banquet. It appears unlikely that anyone then imagined winning an "Oscar" would add even a few dollars to a movie's gross.

So what happened? What robbed these events of their former coziness, turned them into the madhouses they are today? The answer, as far as Cannes is concerned, is simple. What happened to Cannes was a starlet named Simone Silva, who in 1954 happened to attend a picnic that was part of the official festival schedule. As Goldman relates the story, she chose to wear a grass skirt with a scarf tied around her bosom.

Photographers, bored with the sedateness of the party,

kept begging her to just sort of, you know, untie the scarf. Which in time she did. But not before maneuvering herself into the proximity of a movie star.

Not just any movie star, though. Whom she sidled up to was Robert Mitchum, then thought to be a dangerous guy because he had once been busted on a marijuana rap. Well, he was dangerous, but not for the reasons people think he was. He was dangerous because he was a smart, cynical, honorable man who passed his life in a state of perpetual disgust with the hypocrisy, venality, and stupidity of life. Especially public life. Most especially movie star public life. What he did when he saw a young lady exposing herself in front of all those cameras was move to cover her up. His gallantry—or maybe it was simple, old-fashioned moralism—had two effects: it brought a genuine celebrity into her act, and it made at least some of the *paparazzi*'s pictures publishable in family journals. The effect, as Goldman puts it, was electrifying.

"My God, the world wondered, what's going on over there. What are all those beautiful people doing?"

"I want to do it too" [italics his].

And so the Cannes festival ceased to be about promoting Cannes as such. It also ceased to be about presenting prizes to worthy movies, though it continues to do so because that is its official, stated business. It became a giant photo opportunity before that phrase was invented. (It also became a great international movie bazaar, a not entirely unpleasant place to presell your latest project to distributors in Iceland, Argentina, and points between, though that is beside our point here.)

To put it simply. Cannes achieved what all events of this sort must achieve if they are to attract the ogling world's restless gaze. It achieved, or began to achieve—these things take a little time—perfect detachment from ordinary, boring reality in the public's mind. It is now to all other film festivals— many of which, like Telluride, have a higher reputation among cineastes for doing good, useful things like bringing worthy new works to the attention of caring people—what Robert Redford, for convenient instance, is to most of the other actors who get their names above the title: a thing, a world, a law unto itself, unique and unduplicable.

Now, by a nice irony, it is in a position to offer the select few stars of Redford's magnitude the opportunity—which they must all exercise from time to time, for purposes of self-reassurance if nothing else—a perfect context in which to strut their singular stuff. I'll set the scene—the grand staircase at the Palais de Festival, which is where the pictures in competition are screened, with thousands gathered around the staircase to pay homage to the stars as they enter to see their films—and let Goldman take over:

> Redford just standing there.
> Now the left hand rises. A wave. He turns, starts up the red carpet toward the Palais door.
> The crowd becomes silent, all their eyes on him. He was leaving them. Going someplace so splendid, where fountains were golden, champagne always poured, the music, such sweet music, never stopped.
> Redford stopped.
> At the highest Palais stair. And turned one final time to face the thousand. A last generous wave. A quick perfect smile.
> Then—
> —then he was—
> —alas—
> —gone.
> Murmurs. Not angry at all. He had been so splendid for them. . . .

Yes. And this had to do with what? Practically speaking, it had to do with selling the European market *The Milagro Beanfield War*, a dud Redford had gone far over budget directing. He owed the studio this help in recouping some of the cost of his mistake. (It is, as they say, a relationship business, and, big as he is, Redford, like everyone else, must tend to his relationships, doing what he can to stave off for a little longer what Goldman elsewhere makes a point of insisting must come, the day when his phone stops ringing.) But that's all insider stuff. The great unwashed world knows little and cares less about it. What it wants-needs-requires of its favorites is pure essence of celebrity, untrammeled by practicalities, undistorted by the requirements of fictional role-playing, entirely detached from his or her human reality.

So there he is, Mr. (or Ms.) Wonderful, near but not too near, here but not for too long, offering a distant, fleeting glimpse of that perfection which cannot withstand closer, longer scrutiny. Goldman again:

> I know glamour doesn't exist
> I know it's all horseshit.
> But I need it.
> I want my morning fix of stardom. I want to believe what
> I did once. I'm like the people by the stairs. Hell, I *was* the
> people by the stairs, staring up.

It may be that Cannes prospers so, becomes the journalistic zoo that it is every year, because it is itself distant, isolated like a movie star. You can't televise it live or in toto, because in its remoteness it offers no facilities for so doing and because it is a composite of hundreds of events (screenings, receptions, press conferences) spread over two weeks. It forces journalism to cover it the old-fashioned way, artfully (if one dare use that word in this context) picking and choosing those moments that represent its essence to the world beyond, in the process making much of them, making more of them, indeed, than their reality actually supports.

There must (or should) be days when the Motion Picture Academy envies Cannes. For the Academy is stuck with its live telecast of its awards. Well, maybe "stuck" is not quite the right word, considering that the license fees for the broadcast are virtually the sole support of the institution's many good, generally unsung works, most notably its great research facility, the Margaret Herrick Library. But still, stuck in the sense that the show must inevitably disappoint, must inevitably engender hundreds of contemptuous reviews, millions of slighting remarks around the water coolers the morning after.

There are practical reasons for this, of course. The obvious one is the need to broadcast all the draggy minor awards, force the world to listen to acceptance speeches by dozens of nobodies, people who are—ugh—alarmingly like ourselves. This distracts from, vitiates the suspense of, the competition for the major awards, makes us, as an audience impatient, irritable. The less obvious reason for Oscar-bashing is that because of union costs and the reluctance of the star presenters to devote much preparation time to it, the show is always underrehearsed. Also, of course, it takes the form of a variety program, an antique genre that is irrelevant to the modern audience.

But still that's not the main problem. Think about it a minute. What is the most successful moment in every Oscar show, the one that never disappoints? Yes, that's right. It's the opening, the entrance of the stars into the auditorium broadcast on preshows nowadays aired on several venues, but also presented in severely edited form on the Oscar telecast itself as a kind of tease for the show.

Coifed to perfection and dressed to the nines, the beautiful people and their scarcely less resplendent escorts step smiling from the dark depths of their limos, sweep past bleachers full of bedazzled gawkers, flashbulbs lighting their way, then disappear, no more than a few banal words spoken, into the temple from which all but the elect (and those who have paid the scalpers as much as $1,000 per ticket) are excluded. It is Redford on the stairs at Cannes, multiplied by a factor of several dozen, stardom in its purest form.

From there on, obviously, the show must go downhill. Cues will be missed, lines will be garbled, jokes will fall flat, emotions will rise high, stupid things will be said, important things will be left unsaid. In other words, the exigencies of public appearance in a venue that permits no perfecting re-takes will force the stars to expose their quotidian humanity, thus betraying our fantasies about them.

It must be said: a terrible mistake was made in 1953 when it was decided to let television in. Radio, abetted by the print press, had been the Academy's perfect medium—a fly on the wall instead of a hog in the parlor. It served everyone well. It preserved the original spirit of the occasion, that of a privileged private party, while permitting us to feel that we were being permitted access to a glamorous mystery. And it didn't stiffen the stars with fear.

The Miss America Pageant is even worse served by televi-sion, by the need to make a production out of it. I was sur-prised to learn from Goldman that a talent competition had been added to the beauty contest as early as 1938, that is to say, pre-TV. Obviously the thought, even then, was that if the pageant was to attract a live audience to Atlantic City it had to offer something more than a simple anatomical display.

It was the first, but not the last, deviation from the true faith. As Goldman says, girl-watching is a subjective sport. We may argue about who is the most beautiful of them all, but we are at least arguing about the same thing, the same style points, as it were. But how does one compare this amateur vi-olinist with that amateur coloratura? And what about that tap dancer? Or the baton twirler? Literally, this is no contest. For as Goldman also observes, if you are genuinely serious about becoming, say, a concert pianist, you are unlikely to have the time or the inclination to muck about in beauty con-tests.

But it's not a beauty contest, the sponsors cry. Hence the more recent, and still more lunatic, add-ons to the competition—the interviews both before the judging panels and on stage, which are designed to reveal a young woman's character, her grace under pressure, if you will. These have, perhaps, one practical value: they give the pageant's sponsors some idea of how the young ladies will stand up to the year of public appearances that are required of the winner. But no more than the ability to stay on pitch while sawing away on a violin do they test virtue. Indeed, it is clear from Goldman's account that the young women are coached to stay within rather narrow parameters as they answer questions designed to elicit their adherence, or lack of same, to mainstream American values. Indeed, the queasiest moments of the television show are always those in which the host taxes the finalists for solutions to public problems of the moment.

Ironically, the show has only one moment of truth, and it is a moment pageant sponsors would abandon if only television would let them (in these postfeminist days it uncomfortably reminds them of the event's primitive and vulgar origins). That is, of course, the swimsuit competition. It counts for almost nothing in the weighted balloting of the judges, but it is as close as the Miss America contest comes to Redford on the stairs, as close as it comes to owning up to its essence. Goldman:

> What mattered was the same as in movies: star quality. Which . . . cannot be defined, but we do know this: it's somewhere in the eyes.
> And that is what you concentrated on as the girls came down the stage toward you. What the eyes said.
> Some eyes said this: "This is not a nice place."
> Others, this: "Hellllppp."
> And: "You rotten son of a bitch, staring at me."
> "Pig."
> "I want my mommmeeee."
> But some of them, the best actresses of the bunch, had a

slow drumbeat coming from somewhere, keeping them
company as they came closer and closer, all the time whis-
pering . . .

"I want you . . .

. . . oh Daddy yes . . .

. . . so bad . . .

. . . oh Daddy yes . . .

. . . just you, Daddy . . .

. . . please . . .

. . . take me, Daddy . . .

. . . take me all the way . . .

. . . d
    o
    w
    n."

The Miss America contest is not an entrance exam for
celebrity. As we observed at the outset, most of its winners return after their year of false fame to the sheltering anonymity
from which they came. But all who participate, no matter
how quickly they are eliminated from the competition, do
have this one totally isolated moment of near-nakedness
when they are forced to experience, and deal with as best
they can, the central issue of celebrityhood, which is, all
pieties aside, presenting, selling your sexuality, making yourself believe, making the world believe, that it is paradigmatic,
the perfect summary of a universal unspoken yearning. In an
event that goofily insists on its devotion to the cause of learning—all those scholarships it hands around—this is the only
truly educational experience it offers its participants. It is the
successful surmounting of this moment that might just possibly guide and help them in later life.

Put it another way, the long-drawn-out attempt to
clean up Miss America's act, the attempt to wrap it round in
middle-class moralities is a mistake, and probably accounts

for the steady decline of its TV ratings. It is not just that so-phisticated people see through all that—they still tune in to sneer and snort their superiority to these revels. It is not just that the pageant seems increasingly like a rather pathetic par-ody of celebrity occasions. It is that it runs counter to the long-term trends of public life.

This is something that Deyan Sudjic begins to get at, however superficially, in *Cult Heroes.* It is very largely about the fashion industry, about the marketing of its great names— Armani and Lauren, that crowd. What he shows us is that they have achieved what all famous people would like to achieve: utter detachment of the self from public obligation, in some cases from the very work that made them famous in the first place. They make their money by licensing their names, which are, of course, their trademarks, to others. They generally have but small obligations to appear in public in support of their lines of clothing and toiletries, and, indeed, have little obligation to supervise what is produced in their names; vaguely, distantly, they approve and disapprove. Maybe. That issue appears to be in some doubt. What is not in doubt is that they have achieved a new purified, rarefied level of celebrity. They represent, each in his own way, a pure idea of style. They have become, each in his own way, perfect ab-stract symbols of desire. We cannot touch them. We would not, most of us, recognize them on the street. But we can wrap ourselves in their creations, thus partake of their essences yet more intimately than we can those of any other celebrity.

Early in *All-Consuming Images,* a book that soberly and gracefully puts all this in large historical perspective, Stuart Ewen quotes from Oliver Wendell Holmes's remarkably pre-scient essay on photography, which is, of course, the techno-logical base on which illustrated magazines, movies, television rests, and is thus the basis of the modern celebrity system: "Matter in large masses must always be fixed and dear; form is cheap and transportable. We have got the fruit of creation now, and need not trouble ourselves with the core. Every conceivable object of Nature and Art will soon scale off its surface for us. . . ." From this Ewen goes on to argue that it is the very essence of modernism to push toward abstraction, immateriality, ephemerality, evanescence. It is reflected in the disposable nature of mass-produced conveniences, in our clothing, in our art, both high and low. And, above all, in our choice of the celebrities we temporarily admire. Solidity, substantiality is square and dumb. For corporeality implies accountability, responsibility. And who needs that? Or wants it?

Greta Garbo (along with, perhaps, J. D. Salinger and Thomas Pynchon) is, finally, the ideal to which the publicity mechanism must aspire—a shadow of a self who flitted through the shadows of our collective consciousness, uncapturable, unanalyzable, a projection not of Garbo the woman but of Garbo the idea. Maybe the stars who die young and tragically—Dean, Monroe, Presley, Princess Di—achieve by unlucky accident or—to use the word literally—self-destructiveness, this quite bearable, really quite delicious, lightness of being. Certainly we must count it a blessing that corporate PR cannot achieve this status for its big, clumsy clients, who like the Miss America Pageant have missed modernity's thrust.

We may also, perhaps, count it among our blessings that politicians have traditionally been barred from this status also. For we cannot doubt that if a president could, like a dress designer, reduce his essence to a signature, retaining his power while being spared the inconveniences of going to stupefying banquets, of treating politely with the hounding press, the moronic Congress, he would do so. How nice it would be for him if his public life could be all entrances and exits, with the marine band playing "Hail to the Chief" as he hurries about, soberly attentive to what we have all agreed to regard as the world's serious work, even though most issues these days (abortion rights, affirmative action, guys in the military) are as symbolic as the leadership itself. All-American presidents—most particularly the one who took office shortly after this piece first appeared—must now profoundly wish to achieve the condition of Redford on the stairs, an obscure object of desire, glamorously glimpsed. A photo op if you move quickly enough. Otherwise just a memory. But still, if he could, like a fashion designer, reduce his essence to a signature, and retain the illusion of power while being spared the inconvenience of hard legislative work, of decision-making, of public appearance, of (above all) trying to defend the privacy that baying legions are now devoted to penetrating, we cannot doubt he would do so—no matter how much some atavistic part of his soul still hankers to work the rope lines. Who—these days—would not?

1991

Clint on the Back Nine

Sixty-five going on sixty-six. The age of alarming checkups, as David Thomson once characterized it. The age of alarming checkouts, as the obituary page reminds us daily. The age of made-for-cable movies, ghostwritten autobiographies and broody, blinds-drawn stays in the Palm Springs house for many a movie star. The age of self-parody, long silences, and politely put critical disappointment for many a director.

And yes, tributes, retrospectives, life-achievement awards. Given the American propensity to hand around celebratory hardware, our desire to give standing ovations as much to the warmth of our own nostalgia as to its avatar, filmmakers of a certain age and stature can count on those, too. Having neatly sidestepped all the other pitfalls his two professions impose on men and women of his years—having, indeed, high-stepped his way through the demographic briar patch with a run of successes almost certainly unduplicated by any other seventh-decade actor or director in history— even Clint Eastwood, for all his genial elusiveness, cannot

evade our desire—our profound need—to accord him our respects.

Perhaps—all modesty aside—does not want to. For Clint
is a realistic, even fatalistic, man. We've never discussed the
matter, but I suspect he sees the urge to press prizes upon figures like himself as part of the natural order of things, to be
dealt with—how else in his case?—coolly, not as some grand
culmination but as an agreeable interruption in a life still un-
predictably unfolding, something like, say, a round of golf; di-
verting, absorbing, a matter to be taken seriously for the
moment but not dwelt upon for very long.

Except, possibly, as a useful metaphor, Clint likes to refer
to the passage he is now traversing as "the back nine of life,"
adding that he often finds it to be golf's better half, a time
when one starts playing the shots rather than the score, begins to enjoy the day, the stroll, the company, ambling toward
the clubhouse, as it were, an ironic smile on his face, the
double-bogey on eight all but forgotten, the birdie on fourteen happily recalled, the possibility of closing out the round
with a par or two still lively; he is a man visibly content within
that metaphor.

But the public, generally speaking, sees nothing
metaphorical about celebrity. That's why it habitually con-
fuses stars with their roles, a star's life with readily imitable
reality. This is mostly a bad thing. But in the case of Clint
Eastwood, at this moment, it is probably a good thing. For as
we see him looking great and working well, we happily accept
from him the final gift it is within fame's power to confer, a
hopeful, even inspiring, example of grace under the pressure
of the years. He hints to us the possibility of edging toward
the exit unflustered, steady on our feet, all our buttons firmly
attached.

Doubtless we are indulging ourselves in yet another fantasy here. We tend to ignore the fact that stardom nearly always begins with a lucky genetic accident. And that the older

we get the luck of the DNA draw more and more determines how we will be permitted to play life out. Still, it is a pretty thing to think otherwise.

And the rest of this life's achievements tend to support this thought, tend to make us believe that anything may just be possible. For no one's trip to our panegyric podiums has been longer than Clint's, or in its way more picaresque. He began so far back in the pack: getting his first acting work in a studio talent program, day-playing in B pictures: gaining his first recognition as Rowdy Yates—"idiot of the plains," as he was wont to call him in those days—catnip for such jailbait as *Rawhide* could attract to its time slot: gaining his first notoriety as the misnamed Man with No Name (actually Joe, Monco, and Blondie) in Sergio Leone's deliberate, and hysterically deplored, subversions of the whole blessed—that is to say, sanctified—John Ford western tradition.

This was not the route to respectability, as even at the time Clint surely knew, for the road to thinking-people's esteem wound through loftier country—method workshops, off-Broadway austerities, on-Broadway acclaim. Then and only then, work in the movies. Once there, of course, one wants to keep striking rebellious poses. We like to think of moviemaking as a desperate enterprise, a form of high-stakes gambling in which people risk all in pursuit of some impossible dream. We want brutal conflict between the visionary artist and the visionless mogul. We want sudden rises to acclaim and fortune. These make good copy. Ultimately they make undying legends. Among directors, Griffith, von Stroheim, and Welles are the figures that command such historical imagination as is brought to bear on Hollywood's past. They are the dark exemplars of Hollywood's propensity first to flatter genius, then to abuse it, then to crush it. They, along with such victim-performers as Garland and Monroe, are the major source of its black glamour, the engine of the tragic celebrity drama that helps keep the world attuned to its doings.

Two things are usually omitted from our consideration of these scenarios. One is that there is a powerful self-destructive element in them. Hollywood's victims are first usually the victims of their own needs and weaknesses. The other is that most of the older American movies we love best were creations of moviemakers who learned to bend the system to their own ends. Vernacularists, working their own variations on genre conventions, they conceived themselves more as craftsmen than as artists—their art being something generally recognized long after their craft was rather dismissively acknowledged.

Rather anachronistically, Clint chose to be of this group. And paid a price for his loyalty to the genres. No matter how he bent or expanded their conventions—*Thunderbolt and Lightfoot, Dirty Harry, The Outlaw Josey Wales, Tightrope*—he was often given only reluctant credit for so doing. Very often, indeed, the critics didn't even notice what he was doing. And when he abandoned genre entirely—*The Beguiled; Honkytonk Man; White Hunter, Black Heart*—forget it.

It has to be said, of course, that Clint, who in his earlier years, was a demonic and impatient worker, did not make things easy for those few critics who wanted to take him seriously, wanted to identify the main lines of his interest. He would make two and three movies a year, and he did not always choose his projects carefully. He very rarely had them tailored neatly to his specifications, for he did not enjoy the long fitting process required by bespoke movie clothing. He preferred to pick finished goods up off the peg—from freelance writers or from the Warner Bros. store of projects—get the sleeves lengthened, the pants shorted, and shrug into the garment. He thought it was better to be up and doing than to sit around idly, waiting for something that might not necessarily be superior to come along.

This way of doing business suited another idea of his, which was that the stars of an earlier era, the stars of his boyhood, had attained and maintained that status not by finely calibrated calculation but by staying constantly before the public. "Name all of Clark Gable's pictures, Joe," he had once replied to a friend and colleague who had taxed him for his hardworking ways. Meaning, we don't remember all the details of old-fashioned star careers, only the screen presence they established through repetition in contexts good, bad, and indifferent.

So yes, there is *Firefox* and *The Rookie* and two or three *Dirty Harry* sequels too many in his filmography, and several pretty good movies that might have been very good if he had worked on them a little more intensely. I had been aware of this, of course, before I began writing a biography of Clint, and more or less cheerfully accepted his failures as the price one paid for his successes, which derived from the go-ahead, don't-worry-about-the-consequences spirit. I also knew going in that he would have to be defended against the ridiculous charge of fascism, leveled at *Dirty Harry* by Pauline Kael and for some time an issue that dominated discussion of all his work. But even I was surprised at what turned up in my research, the heaps of critical calumny piling up around my desk. That the tenor of his reviews began to change sometime in the eighties was a relief to me—as surely it was to him. That other reviewers, other thoughtful moviegoers, began to respond to those qualities the mass audience had always liked about his screen character—his impatience with temporizing, his ironic coolness under fire, his acceptant loneliness, which encompassed both a bemused tolerance for human eccentricity (including his own) and a reluctance to sue too obviously for the audience's affection—offered evidence that the largest goal of his enterprise, a reexamination of the images by which popular culture tries to understand heroic masculinity, was beginning to get through to the people who counted. Still, given the venom of the earlier attacks on him, we may imag-

ine that *Unforgiven* was a title that held a certain resonance
for him.

Not that Clint ever seemed to care much for the forgive-
ness of strangers, critical or otherwise. He may have been, as a
maker of westerns, the Anti-Ford. But he lived by a Fordian
axiom: "never apologize, never explain—it's a sign of weakness." David Thomson, paraphrasing Clint's old friend and
mentor, Don Siegel, wrote that he "had an uncanny urge to
make heroic figures into antiheroes." Refusing ingratiation,
refusing to seek our love and sympathy, "He wondered, instead, just how far he could stretch the audience's support."

With this assessment, Clint agrees. "I've always had the
theory that actors who beg their audience to like them, and
say, 'Oh, God, come like me.' or 'Am I not cute?' are much
worse off than actors who just say, 'Fuck you, if you don't like
this, don't let the door hit you in the ass.'"

In an age when celebrity fawns all over us, ever eager to
share its pain (but never ours), this was a refreshment, implicitly perceived by many as a return to classic American taciturnity. "No movie star of his magnitude," Richard Jameson
wrote over a decade ago, "has ever been so private at the center of his celebrity, or played so openly and artfully with the
mysteriousness, the essential unknowability of his personality." The late Harold Brodkey thought he perceived something Garboesque in Clint's screen persona—taciturnity does
have its downside, especially when it falls under the gaze of
the nattering class— but Garbo's silences concealed an emptiness, or, anyway, a profound passivity and a curious detachment from reality, that could not be further from his truth.

For he is an activist. It's not just that he has directed the
majority of his films over the last quarter-century but that he
has been the de facto, if not always credited, producer of them
all. Nothing moves in his movies without his approval, and
that's not because he worries about, say, placing his good side

before the camera. It's because he has something on his mind: "America's daunting ideas about manhood," as Janet Maslin once nicely put it.

In *In the Beauty of the Lilies* John Updike calls the male stars of the thirties and forties "beasts of burden," numbly, dumbly laden with Protestantism's righteous furniture, doomed eventually to buckle under its weight. Clint, in discussing these men, identifies not with the likes of John Wayne, so proud of his mulishness, but with Cagney, Bogart, Garfield, Mitchum, even (surprisingly, but correctly) James Stewart, all of whom in their different ways registered their restiveness, their inchoate anger, with this mysterious obligation to dauntlessness.

There came a moment when it would no longer do. Maybe it crystallized at the climax of *Red River,* when Montgomery Clift, exemplar of the new masculinity, was obliged to duke it out with the Duke, exemplar of the old, until both collapsed under the symbolic strain of the effort. Maybe it came later, watching Brando's inarticulate sensitivity shade over into masochism or Dean's callow imitation of it. In any event, Clint and the other young actors in the Universal talent program began to joke about "taking our man pills" when they were obliged to emulate traditional male ways in their acting classes. Seven years of gulping acquiescence to Eric Fleming's booming, almost parodistic, representation of that spirit brought Clint near to desperation. Near enough, at least, to take the $15,000 and the ticket to Rome that became his ticket to stardom.

The first thing he saw in the *Fistful of Dollars* script was a parody of the parody—a character whose silences were so deep, whose skills with his weapons were so uncanny, that he constituted a critique of the stoical convention. Mere anarchy was here loosed upon the world of the western, and at a stroke the genre was converted to postmodernism, the mainstream critics reduced to a tizzy.

Not that I've ever heard the PM word escape from Clint's lips. He just thought there was something more—well—realistic to this approach, something that squared with his own experience of life, which from childhood on had taught him not to count too heavily on anything, especially when promises are made by institutions and their representatives. That, of course, is what Dirty Harry Callahan is all about. The man is not a "fascist." He's an anarchist who can't quite admit it. Which is one of the several things that pisses him off—and also depresses him. Clint has always said he found something sad about Harry.

What happened in the Leone pictures and the *Dirty Harry* pictures was that heroic action finally got detached from humanistic principle, from the optimistic faith in the community's future that had previously sustained and rationalized the bloodlettings of that final shootout to which the hero so reluctantly came. San Miguel is not going to rebuild the church and bring in a schoolmarm after the stranger in the serape cleans the place up and departs. San Francisco isn't going to make its police department more responsive to community needs after Harry Callahan finally offs Scorpio.

Or, to put the point more generally, Clint has taken the presentation of the heroic male deeper into the country of disaffection than he had ever ridden before. Since Howard Hawks placed it at the center of his adventure films, male bonding has been a great recurring motif in American movies, but it is a rarity in Clint's. His great theme has been the opposite: the difficulty men have in making connections of any kind—with communities, with women, with conventional morality, with other men. When we speak of Clint's screen character we are speaking of an isolation more radical, more rebelliously withdrawn, than anyone has ever offered in a protagonist of movies intended for, and embraced by, a popular audience.

We are also talking about self-consciousness—the very

hallmark of the PM sensibility. In the past when a man had to do what a man had to do, his course was obvious to him. For at least a quarter of a century, in real life, a man has been obliged to think that matter over rather carefully. And for much of that time Clint has been exploring the ways a man can fail to do what he's supposed to do: through sexual arrogance (*The Beguiled*), through self-absorption (*Play Misty for Me*), through self-destructiveness (*Honkytonk Man, Bird*), through pride (*White Hunter, Black Heart*), even through sheer stupidity (*The Gauntlet*) and the lure of perversity (*Tightrope*), requiring in the last two instances the aid of good women to right himself. These are realms no predecessor in his line of screen work dared to traverse—or even thought about traversing. One thinks of William Goldman's axiom— "stars will not play weak and they will not play blemished"— and frankly marvels at this one's willingness to do so.

What is true of those films is true, in a slightly different way, of the films that cling more closely to genre convention. Action movies have always resembled action painting in that their pleasures are to be found on their surfaces, in the tensions arising from the arrangement of abstract elements (the good, the bad, the ugly, as it were). When, starting sometime in the sixties, movies began to acknowledge this fact openly, a sort of cultural crisis—otherwise known as the sex-and-violence controversy—was at hand. Or maybe it wasn't a cultural crisis; maybe it was only a critical crisis, since movie reviewing in this country has always been operated as a branch of moral rather than aesthetic philosophy. Doesn't matter, really. What does matter was the dawning realization among filmmakers that the audience really doesn't care a rap who shoots whom or why as long as the matter is handled with a certain panache.

This context radically alters the nature of screen heroism; it encourages us to root for our guy on the basis of his superior style, not his heavier moral weight (Dirty Harry's wisecracks, or Josey Wales's—"Dyin' ain't much of a living, boy"—are not idle verbal decor, they're the heart of the matter). Talk about your "daunting ideas." What could be scarier than the notion that there are no reliable guides to masculine assertion, that we succeed or fail in this matter by the degree of cool we bring to our moments of crisis?

This is, in fact, more than scary. This obligation to style, the imperatives of which are all improvisational rather than moral, is profoundly subversive of all the codes that have traditionally been evoked to justify violently heroic measures. And as the official honors begin to accumulate around the deeply unofficial figure of Clint Eastwood—paperweights under which to bury all those old appalled reviews—irony also begins to accumulate. It's as if somebody decided to appoint Harry Callahan chief of police.

It's possible, of course, given America's problem with long-term memory loss and our infinite capacity to compensate for it through reinvention, that what we are really talking about here are late-life achievement awards. For Clint's recent movies are much more acceptable to the sentiments of the mainstream than the rest of his filmography is. *Unforgiven*, often described by critics as a "revisionist" western, is in fact a revision of a revisionism, stylistically postmodern, but also, as Gilbert Adair observes, post-postmodern in the way Clint's Bill Munny evokes old-fashioned heroic guilts, regrets, hesitations before at last he draws a vengeful gun. *In the Line of Fire* offers us a kind of Cleanly Harry, a law-enforcement lifer who feels he has not lived up to the highest ideals of his service instead of vice versa, a man no less in need of redemption—to be sure, for a sin of omission rather than commission—than Bill Munny is. *A Perfect World* presents us, in Kevin Costner's character, a criminal redeeming himself (and ultimately condemning himself) through the embrace of what can only be described as, yes, "family values." *The Bridges of Madison County* is what it manifestly is, Clint's first flat-out romance. To be sure, he rides off into the rain alone at the end, but remember that he's the one who proposes making something permanent of the affair.

David Thomson, one of Clint's warier sympathizers, thinks slightly ill of him for these reconciliatory moves. Death, he believes, would become him—or, anyway, a more forthright acknowledgment of its growing shadow. "Gary Cooper has seen doom ahead some time in the mid 1940s, and it gave him grandeur. Eastwood wants to suffer in his recent films—but it's still a reach, just a little beyond his experience or imagination."

There's some truth in that. But some untruth also. Implicitly was a sort of stunned pathos in Cooper's slo-mo collapse, a weary bitterness in his tentative embrace of anti-heroism—that seemed to surprise him as much as it discomfited us. A hero must today show a certain vulnerability. But we can have too much of a good thing.

Going in the opposite direction, opting for reconciliations that are, one must say, not easily come by, choosing to wear his age well and openly instead of trying to disguise it, or worse, evoke sympathy for it, Clint remains true to what has always been his primary obligation—the obligations to style. Younger, smoldering with anger but struggling to control it, he confronted the chaos attendant upon our culture's redefinition of maleness with the willed application of a sometimes violent irony. Confronting age—that universally redefining force—irony, slightly sadder in its expression, more gently wielded, remains his weapon of choice. And if it lacks doomy grandeur, it is not without gallantry. Or instructive power.

1996

The Narrative Crisis

You are talking to a friend. The conversation turns to movies. You mention something you happened to see last week. Your acquaintance asks you how it was. You respond: He is . . . She is . . . And then they . . . You won't believe this . . . And the ending . . . I'd spoil it if I told you . . . Or words to that effect.

It is curious, this emphasis on story in an era when a measure of cinematic sophistication is supposed to be one of the hallmarks of a civilized person, when we are supposed to decorate our remarks about whatever movie is on our minds with a word or two about the direction or the cinematography or even the editing or the art direction—matters that rarely arose when people talked about movies in earlier times. But in our narratives of the movie narrative we have experienced, these remain minor points. The story and how it affected us is still the thing that usually preoccupies us—just as it did when we were in high school.

That preoccupation corresponds with the principle concern of the principal creators of movies—producer, writers, and directors. They talk about movies in anticipation as we talk about them in immediate retrospect—as a story. For typically they begin the production process by teasing the interest of studio executives with storytelling of the crudest possible kind. It is generally agreed that the best—that is, the most easily salable—movie concepts are those that can be summarized in a single irresistible sentence. But in any case, the pitch should not take up more than a couple of minutes of the executive's time or a couple of pages of paper heavily laden with active verbs. The movie's would-be creators will receive their first money—and very often their last—for developing a "treatment" of this idea, offering a little more detail about it. If accepted (usually only after much "input" from its buyer) it will lead on to the first-draft screenplay and its many subsequent revisions and "polishes." At every step of the way through these brave beginnings, everyone will concentrate on clarifying and vivifying the story. That emphasis will continue to be honored (though once stars are engaged and the director is free of supervision on location, ego considerations start looming larger and larger) through shooting and editing and scoring and previewing, both in house and in public.

When the picture is finished the marketing department—which, you may be sure, has not been silent up to now—goes to work in earnest, reversing the process. That is to say, it now begins boiling the story back down to its essence—and beyond. The original concept must now be reduced to a few key images, a few strong lines of voice-over narration for the trailers and TV commercials, to even less than that for the print ads—a headline and a single image. In the best of all possible marketing worlds, the movie will inspire some simple, summarizing graphic treatment, adaptable to all media, by which it can be instantly recognized the world over, even by subliterates.

The job of the marketeers, as we all know, is to get a picture to "open," do well on its first weekend. If it does draw a large (and reasonably satisfied) audience in its first three days, it should generate "word of mouth" sufficient in quantity and quality to give it "legs," that is, to keep drawing customers in for the weeks and months it takes to recoup its costs and turn a profit. Everyone agrees that it is word of mouth that makes the difference between a flop and a hit, a hit and a mega-hit.

And what constitutes good word of mouth? Why, in effect, getting early viewers to pitch the story to other potential customers with the same brevity, clarity, force, and enthusiasm that, so many months ago, its original creators pitched it to studio executives. The difference is merely one of scale. The moviemakers required a decision to spend (on average these days) something north of $50 million to realize their dream. We require of our pals only, at most, a seven- or eight- or nine-dollar investment in our enthusiasm.

But modest as that commitment may seem, multiplied by millions, it is crucial to a movie's success. Consider, for example, the sad case of *L.A. Confidential.* A morally and narratively complex *film noir*, it was, beyond question, the American movie that was best received by reviewers in 1997, going on to sweep virtually all the significant year-end prizes awarded by critics' groups. It also received a raft of Academy Award nominations, which to be sure was swamped in *Titanic*'s wake, though two major Oscars were found in the wreckage.

Normally, one would expect a movie so unanimously admired to be a large box-office success. Yet it was not. It probably achieved modest profitability when all the takings from the ancillary markets were counted. But everyone agrees that it should have done much better, especially when you consider that it was, among other things, a sexy and violent movie.

What went wrong? Very simple, one if its producers told the *Los Angeles Times.* The research showed that "people found it hard to describe the complicated story line concisely to friends." That, more than the picture's lack of important stars, and turmoil in the marketing department at the studio (its chief got fired largely because of *L.A. Confidential*'s failure), is what doomed the movie to "disappointment."

How quickly one comes full circle in today's movie game. And what a constricted—not to say ironic—circle we describe. More ironic than it appears to be at first. Because, for all this emphasis on storytelling at every moment of the filmmaking and marketing process, the most common complaint you hear these days from reviewers and from thoughtful moviegoers is that Hollywood seems to have lost or abandoned the art of narrative. We implicitly recognize, I think, that movie people are deluding themselves. Fussing their way through a project, they are generally not refining stories at all, they are sprucing up "concepts" (as they like to call them), refining gimmicks, making sure there are no complexities to fur our tongues when it comes time to spread the word of mouth.

It might be argued that this represents more of a geriatric grumble than a full-scale crisis. American movies, after all, have reached new heights of profitability in recent years. But their prosperity is based on two factors. One is the growth of the international market, which remains, ever more than the domestic one, a mass market, but one that demands easily translatable, that is to say sub-verbal, thrills—lots of chases, lots of explosions, lots of spectacular special effects—stuff you do not need much subtitling to understand.

Meantime, in the domestic market only a very few movies (*Titanic* is the best recent example) achieve event status, meaning they cross all demographic lines, becoming must-see fare for young and old, men and women, rich and poor. In general, movies in the United States do not enjoy vast popularity. The most recent (1999) survey indicates that in any given month only about one-third of the population goes to the movies, but that 59 percent of the 18- to 29-year-olds do. Ever. In other words, the financial success of the industry is based on the intense interest of a relatively small portion of their potential audience, which often returns to a particular favorite over and over again (as young women did with *Titanic*). Repeat business is perhaps the prime factor that drives a very few releases from hit to mega-hit status, but in any case almost any film that succeeds in the domestic market does so because it appeals to an essentially youthful crowd, which does not have very sophisticated tastes or expectations when it comes to narrative. As a result, movies are not reaching their full economic—let alone aesthetic—potential, are no longer truly a mass medium, appealing equally to every segment of the great audience.

It has to be admitted, of course, that American movies have always trafficked mainly in the broadly melodramatic and the broadly comedic, have always, therefore, dealt heavily in the improbable—improbable heroism, improbable goofiness, improbable romantic annunciations and renunciations of every kind. But precisely because these non- and anti-realistic factors were so important, much care was taken to justify logically the extremes to which we were being taken. The dramatic movie of what the young film scholars now refer to as "The Classic Age" built toward its single central crisis slowly and sensibly, anticipating our questions as it went along, generating suspense by letting us see dangers looming, a lovely flood of relief when they were at last surmounted. It was essentially the same with lighter fare. A simple premise was set up, and then exquisitely wrought complications were introduced until everyone was totally unbalanced by the accumulated weight of these increasingly giddy inventions.

Nowadays the opposite is generally true. The typical action-adventure movie (something like one of the *Lethal Weapon* series, for example), seems less scripted than shuffled, as if it were a deck of cards, with chance determining the appearance of its ace sequences. Comedies are nowadays often shtick compilations, in which only the smallest effort to develop comic momentum is made. What we get in both cases is not narrative as it has been traditionally defined but a succession of undifferentiated sensations, lucky or unlucky accidents, which often have little or nothing to do with whatever went before or is about to come next. To create the illusion of forward motion, the music gets louder and the action grows more frenetic as the climax approaches, but there is, in fact, no authentic emotional buildup, consequently no catharsis at the movie's conclusion.

One leaves these movies—indeed, most current American movies—feeling drained or battered or both. And sometimes just plain jerked around. For the traditional function of narrative has been inverted. Instead of the major dramatic incidents growing naturally out of the story, that is, out of the interaction of plausible characters within a recognizable moral and physical landscape, the opposite occurs. Now everyone, everything, must serve the pitchable, promotable showpiece sequences, never mind what that costs us in belief, in genuine feelings for characters or a satisfying sense of conclusion. A friend of mine, a distinguished screenwriter, recently spent several months rewriting a carefully wrought script to accommodate the big action sequence his director dreamed up (and sold to the studio) while the writer was otherwise engaged—engaged, it should be said, in rewrites designed to make sure his scenario was logically persuasive.

Notable, noble exceptions aside, a screenplay today is less a dramatic structure than it is a linking rationalization for gaudily improbable behavior. Where once it was a movie's power source, it is now merely a power line, transmitting without too much resistance the juice generated by one wow sequence on to the next. And the next. Until the whole works short-circuits, with much flashing, crashing, and bashing. Hmm. Looks like an ending. Must be one.

There is a tendency to blame television for the episodic nature of screen narrative today. Since the medium requires a commercial interruption every eight minutes or so, it obvi ously discourages complex narrative. Equally obviously, it has encouraged several generations of writers to think in terms of short, punchy sequences, strong enough to keep viewers tuned in, anticipating more of the same during the commercial breaks, while not requiring them to bear a lot of complicated information in mind in order to follow the story when it resumes. More obviously still, TV has reduced the audience's expectations of coherence in the development of a plot, as well as its capacity to deal with the more subtle layerings of a more sophisticated kind of storytelling. It was the genius of *Seinfeld* to solve this problem by virtually eliminating plot—vestiges of which continue to cling to most TV comedies—in favor of loosely linked anecdotage, encouraging us not to expect new story developments but small fresh predicaments for each of its highly stylized characters to respond to in ways that exquisitely fulfilled our well-schooled expectations. If these figures had ever "developed" in traditional fashion, the program would probably have failed.

In short, the familiar argument that television has disastrously reduced the national attention span is indisputable. But there is rather more to be said on this subject, some of which derives from a less obvious aspect of television's influence on how movies are made, some of which derives from much broader cultural influences now working on the movies. First things first. It is important to understand that when TV replaced the movies as the most significant instrument of mass entertainment in the United States in the early fifties, its initial accomplishment was not "reordering our sensorium"—that took a little more time—but reordering the way the motion picture industry did business.

For one thing, genre filmmaking virtually disappeared. Most of the basic movie forms, forms which had been the backbone of Hollywood's business for over two decades— westerns, detective stories, domestic comedies—moved over to television, which perhaps did not produce them as handsomely but could make them more efficiently than the movies had. These were, of course, highly conventionalized—not to say ritualized—forms. Their stylizations had been a huge help in sustaining narrative. Maybe you couldn't phone a genre script in, but if you got stuck it was easy enough to refer, say, to previous lost-patrol movies or submarine-stuck-on-the-bottom movies or whatever, and solve your narrative problem. If even that was too much bother, you could count on the audience, which by and large knew these forms as well as the screenwriters did, to fill in the gaps. The movies as Gestalt therapy.

Along with genre films, another type of narrative-intensive movie also used to be produced on a regular basis—adaptations of popular and classic novels and plays. Even in their radically simplified and sentimentalized screen versions, these enterprises kept the tradition of the well-made plot alive and informed our expectations as well. They also linked the movies to an older cultural tradition—to the mega-narrative of history, if you will—and that was no small service, either.

All that is now changed. To be sure, best-sellers, ranging from the works of John Grisham and Tom Clancy to curiosities like *Midnight in the Garden of Good and Evil* and *Primary Colors* are still made into movies. But I'd like to suggest that the narratives offered by the former are every bit as spasmodic as those presented by the typical modern American movie, quite illogical and full of what Hollywood has learned to call "whamos," bursts of lunatic activity that ideally should succeed one another at intervals of roughly ten minutes. In adapting these books for the screen, it should be noted that one of the things that makes them appealing to readers is that the shovelsful of information they present on topics that interest us—how a law firm works or doesn't work, how the national security system functions or malfunctions—are always eliminated, which starkly reveals their narrative poverty. Or one should say narrative desperation.

But at least these adaptations are successful at the box office. The curiosities, which depend entirely on imparting information, whether they be exotic like *Midnight* or insider-ish like *Colors*, are not. There's just not enough interesting narrative to sustain them. Meantime, fictions that depend for their success on traditional, somewhat more complex narratives aren't often converted to the movies in the United States. Works of this kind have migrated to television—to the miniseries in the case of popular fiction of the Sidney Sheldon–Danielle Steele school, to British television and then to PBS in the case of the classics. What few classical fictions—the recent *Les Misérables*, for example—or modern novels of true narrative complexity –the lovely *Oscar and Lucinda*—make it to the movies under foreign auspices.

Another force for narrative coherence has also dwindled in recent decades. That's the star system. As it functioned under the old studio system, with players under long-term contract and pretty much obliged to do what the moguls told them to do (which was to appear in genre films tailored to their images), it helped us to fill in a lot of blanks. Playing types, making their familiar and beloved moves three or four times a year, stars once supplied a lot of what might be missing in any given screenplay. More than that, their careers themselves functioned as a sort of mega-narrative. Discussing the not-so-distinguished *China Seas* in his very good book on *The Hollywood Studios*, Ethan Mordden observes that we view the picture "cross-contextually, combining reflections of Gable's amused tolerance of Harlow in *Red Dust* with Harlow's charming exploitation of Beery in *Dinner at Eight*, meanwhile thinking back to the three stars in *The Secret Six* (1931) playing the same mutual perspective in a city setting.

It's like the serial publications of Dickens and Thackeray: the fascination of the whole redeems the weakness of an entry here and there."

More important to the present argument, the stars often provided the organizing concept of a movie, a simple method of describing it attractively. "It's—you know—a Bette Davis picture," we would say. Or, "It's Tracy and Hepburn—I always love them." Or, "Alan Ladd's in it, but its pretty good anyway." Maybe they did not provide true coherence any more than genre picture-making did, but they and their equally familiar supporting players certainly provided an awfully good illusion of that quality. And when the studios phased out their long-term contractual arrangements with them (around the same time they cut back genre production), something was lost.

Not the least of which was the ability to force these actors to go on repeating themselves, which may have been hard on their egos but was good for our sense of narrative stability. Those of the stars who survived into the new Hollywood era (and their successors, of course) could no longer be ordered to do anything. They could only be wheedled and wooed—with the promise of roles that would "stretch" them, with the promise that they might have script approval (along with director and costar approval, of course). Much of the time, naturally, power flowed in exactly the opposite direction, with the stars, aided and abetted by their newly powerful agents, bringing properties, and very often all the above-the-line personnel for a project, to the studio, which in return for financing might get some budgetary control but not much creative control over the picture.

When an actor has this much power over a picture, you can imagine what happens to narrative logic. There are certain things he or she won't do. There are certain things he or she must do. No matter what the original script called for or the director suggests or the desperately rewriting writers beg for. See any Barbra Streisand vehicle. Any Dustin Hoffman or Robert Redford picture. It's as Joan Didion put it many years ago: "To understand whose picture it is, one needs to look not particularly at the script but at the deal memo."

And that says nothing about the *auteur* theory as it's been corrupted in Hollywood's workaday understanding of it. For if the stars do not have creative control of a movie, its director may have, or may be permitted to think he has. In either case, that means he gets to start putting his stamp on a film while it is being written (or rewritten at his behest)—something that never happened in the old studio days, when he was handed a script a few days before the start date and was obliged to shoot it pretty much as written.

Nowadays a director has far more time to pursue his natural and legitimate interest in clarifying story lines, making them "work" when actors are on their feet in front of the camera, and there's nothing wrong with that; it's the traditional heart of his craft. But today's *auteur* is often a man with something else on his mind, a man using the movies "to make personal statements." Which may or may not coincide with the main thrust of a script. If they do not, he, like his stars, has at his disposal a hundred ways of subverting that thrust in order to make sequences representing his "vision." That a certain confusion must result from this effort is obvious.

But ego mischief of this kind aside, it must also be admitted that a director is, or should be, the man in charge of a movie's movieness, a man with the skill and the will to create, using techniques utterly unique to his medium, a purely cinematic "text" out of the more conventional materials at hand. Another way of putting that is to say that, whether he knows it or not, he is the chief modernist in residence on the set.

Up to now the forces we have identified as subverting traditional narrative have been generated largely by conditions within the movie industry itself as they have developed over the last three or four decades. But when we start to think about the influence of serious and greatly gifted directors, we start to link the narrative crisis of movies to larger and more long-standing cultural issues.

It was really only an accident—because Griffith and the rest of the pioneers didn't know what else to do with their new medium—that movies took as their narrative models nineteenth-century popular fiction and theatrical melodramas (though it must be said that the efficiency with which they could convey the essence of these tales was something of a miracle). It was also an accident that, just as the silent cinema was achieving a high degree of sophistication in the realm of purely visual storytelling (Gance's *Napoleon,* Vidor's *The Crowd,* Murnau's *Sunrise*), talking pictures applied reverse thrust to the process, sending filmmakers back to highly verbal material for their sources. What is not accidental, what is in fact inherent in the basic technology and technique of moviemaking, is the capacity to fragment and rearrange time, to move instantly from place to place geographically and emotionally, to find and direct our eyes toward what an early film scholar called "the visual hieroglyphs of the unseen world"— to enter naively, almost childishly, that surreal landscape, that dream state that more self-conscious modernists must work so hard, with such conscious effort, to enter.

The movies, in short, have almost as a birthright their versions of modernism's most treasured tenets. Somewhere Didion, who has done plenty of time as a screenwriter, has recorded her delight at discovering the essence of what Conrad was trying to convey in one of his novels in a parentheses. I would propose that something akin to that often occurs amidst the hubbub of a movie story when a couple of characters exchange silent glances. I don't know how many directors are aware of E. M. Forster's weary and grudging admission that "Oh, dear, yes, a novel must have a plot." Or T. S. Eliot's more famous remark that plot is the piece of meat the burglar throws the watchdog in order to distract him. But instinct,

and a sense of their own form's imperatives, informs them on
this point.

It is possible that, if we are willing to admit it, we in the
audience possess the same instinctual information. Story
may be everything to us as we make our decisions over what
movies to see. It may be everything while we are in the theater wishing, above all, to be pulled out of ourselves, absorbed
in another world. It may be everything in the immediate af-
termath of a movie, when we are trying to sort out its meaning, its place (if any) in our inner lives. But as the months and
years mount up, its significance diminishes to the vanishing
point. Can you actually recount the story, except in the
vaguest possible terms, of movies you saw last month, last
year, last childhood? I doubt it. No, I know it, for part of my
job as a movie reviewer is recounting plots, and it is the hard-
est, most boring, and, above all, most error-prone part of the
work.

Memory is both a deconstructionist and a reconstruc-
tionist as far as movies are concerned. What it tends to retain
are images, possibly a snatch of particularly vivid dialogue (in
increasingly short supply these days), an overall sense of the
movie's drift. But all of this we often reshuffle, improve upon,
remaking the movie in a form more pleasing to various minds'
eyes—and perhaps a lot of different souls' needs. That is why
movie dialogue, for example, is constantly misquoted, even
enters the common culture in erroneous form. (Bogart, as we
all know, never said, "Play it again, Sam," in *Casablanca*. But
we also all know that he should have said it—it's a better,
more succinct line than the mouthful of words he actually uttered.)

Modernist criticism recognizes this. Helen Vendler
summed up the point—perhaps everything useful in current
critical theory—very succinctly in her superb essay on Roland
Barthes, when she observed that he came at last to believe
that writing is not so much an "authorial production" as it is

291

"a shimmering forcefield of signifying, into which the reader enters and by which the reader is 'traversed.'" As she puts it, "Through the text the reader becomes a writer, producing meaning." Substitute "movie" for "text" in that sentence and you have a fair summary of what is beginning to happen at the upper levels of the movie world today. Indeed, I think the Barthesian formula is more applicable to movies than it is to literature. For a book is, after all, the product of a single author who is capable of exercising ... well, yes ... near-authoritarian control over his materials. Despite the claims of some directors, most movies have many authors, none of whom has absolute authority over the finished work. What these many hands are most likely to produce is exactly a "shimmering forcefield," not a coherent or fully explicable narrative, something endlessly open to whatever interpretation we care to place on it.

Oddly enough, it seems to me that the typical action movie tacitly acknowledges this fact—in an entirely primitive way, of course. In the hands of someone like John Woo, leader of the Hong Kong action school, plot, as we conventionally define it, is reduced to total irrelevancy, total incomprehensibility. We attend his films to witness his masterful orchestration of individual sequences, like the concluding chase in *Face/Off*. These in turn are appreciated critically almost as if they were action paintings, as abstract exercises in filling a two-dimensional canvas as richly and colorfully as possible. Their connection to whatever narrative may precede or succeed them is rarely mentioned, and their connection to any reality—or any meaningful emotion—outside the frame of the movie is ignored, because, of course, they make no such connection.

The defense for the state this art has attained is, naturally, that movies are "a visual art," that they are at last shrugging off the bonds of literary and theatrical narrative they inherited from nineteenth-century popular culture and

are at last beginning to obey their own imperatives. This ar
gument, as David Denby has observed, is particularly advanced by young media types (and some academics) brought
up on quick-cut music videos, which are nothing but "shimmering forcefields," the aim of which is merely to suggest the
emotional tone of a pop song and have no narrative obligations.

It's a nonsensical argument, of course. No matter how
brilliantly one shoots and edits a music video (or a commercial) it is a useless model for a movie demanding our attention
for something like two hours. We must have some sort of suspenseful forward motion to engage and divert our minds for
that length of time, and narrative is the only device capable of
so doing. Indeed, I know of only two feature-length movies
that (in my minority estimation) successfully diminished narrative to a minimal level yet imparted the kind of information
we need to sustain interest in its leading character's journey
through purely visual means. These were Stanley Kubrick's
2001: A Space Odyssey and his even more challenging *Barry
Lyndon*.

Neither film, it should be observed, particularly pleased
the better critics, whose biases are ever toward the literary, especially when the dialogue track prates humanistic pieties.
Their lack of regard for *2001* was especially ironic in that the
movie actually took them where they always want to go—toward transcendence, toward rebirth. As for *Barry Lyndon*,
how they hated it for not being *Tom Jones*. Or, for that matter, Thackeray. But, in this instance, of course, Kubrick was
actively subverting stories of that kind. Through his anti-hero
protagonist, he was projecting a modern sensibility, up to its
usual trick of trying to create an identity out of his surroundings, projecting backward in time, into, yes, a forcefield, in
which that sensibility (and the rest of us, observing the world
through his alternately puzzled and bedazzled eyes) strained
to pick up clues to right behavior from the folds of the

draperies, the light in a candlelit room, the rustle of a skirt. It is demonically sub- and anti-verbal but brilliantly imagistic moviemaking, carefully designed to subvert conventional expectations, and trying to compensate for that disappointment with its ravishing *mise-en-scène*.

These movies are signposts on a road not taken by the best American filmmakers. For which, I think, we must all be grateful. Kubrick is Kubrick, and it is best for other directors and for the audience if he remains inimitable. The modern American main line begins elsewhere, possibly with *Bonnie and Clyde*. It surely includes *The Wild Bunch, The Godfather, Chinatown, Taxi Driver, Raging Bull, Blue Velvet, Unforgiven, Pulp Fiction, Fargo*. It could be vastly extended. And its end is not in sight.

All of these movies are, to be sure, violent movies, therefore disturbing to some critics. This often leads to not very illuminating controversies about them, which I'll consider in a moment. Right now, I want to concentrate on the more important fact that all of them are also narratively complex, some of them very densely so. All of them are, as well, emotionally complex. And all of them are acutely, wittily aware of the genre traditions—westerns, gangster movies, road pictures, what-have-you, out of which they grew. Indeed, they build their "forcefields" out of our awareness of those traditions, gaining richer textures, deeper resonances in this process. In fact, as the history of the movies lengthens they become, at least at their higher, more self-conscious level, more like literature—posing for their creators and for the knowing audience the challenge of cross- and historical reference, maybe even "the anxiety of influence." Quotation can, of course, be a form of laziness, a way of adding spurious knowingness, false richness, to a work. But a quotation, we should always remember, can also function as a building block, vital in establishing the foundations on which art's extensions rest.

Consider, in this regard, *Bonnie and Clyde*. There had been couple-on-the-run movies before—the likes of *You Only Live Once* and *Gun Crazy*—but none had taken up the theme of outlaws-as-celebrities in the way this movie did. And none had shown so vividly the often comically careless violence inherent in the relationship between the lawless and the lawful. Something similar might be said about *Chinatown*. It has all the elements of a classic late-forties *film noir*—a mysterious woman leading a private eye through a labyrinthine plot, which eventually takes him to the corrupt power elite of his city (Los Angeles, naturally). But the crimes he uncovers—incest and an analogous rape of the landscape by that elite—dwarf in their horror on the one hand, in their vastness on the other, anything the genre had previously dealt with.

Now think for a moment about *Blue Velvet*. Considered purely as plot, it is like a mystery novel written for teenagers—nice kids in a nostalgically realized small town (you can imagine Sandra Dee and Bobby Darin in the roles, because the director, David Lynch, shoots their sequences in the fifties manner) stumble on criminal behavior in this unlikely venue and set about restoring order. But this criminality is insanely violent. It is never important how *Blue Velvet*'s "story" works out (quite conventionally, as it happens). Its meaning lies in the constant, insistently jarring juxtapositions of escapist dreamscapes with those ugly realities of life that we do our best not to think about, that in fact are what we typically go to the movies to escape. The boldness with which Lynch rubbed our noses in this contrast was what made his movie so controversial. The mixture of a nostalgic style—something that sweetly promises escape from the violence of contemporary life and the "violence" of contemporary movies—with intensely realized passages of profoundly sadistic behavior—much more disturbing than the destruction of hundreds of anonymous extras in a whammo sequence—was marvelously dislocating. If you had the stomach for it.

Let's look, too, at *Unforgiven*. It is full of classic western tropes: the good bad man who has put away his guns and is now obliged to strap them on again; the corrupt town in need of cleansing; a murdered pardner whose death requires vengeful retribution. But the point of the movie is to subvert our traditional responses to those activities, to make us see that they lead not to moral satisfaction but instead push us further into moral squalor.

Unforgiven, unlike *L.A. Confidential,* was a critical success that became a commercial success as well. That's partly because it had a major star in the leading role, supported by well-known costars; partly because its narrative was somewhat more straightforward, simply describable; mainly, I think, because, whatever its moral complexities, it did contain enough moments of vividly murderous action first to intrigue the mass audience, then to satisfy it. You could cut a swell, quite misrepresenting trailer for this film, making it appear to be the kind of tough, gritty western in which its star-director, Clint Eastwood, had always pleased the people. In other words, it was capable of being deconstructed—however falsely—as a pure action piece, not different in anticipation, or even, in the memories of dullards, as dumb, bloody fun.

The same, I think, might be said of Quentin Tarentino's *Pulp Fiction.* But like the equally amoral *Goodfellas,* its real interest lies in the way it places at the center of our attention the kind of second and third heavies who have typically lurked in the corner of the gangster film's frame, and allows us to see that they have, of all things, inner lives—primitive, to be sure, but palpable. It's a profoundly disturbing thought—or should one say cross-reference? The film has been criticized for seeming to celebrate the absurd cool of these hit men, the affectlessness with which they conduct their business. The literary critic Roger Shattuck claims that since all of its references are to other movies, *Pulp Fiction* encourages us to aestheticize violence, to affect an affectlessness of our own as we confront its symbolic representation of the bloody realities of our times.

Immersed as I am in the movie culture, I would, of course, argue the opposite. Every one of the movies I've been discussing aestheticizes violence in one way or another. But in the process all of them do so with shocking and unforgettable immediacy. They do not make violent death merely an element in a composition; they make it something we feel and remember.

But even if we chose to concede his point, we might want to direct Shattuck's attention to *Fargo,* in which the Coen Brothers brilliantly juxtapose violently modernist anarchy with traditional American small-town values, permitting the latter, as personified by the sweet-souled (and pregnant) police chief, Marge, to triumph not merely over the bad guys from the big city but over the criminal infections that have leaked out of it into her snowy, peaceful territory, causing some of its citizens to swoon into temporary insanity.

All right, I'll admit it, I don't give a hoot about media violence as a social issue, no matter how many insane little twerps go into court claiming that a movie or a TV show made them do whatever they did. Maybe—job-related illness about to be evoked here—after thirty-odd years of reviewing them I am incapable of seeing violence in anything but aesthetic terms. Maybe I and my fellow reviewers have a class-action case we could bring against our employers; surely loss of sensitivity must be worth as much in hard cash as, say, hearing loss is to a foundry worker.

But seriously folks. . . . The question of violence *is* an aesthetic issue, and it is, I believe, directly related to the issue of narrative coherence. To the degree that violence is sited in conscientiously constructed movies and is carried out by characters whose motives are socially or psychologically explicable, we can—and should—endure it in a morally balanced and intelligent way. I understand, of course, that modernism, maybe even postmodernism (whatever that actually is) has crept in on its little cat feet in all the good movies I have all too briefly mentioned here. I understand as well that the seeming randomness with which it arises in these movies, and the moral indeterminacy with which these films sometimes regard it, represents, if you will, a pressure from above that is as serious as the pressure arising from below, from purely commercial ventures, on narrative coherence. I am concerned that the matrix of cross-references to genre conventions, which the best movies rely on to keep us oriented morally as well as narratively, may not be strong enough to sustain us, or the medium, for very long. I am worried about the movies' self-referentiality, especially as it's practiced by such deeply knowing directors as Scorsese and Tarentino. It may ultimately prove to be a blind alley.

On the other hand, the self-conscious movieness of the better movies of the last two or three decades may also be only a passing phase. Certainly we see an artist like Scorsese trying to grope his way out of it with works like *The Age of Innocence* and *Kundun.* In any case, better this kind of self-consciousness than the aspiration to make movies into a branch of literature—more properly, or anyway more usually, a branch of subliterature—which was the prevailing desire among moviemakers and critics alike until sometime in the 1960s.

That aside, who can doubt that the truly memorable movies of recent times are, indeed, "shimmering forcefields," offering the sophisticated moviegoer—through their genre references and their glancing "homages" to the stylistic tics of past masters—opportunities for "authorship" of a far more sophisticated and memorable sort than those presented by the typical big-scale action film, which invites us merely to fill in its gaping narrative and logical gaps. Moreover, since conventional narrative—shepherding us into line, marching us along to some simple emotional point, like the execrable *Ti-*

tanic—is an authoritarian imposition on reality (analogous, let us say, to the impositions of the Marxist interpretation of mysterious, multifarious history), we have to be grateful for the bravura of the best of the contemporary directors, for the eclecticism of their borrowings, and for their frequently electrifying techniques, which often enough are themselves totally enrapturing—beyond good and evil as it were.

Often enough? No. Not often enough. The trouble is, of course, that films of the kind we've been talking about are rare and in the marketplace remain essentially a minority pleasure—and perhaps an endangered one, for many of the best filmmakers are being snowplowed to the margin. Even when their pictures make money—and some of them do—they don't make enough money, therefore aren't worth the trouble, particularly for a major studio. For some years now, as the entertainment press constantly reports, the studios have been growing increasingly less interested in picking up small change. They would rather put their money and their bullying marketing machinery behind movies they deem to have the kind of blockbuster potential the large-scale action movie has in the dumbed-down world market.

In this context, which is not about to change, the visionary—and enormously witty—possibilities of modernist and postmodernist filmmaking are going to remain a sometime thing, accidents that occasionally slip through the system's filters. In the meantime, seeking an idle evening's entertainment, we are left without the consoling coherences of old-fashioned movie narrative, are too often left with the less elevated forms of anarchy and abstraction. Picking through the emotional and intellectual rubble something like *Twister* leaves in its wake, we keep wondering what hit us. And why we keep letting it hit us.

1989

Author's Note

The place I've most often and most happily written essays about the movie has been *Film Comment,* and I owe a special debt to its editor, Richard T. Jameson, for his friendship, his encouragement, and the leisurely conversations that have improved many of these pieces, not to mention the quality of my life. "Mind Slips" and "Real Reality Bites" as well as the essays about Irene Dunne, Bette Davis, Laurence Olivier, Satyajit Ray, Federico Fellini, and Clint Eastwood appeared originally, in slightly different form and under other titles, in *Film Comment.*

The pieces on Frank Capra, Sam Fuller, and Richard Brooks appeared first in the *DGA News* as salutes on their passing. All have been considerably expanded for publication in this book. "The Star on the Stairs" and "The Narrative Crisis" were first published in the *Gannett Center Journal,* whose editor at the time, Huntington Williams III, suggested both topics. The latter essay has been somewhat updated for republication here. The article on King Vidor was written as a program note for a retrospective of his films in Rome. "*Auteur* of Our Misery" appeared in the *Atlantic,* where Jack Beatty proved to be a sensitive and sympathetic editor. A very much briefer version of the Charles Laughton essay appeared originally in the book *Close-Ups,* which Danny Peary edited for Workman Publishing. "Time Out" appeared in my hometown newspaper, the *Milwaukee Journal,* as part of its coverage of the Green Bay Packers' return to Super Bowl glory in January 1996. "Cinema Paradiso" was first given as a paper at a Woodrow Wilson Center conference called "Popular Culture: America and the World." It was organized by Michael Kammen, the historian, who made several valuable suggestions to me. The piece later appeared, in slightly different form, in the *Wilson Quarterly.*

Two articles require a little longer explanation. "Garbo: The Legend as Actress" was commissioned by Simon and Schuster as an afterword to a book about her by Antoni Gronowicz, which the house published after both the author and his subject died. Before her passing, Garbo had broken her famous silence to denounce Gronowicz as a fraud, his book as a hoax. The book's editor assured me, however, that the publishers had checked out his tale—to the point of engaging private detectives—and believed it to be authentic. In any case, I was not obliged to endorse his work, only to supply what the publisher's thought was missing from it—a critical overview of her work. This I did, only to become convinced by biographically astute reviewers and by Barry Paris's superbly detailed biography of Garbo that Gronowicz's work was, to say the least, highly suspect. But since I relied largely on my own research for my essay, I have no hesitation in reprinting it here, revising it only to add one or two later ideas and to withdraw from it a couple of critical notions based on information gleaned from the Gronowicz book, which Paris persuasively disputed.

Finally, the essay on my friend and colleague Andrew Sarris appears here for the first time. It was requested by the editor of a *festschrift* in Andrew's honor, and accepted by him with the pleasantest of thanks. Alas, its scheduled publication date has long since come and gone, and neither I nor any other contributor to that volume whom I have talked with has heard anything further from him. I am very glad to have this opportunity to print these reflections on a treasured friend.

I am equally pleased to have this opportunity to thank Ivan R. Dee for proposing this collection to me and for the firm but tactful editorial pencil he has applied to the manuscript. He has made this book better than the one he bargained for.

R. S.

Best known as a film critic for *Time* magazine for more than two decades, Richard Schickel is also the author of more than twenty books, most of them about the movies. They include biographies of D. W. Griffith, Clint Eastwood, Marlon Brando, Cary Grant, Douglas Fairbanks, Sr., and James Cagney; a definitive study of Walt Disney and his works; and a pioneering consideration of the celebrity system. Mr. Schickel has also written, directed, and produced a wide variety of television programs, many of them documentaries about film and filmmakers. He has been nominated four times for an Emmy, has held a Guggenheim Fellowship, and has taught film history and criticism at Yale and at the University of Southern California. He lives in Los Angeles.

Theatre and Drama

Linda Apperson, *Stage Managing and Theatre Etiquette*
Robert Brustein, *Cultural Calisthenics*
Robert Brustein, *Dumbocracy in America*
Robert Brustein, *Reimagining American Theatre*
Robert Brustein, *The Theatre of Revolt*
Stephen Citron, *The Musical from the Inside Out*
Irina and Igor Levin, *Working on the Play and the Role*
Keith Newlin, ed., *American Plays of the New Woman*
Louis Rosen, *The South Side*
David Wood, with Janet Grant, *Theatre for Children*
Plays for Performance:
  Aristophanes, *Lysistrata*
  Pierre Augustin de Beaumarchais, *The Barber of Seville*
  Pierre Augustin de Beaumarchais, *The Marriage of Figaro*
  Anton Chekhov, *The Cherry Orchard*
  Anton Chekhov, *The Seagull*
  Euripides, *The Bacchae*
  Euripides, *Iphigenia in Aulis*
  Euripides, *Iphigenia Among the Taurians*
  Euripides, *Medea*
  Euripides, *The Trojan Women*
  Georges Feydeau, *Paradise Hotel*
  Henrik Ibsen, *A Doll's House*
  Henrik Ibsen, *Ghosts*
  Henrik Ibsen, *Hedda Gabler*
  Henrik Ibsen, *The Master Builder*
  Henrik Ibsen, *When We Dead Awaken*
  Henrik Ibsen, *The Wild Duck*
  Heinrich von Kleist, *The Prince of Homburg*
  Christopher Marlowe, *Doctor Faustus*
  Molière, *The Bourgeois Gentleman*
  The Mysteries: Creation
  The Mysteries: The Passion
  Luigi Pirandello, *Six Characters in Search of an Author*
  Sophocles, *Antigone*
  Sophocles, *Electra*
  Sophocles, *Oedipus The King*
  August Strindberg, *The Father*
  August Strindberg, *Miss Julie*

American History and American Studies

Stephen Vincent Benét, *John Brown's Body*
Henry W. Berger, ed., *A William Appleman Williams Reader*
Andrew Bergman, *We're in the Money*
Paul Boyer, ed., *Reagan as President*
William Brashler, *Josh Gibson*
Robert V. Bruce, *1877: Year of Violence*
Douglas Bukowski, *Navy Pier*
Philip Callow, *From Noon to Starry Night*
Laurie Winn Carlson, *A Fever in Salem*
Kendrick A. Clements, *Woodrow Wilson*
Richard E. Cohen, *Rostenkowski*
David Cowan and John Kuenster, *To Sleep with the Angels*
George Dangerfield, *The Era of Good Feelings*
Clarence Darrow, *Verdicts Out of Court*
Allen F. Davis, *American Heroine*
Floyd Dell, *Intellectual Vagabondage*
Elisha P. Douglass, *Rebels and Democrats*
Theodore Draper, *The Roots of American Communism*
Edward Jay Epstein, *News from Nowhere*
Joseph Epstein, *Ambition*
Peter G. Filene, *In the Arms of Others*
Richard Fried, ed., Bruce Barton's *The Man Nobody Knows*
Lloyd C. Gardner, *Pay Any Price*
Lloyd C. Gardner, *Spheres of Influence*
Paul W. Glad, *McKinley, Bryan, and the People*
Sarah H. Gordon, *Passage to Union*

Daniel Horowitz, *The Morality of Spending*
Kenneth T. Jackson, *The Ku Klux Klan in the City, 1915–1930*
Edward Chase Kirkland, *Dream and Thought in the Business Community, 1860–1900*
Herbert S Klein, *Slavery in the Americas*
Aileen S. Kraditor, *Means and Ends in American Abolitionism*
Hilton Kramer, *The Twilight of the Intellectuals*
Hilton Kramer and Roger Kimball, eds., *The Betrayal of Liberalism*
Irving Kristol, *Neoconservatism*
Leonard W. Levy, *Jefferson and Civil Liberties: The Darker Side*
Leonard W. Levy, *Original Intent and the Framers' Constitution*
Leonard W. Levy, *Origins of the Fifth Amendment*
Leonard W. Levy, *The Palladium of Justice*
Seymour J. Mandelbaum, *Boss Tweed's New York*
Thomas J. McCormick, *China Market*
John Harmon McElroy, *American Beliefs*
Gerald W. McFarland, *A Scattered People*
Walter Millis, *The Martial Spirit*
Nicolaus Mills, ed., *Culture in an Age of Money*
Nicolaus Mills, *Like a Holy Crusade*
Roderick Nash, *The Nervous Generation*
Keith Newlin, ed., *American Plays of the New Woman*
William L. O'Neill, ed., *Echoes of Revolt: The Masses, 1911–1917*
Gilbert Osofsky, *Harlem: The Making of a Ghetto*
Edward Pessen, *Losing Our Souls*
Glenn Porter and Harold C. Livesay, *Merchants and Manufacturers*
John Prados, *The Hidden History of the Vietnam War*
John Prados, *Presidents' Secret Wars*
Patrick Renshaw, *The Wobblies*
Edward Reynolds, *Stand the Storm*
Louis Rosen, *The South Side*
Richard Schickel, *The Disney Version*
Richard Schickel, *Intimate Strangers*
Richard Schickel, *Matinee Idylls*
Edward A. Shils, *The Torment of Secrecy*
Geoffrey S. Smith, *To Save a Nation*
Robert W. Snyder, *The Voice of the City*
Bernard Sternsher, ed., *Hitting Home: The Great Depression in Town and Country*
Bernard Sternsher, ed., *Hope Restored: How the New Deal Worked in Town and Country*
Bernard Sternsher and Judith Sealander, eds., *Women of Valor*
Athan Theoharis, *From the Secret Files of J. Edgar Hoover*
Nicholas von Hoffman, *We Are the People Our Parents Warned Us Against*
Norman Ware, *The Industrial Worker, 1840–1860*
Tom Wicker, *JFK and LBJ: The Influence of Personality upon Politics*
Robert H. Wiebe, *Businessmen and Reform*
T. Harry Williams, *McClellan, Sherman and Grant*
Miles Wolff, *Lunch at the 5 & 10*
Randall B. Woods and Howard Jones, *Dawning of the Cold War*
American Ways Series:
    John A. Andrew III, *Lyndon Johnson and the Great Society*
    Roger Daniels, *Not Like Us*
    J. Matthew Gallman, *The North Fights the Civil War: The Home Front*
    Lewis L. Gould, *1968: The Election That Changed America*
    John Earl Haynes, *Red Scare or Red Menace?*
    D. Clayton James and Anne Sharp Wells, *From Pearl Harbor to V-J Day*
    John W. Jeffries, *Wartime America*
    Curtis D. Johnson, *Redeeming America*
    Maury Klein, *The Flowering of the Third America*
    Larry M. Logue, *To Appomattox and Beyond*
    Jean V. Matthews, *Women's Struggle for Equality*
    Iwan W. Morgan, *Deficit Government*
    Robert Muccigrosso, *Celebrating the New World*
    Daniel Nelson, *Shifting Fortunes*
    Thomas R. Pegram, *Battling Demon Rum*
    Burton W. Peretti, *Jazz in American Culture*
    John A. Salmond, *"My Mind Set on Freedom"*
    William Earl Weeks, *Building the Continental Empire*
    Mark J. White, *Missiles in Cuba*